AMERICAN LITERATURE

by Guy E. Smith, Ph.D.

About the Book

1. Designed for nonspecialized students and general readers. Emphasis in the main section is on the works that make literature, with biographical and historical backgrounds woven in to make a unified and complete review of the major literary contributions of American writers. In this section 20th century writing is given an especially detailed treatment.

2. Separate sections of plot summaries of the major works and a dictionary of literary terms to enable the student or general reader to find in a few seconds essential review information about works he has read and definitions which may be difficult to locate quickly in voluminous histories and anthologies.

3. Sections that stand out from the main text, giving careful and detailed treatments of the literary trends and movements as well as the political and social backgrounds within which the types of works are produced.

About the Author

1. Dr. Smith has taught both classical and modern languages and literatures for 25 years. He has been employed in the Department of Languages, University of Utah, for the past nine years.

2. His publications have included articles in various professional educational journals, and translations. His 1957 publications include *English Literature: To Romanticism*, *English Literature: After Neoclassicism* (Littlefield, Adams and Company), and *The Disinherited Lady*, translated from the Spanish of Benito Pérez Galdós (Exposition Press). At present he is completing a manuscript in English of the Galdós masterpiece, *Fortunata y Jacinta*. He has partially completed his projected series of review handbooks on various of the world's literatures.

AMERICAN LITERATURE

A Complete Survey

with

Plot Summaries of Major Works
Dictionary of Literary Terms

By

GUY E. SMITH, Ph.D.
University of Utah

1962

LITTLEFIELD, ADAMS & CO.
PATERSON, NEW JERSEY

ACKNOWLEDGMENTS

In the section on 20th century poetry, permission to quote representative selections is gratefully acknowledged to the following publishers, agents, and individuals:

1. The Macmillan Company for permission to quote from "The Callyope," "General William Booth Enters Into Heaven," "Abraham Lincoln Walks at Midnight," and "The Congo," from *Collected Poems* of Vachel Lindsay. Copyright, 1925, by The Macmillan Company. (*See pages 164-65.*)

2. Mrs. Ellen C. Masters for permission to quote "Abel Melveny," from *Spoon River Anthology* by Edgar Lee Masters. Published by The Macmillan Company. (*See pages 166-67.*)

3. Harcourt, Brace and Company for permission to quote from "Portrait," from *Smoke and Steel* by Carl Sandburg. Copyright, 1920, by Harcourt, Brace and Company, Inc., renewed, 1948, by Carl Sandburg. Used by permission of the publishers. (*See page 168.*)

4. Henry Holt and Company for permission to quote from "Chicago," "To a Contemporary Bunkshooter," and "Fog," from *Chicago Poems* by Carl Sandburg. Copyright, 1916, by Henry Holt and Company. Copyright, 1944, by Carl Sandburg. By permission of the publishers. (*See pages 167-69.*)

5. Houghton Mifflin Company for permission to quote from "Patterns," by Amy Lowell. (*See page 171.*)

6. Alfred A. Knopf, Inc., for permission to quote "Let No Charitable Hope," from *Collected Poems of Elinor Wylie.* Copyright, 1923, 1932, by Alfred A. Knopf, Inc. (*See page 173.*)

7. The Macmillan Company for permission to quote "Meadowlarks," copyright, 1948, from *The Collected Poems of Sara Teasdale.* Copyright, 1937, by The Macmillan Company. (*See page 174.*)

8. Messrs. Brandt and Brandt for permission to quote from "Invocation," from *John Brown's Body* by Stephan Vincent Benét. Published by Rinehart and Company. Copyright, 1927, 1929, by Stephen Vincent Benét. Copyright renewed, 1955, 1956, by Rosemary Carr Benét. (*See page 175.*)

9. Henry Holt and Company for permission to quote from "Mending Walls," and "Stopping by Woods on a Snowy Evening," from *Complete Poems of Robert Frost.* Copyright, 1930, 1949, by Henry Holt and Company, Inc. Copyright, 1936, 1948, by Robert Frost. By permission of the publishers. (*See pages 177-78.*)

Preface

American writings, from the settlement of Jamestown in 1607 to the present day, form a relatively short chapter in the history of world literatures. In its beginnings our literature was Colonial and English and was largely restricted in its scope to the hard reality and the dogma of our Puritan forebears. But, from its beginning, it reflected a new life and new independent ideals. American literature is young and it is built upon broad foundations of political, religious, and social freedom. It has widened into the broad world stream of great literature in its short history and has remained a faithful medium for the recording of the rapidly developing advances of American life and thought. In the past century and a half, American writings have come to command world interest and recognition; they have, at the same time, retained and deepened their capacity to depict the shifting American scene in all of its rich and varying aspects.

This book is designed to review the literary story of the United States for the student or for the general reader. Its single aim is to create an interesting and accurate view of the writings which have combined to form a body of literature which, in its brief course, has won its place beside the finest modern literary expression of Western civilization.

Designed for general students and nonspecialists

This volume seeks to give the nonspecialized student and the general reader a conveniently manageable manual of essential information, unified but uncrowded by detail. It is compiled primarily for the student who needs help in supplementing his reading and lecture notes or who desires a handy organization of essential data, or who wishes a quick reference manual wherein he may find in a few seconds a particular fact or definition. The plan also provides the student with detailed summaries of the major works, thus giving him a reference outline of the books he reads as well as the content of many important selections he will not have time to read in their entirety. The book is also designed for the nonstudent who desires to acquire a working knowledge of this essential branch of our cultural heritage and who has not the time to wade through many books and to sift out the requisite information from many detailed discussions. And, third, the work would not be out of place as a handy reference manual on the shelves of the specialist in literatures.

Emphasis on literary works

The major emphasis here is on the writings that make literature and whatever additional data can be considered absolutely essential for an understanding and appreciation of them. This leaves little room for the amassing of biographical and bibliographical detail. My task has been one of meticulous sifting and elimination of masses of material and to organize the elements of prime importance into a unified whole with plentiful aids for the busy student who must meet examination deadlines.

Divisions of the manual and their use

The specific plan of this book is as follows:

1. The main section gives a continuous presentation of the story of the literary development of the United States from its beginnings to the present time. The contemporary period is given extensive coverage, amounting to about one-third of the section. Detail is suppressed to give unity and an uncrowded view of particular periods. Historical and general cultural notes are used to preface each period of literary development to provide a picture of the political and social setting within which the literary men of genius worked upon their masterpieces.

2. Minor works will be discussed in the main section. However, as each major work is introduced, a number or a note in parentheses, (248), will indicate that a summary of its contents will be found in Appendix A. There additional data of a critical and comparative nature ·will be included as needed to develop appreciation or understanding of the importance of the work discussed. The summaries are arranged in the order in which the works were introduced into the main section.

3. As literary terms are introduced into the main section,

an asterisk (*) will indicate that full information relative to this term will be found in Appendix B, in its alphabetical position. This appendix will thus provide a detailed dictionary of the terms used in discussing literatures, presented in nontechnical language. This alphabetically arranged section, with cross references, is calculated to save the student laborious searching for essential definitions in voluminous histories or anthologies. Many common literary terms, not included in the main discussion section, will also be found there.

A unified review—not an encyclopaedia

All nonessential matter has been deliberately omitted. The volume is designed as a complete and informative coverage of the subject for the nonspecialized reader and has no value as a guide to research and to sources. Many histories, anthologies, and bibliographical guides are available for advanced and detailed study of particular aspects of American literature.

Last, the volume has a complete index in which titles of works are indicated in italics and references to major items throughout the book are highlighted in boldface type.

Literature: an essential key to culture

The writer, after many years of study and teaching in the fields of languages and general literatures, still considers that no degree or diploma can represent true cultural achievement in the United States unless its holder possesses a comprehensive knowledge of the two great bodies of literature written in England and in the United States. He sincerely hopes that this volume and his similar manuals of English literature will prove aids to students and nonstudents alike in both areas of great literary accomplishment in the English language.

G.E.S.

TABLE OF CONTENTS

PAGE

AMERICAN
LITERATURE

Chapter I

THE COLONIAL PERIOD
(1607-1765)

American literature begins, of course, with the first writings of the little group of English settlers in Jamestown, Virginia, in 1607. From this date until the calling of the Stamp Act Congress in 1765, the beginnings of our literature must be judged only from an understanding of the harsh primitive physical environment which confronted these early dissenting groups of colonists and the stern principles which they adopted to insure their survival.

Nature of Colonial Literature

To a present-day reader the efforts of the early Colonial writers may seem puny and feeble in comparison with European literatures of the same period. In Europe, by 1607, literatures had reached their most glorious period since classic Greek and Roman times. In England, by 1607, Spenser had been dead only 8 years. Shakespeare was at the height of his career and Bacon had already written some of his most famous essays.

But in Colonial America, the transplanted Englishmen had stripped off the garments of this European heritage of aesthetic grandeur and had gone to work to attempt to carve out a new civilization from an unfriendly wilderness. The task of these hardy settlers was to feed their families and themselves, to clear the forests and to build homes, to overcome hostile Indian tribes, and to organize a new religious, social, and economic life that would insure their survival and progress for their descendants. We, their descendants and the heritors of this Puritan tradition, realize that this formative work consumed the interests and the energies of the colonists to the extent that there was little time or incentive for the development of an artistic literature.

From an aesthetic and comparative point of view there is little that may be called artistic literature in the Colonial period. There is a great deal of historical, geographical, and theological writing and some rather crude and artificial poetry, but little that is imaginative and which has a purely literary appeal to the modern reader. The values in our Colonial literature are to be sought in its sincere portrayal of the struggle of the small bands of Europeans to achieve social solidarity through compromise within an uncompromising wilderness and an atmosphere of conflicting ideologies.

HISTORICAL AND CULTURAL NOTES

By 1600, both the Spanish and the French had established settlements in North America. When the English established their first permanent claims in the New World, the Spanish already possessed the southern portions of the continent and were established in Mexico and as far north as St. Augustine, Florida, and Santa Fe, New Mexico.

Major English Settlements: Virginia and Massachusetts

After several unsuccessful attempts by Sir Humphrey Gilbert and Sir Walter Ralegh, the first permanent English settlement was made in Virginia (named for the "virgin queen" Elizabeth), at Jamestown, in 1607. The cultivation of tobacco was the first guarantee of success for this struggling settlement.

In 1620, a small body of religious dissenters from England secured from the Virginia Company permission to colonize a portion of the north Atlantic seaboard. This group, consisting of 101 men, women, and children, landed their single ship, the *Mayflower,* near Cape Cod, later founding the colony of Plymouth. It is from these 2 centers that the English settlements, or "plantations" developed, eventually numbering 13. These colonies became the first of the United States of America after the war for independence from England, which began with skirmishes with the English at Concord and Lexington in 1775 and ended with recognition of American independence by the Treaty of Paris in 1783.

The political history of this long period is well known to American students and need not be repeated here. Our concentration will be upon those elements of major importance to the creation of a fruitful and differing segment of the American contribution to literature—seedlings for a great and independent literature written in the English language.

Forging of the American Character

Almost one-half of the period of American history from Jamestown to the present day consists of the forging of a new nation and the gradual development of American ideals and character from an amalgamation of a European inheritance and the influence of a New World environment. Throughout this long period, the influence of England upon the development of American institutions and character is the principal one, but it is by no means the only important element that entered into the establishment of the United States of America. The major elements present in this long formative Colonial period which contributed both toward a lack of cultural achievement for a century and a half and toward the future creation of a distinctive and recognized American character in the life and literature of the United States are:

The nonintellectual character of the settlers. The groups of Englishmen who settled in America represented the middle and lower classes of English society. In the early period they were either religious dissenters (as in Plymouth) or adventurers and restless men intent upon gaining fortunes (as in Virginia). Aside from a few of their leaders they were not from the aristocratic nor the intellectual groups in the mother country. They had received little influence from the spirit of renaissance humanism and had little appreciation for the fine arts. They were literal-minded men who regarded literature as idle frivolity and many considered imaginative and fanciful writing as a tool of evil forces bent upon diverting the minds of men from their duties and obligations.

Influence of the frontier. The colonist arrived in America accustomed to a European mode of living. His clash with the rude and primitive wilderness conditions soon stripped from him many of his civilized habits. He must accept the hard conditions of the wilderness or perish. He became practical and resourceful and developed the traits of energetic expediency that a harsh and merciless environment forced upon him. The early settler had little time for indulgence in profound study or for imaginative pursuits. He was a practical man who sought mastery over his material environment and demanded only the learning and culture which were absolutely necessary to give his society the solidarity which it needed to face its hard tasks with a minimum of loss of time and energy.

Diversity in Colonial societies. The 13 original colonies were by no means alike, nor were they all made up of English settlers. To begin with, the extreme diversity of geographical and climatic conditions of the Atlantic seaboard caused entirely distinct types of societies to develop in the north and the south. New England, with its forbidding rocky hillsides, led the colonists to concentrate into township groups in the narrow valleys. In Virginia and other southern colonies the settlers were widely separated on large plantations. There was little actual personal or commercial connections between the early colonies.

There were extremely marked religious differences among the colonial groups. The American colonies early became refuges for various dissenting and disgruntled religious groups in England and on the continent. All the dissenting religious sects of Europe were to be found in the various colonies. Each group sought isolation from the other and there was little tolerance to be found anywhere.

Several of the colonies were not settled by the English. New York was colonized by the Dutch, Pennsylvania by Germans, Delaware by Swedes, and North Carolina by the Scotch-Irish. And aside from the religious and racial differences, there were other distinctions to be found in the purposes for colonization. Georgia was occupied by James Oglethorpe as a refuge for debtors freed from the prisons of England, under bond to work out their freedom over a period of years; Virginia was settled purely as a commercial enterprise by adventurers and fortune seekers from every station of society. The importation of Negro slaves to do the work in the southern colonies soon resulted in an almost equal numerical division between Negroes and whites in Virginia, South Carolina, and Georgia.

The major element of unification. From the foregoing facts, it would seem evident that there was little in the Colonial period to provide promise of either a unified nation or of a people of the necessary spirit of hope, vision, and enthusiasm to create a literature. But the very conditions of the American frontier developed a feeling for freedom and independence. It created a people who were highly individualistic and self-determined. Gradually there developed among these diverse breeds of pioneers a sense of union, and their feelings of dissent and opposition turned first toward the obtaining of absolute independence from England. It was only then, toward 1775, that these peoples began to feel a new spirit—a spirit of Americanism —which took pride in its own particular political and social institutions. And this spirit, slowly, led these peoples to a desire to create a literature of their own, a body of writings which would reflect the hopes and aspirations of a new nation and would command the recognition and admiration of the literary world abroad.

DIVISIONS OF COLONIAL WRITING

It is perhaps better to classify colonial expression as *writing,* rather than *literature.** There is not only nothing of much artistic value in the period; there is seemingly little influence which this early expression exercised upon the body of native American writing which was to begin after 1776 and to continue uninterruptedly to the present day. Some critics, indeed, do not consider that what appeared before the Revolutionary period is *American.* Its models were English, the prose showing the same elaborated and ornate *euphuism** that prevailed in English prose of the day; its writers considered themselves to be Englishmen, and its content is almost entirely factual prose reports of an historical and geographical nature, letters, sermons and long dry theological argumentations, and textbooks for the early schools. Artistic literature was not only absent, but it was largely under official ban in most of the colonies. As late as 1774, the Continental Congress classified drama along with such social evils as gambling, horse-racing, and cock-fighting.

Descriptive Prose Writing

The early English colonists and explorers, especially the leaders, were anxious to make reports to superiors in England and to leave permanent records of their adventures and findings, descriptions of the rude scenery and the strange appearance and customs of the savage natives. Some were interested in recording the struggles of the colonists to establish themselves and to organize their social and political institutions. These early writers concerned themselves little with style, but their accounts are invaluable to the historian and are the most interesting writings of the Colonial period to the reader who desires to relive vicariously the experiences of our first American frontier along the narrow and forbidding strip of Atlantic seaboard.

Captain John Smith (1579-1631)

Smith was a true soldier of fortune who had run away from home when he was 15. He joined the Virginia Expedition in 1607. He proved to be an excellent soldier and seemed to have a personal manner which caused the Indians to be very friendly with him. In 1608 he sent back to London his _A True Relation of Occurrences and Accidents in Virginia._ This is American literature's first book. In his account, Smith makes no mention of the legendary and famous rescue by the Indian princess Pocahontas.

Smith returned to England after 2 years and wrote several other accounts of life in Virginia. In 1623 he recalled the Pocahontas incident in his _General History of Virginia._ In all his accounts Smith is the hero and central figure. He wrote in an energetic style, with a great fondness for the conceits and alliterations which were common to the prose writers of the Elizabethan Age in England.

William Bradford (1588-1657)

Bradford, at the age of 32, was among the passengers of the _Mayflower._ In 1621 he was made governor of Plymouth. His _History of Plymouth Plantation_ covers the years 1620-1647. It remains today the best authority for the early years of the colony. It is a very readable and straightforward account of the religious causes for the migration, the trials and tribulations of the early years of the settlement, and of the daily lives of the inhabitants.

John Winthrop (1588-1649)

Winthrop, like Bradford, was from a prosperous and well-educated family in England. He came to America in 1630 and was governor of the Massachusetts Bay Colony for 12 years. In addition to his very informative _The History of New England from 1630 to 1649,_ he wrote many _Letters_ to his wife and kept a daily personal _Journal,_ both of which were published many years later. These personal writings give great insight into the mind and emotions of an early Puritan. Winthrop came near to being impeached as governor in 1645 for his liberal principles. After that he is said to have become more austere and rigorous in his administration. Unlike Bradford, Winthrop's writings dwell a great deal upon miracles, monstrosities, and apparitions in the depiction of his religion.

Thomas Morton (1590-1646)

A rather differing early account was *The New English Canaan* (1637) by Thomas Morton. On a May day, in 1626, Morton and a group of roistering Cavalier traders from England established a colony at Mount Wollaston (just south of Boston at Braintree, also known in literature and legend as Merry Mount). This group did everything they could to shock and disturb the nearby Puritans. They danced around a Maypole, gave guns to Indians, and engaged in various daring Cavalier pranks.

Governor Bradford sent Miles Standish to arrest Morton and his band. They were forcibly returned to England where Morton retaliated by writing his very coarse and satirical account of the Puritans. His book ridicules the Puritan faith and manners. Among a mass of gross exaggeration he stated that the Puritans closed their eyes when they prayed, "because they think themselves so perfect in the highe way to heaven that they can find it blindfold." Several items of American literature have been written upon Morton's escapade, including short stories by Hawthorne and Motley and an opera by Howard Hanson.

William Byrd (1674-1744)

In the latter part of the Colonial period a number of able historians and chroniclers rose in various of the settlements. The most worthy of the attention of the average reader is Colonel William Byrd, a Cavalier gentleman of Virginia. Byrd was an aristocratic planter, educated in England. He was widely read and cultivated literature as an elegant pastime. His manuscripts, unpublished for more than 100 years, are regarded today as some of the best prose of the entire period.

Especially well written and witty is his *The History of the Dividing Line Run in 1728*. This account records the author's experiences as a member of a survey commission appointed to settle a boundary dispute between North Carolina and Virginia. This account is filled with very vivid descriptions of the North Carolina swamplands and of the animal and plant life of the region. But the most interesting features of his account lie in his lightly satirical and witty portrayals of the crude North Carolina frontiersmen and his amusing tales and incidents which give his account the atmosphere of light (and "tall") fiction in many portions of the book.

Colonial Poetry

Early Colonial poetry is scarcely worth mentioning aside from its historical interest. There is certainly nothing about the quality or the inspiration of the verse that merits attention in a literary discussion. Of great fame historically and as a collector's item is _The Bay Psalm Book_ which ran into 70 editions by 1752. This book, in which an attempt was made by 3 authors to render the psalms into rhyme and meter so that they could be sung, is the first *book* to be published in America (first published in Cambridge in 1640). This collection today is considered one of the English language's best examples of bad poetry. A classic sample from this famed popular collection illustrates well the condition of poetry during the first 150 years of the history of our literature.

> Psalm CXXXVII
> The rivers on of Babilon,
>   there when wee did sit downe,
> Yea, even then wee mourned when
>   we remembered Sion.
>
> Our harp wee did hang it amid
>   upon the willow tree,
> because there they that us away
>   led into captivitee,
>
> Required of us a song, and thus
>   askt mirth us waste who laid,
> Sing us among a Sion song,
>   unto us then they said.
>
> The Lord's song sing, can wee, being
>   in stranger's land? then let
> lose her skill my right hand if I
>   Jerusalem forget.

Two Colonial poets: Bradstreet and Wigglesworth

Two names only need be remembered as representative of the age, those of Anne Bradstreet (1612-1672) and Michael Wigglesworth (1631-1715), both of whom were proudly hailed as among the greatest poets of all time by their fellow colonists in New England.

Anne Bradstreet, in spite of ill health and caring for a household of 8 children, found time to compose a considerable volume of poems which was published in London in 1650, a very brief version of the title being *The Tenth Muse Lately sprung up in America. Severall Poems, compiled with great variety of Wit and Learning, full of delight . . . By a Gentlewoman in those parts.* Anne showed learning and a good command of metrics but she had little of a poetic genius. Her subject matter covers a surprising range of material from classic discourse in heroic couplets* on *The Four Elements* to a theme as timely as *Upon the Burning of Our House.* In her simple themes of her own daily life and feelings, Anne is at her best, and at times is lyrically tender, but for the most part, she is bookish and cramped. She, however, represents the beginning of lyric poetry in America.

The most characteristic of all the Puritan poetry and the most popular poem of the entire age was Wigglesworth's *The Day of Doom* (1662). This is also one of the most terrifying poems ever written. It breathes fire and brimstone from every stanza and portrays for the sinner (apparently anyone who has committed the crime of being born) a yawning hell of blazing sulfur. It was written by a minister and a Harvard graduate, who is described as a gentle soul.

Cotton Mather characterized Wigglesworth as "a little feeble shadow of a man." Wigglesworth's book-length poem (if it may be characterized as poetry because it has a jingling rhyme) was the best seller of Colonial times and countless school children were required to memorize long passages of it. There were no doubts in the gentle Calvinist's mind as to the fate of adult sinners.

> They cry, they roar, for anguish sore,
>   And gnaw their tongues for horror.
> But get away without delay;
>   Christ pities not your cry;
> Depart to hell, there may you yell
>   And roar eternally.

He dealt more gently with children who die in the innocence of infancy, since they have little time either to sin or to repent.

> Yet to compare your sin with their
>   Who liv'd a longer time,

> I do confess yours is much less,
>   Though every sin's a crime.
> A sin it is, therefore in bliss
>   You may not hope to dwell;
> But unto you I shall allow
>   The easiest room in Hell.

Theological Prose

By far the bulk of Colonial writing and that which best characterizes our Puritan forebears is a long list of sermons, philosophical and theological tracts, and church histories which come out of the age. Worthless as literature, this bone-dry and almost fantastically absurd mass of prose is of worth today only to the historian and antiquarian.

The Mathers and Puritanism

Four generations of the Mather family of Boston, all ministers and all in the front line of theological writing, illustrate the gradual declining power of the original Puritanical theocracy in New England during the Colonial period. The famed Mathers and the dates of their lives are:

1. Richard (1596-1669)
2. Increase (1639-1723)
3. Cotton (1663-1728)
4. Samuel (1706-1785)

Their writings are theological for the most part and range from the most bombastic of argumentation to little homilies and essays, handbooks for preachers, and ecclesiastical history. Their work reflects, generation after generation, the desperate, but gradually unsuccessful, efforts to keep the American mind perpetually in the darkness of Puritan control.

The mass of writings of the Mathers revolves around the basic tenets of Puritanism: that all men are born in sin and deserve damnation, that man is naturally bad and that the political state governs all forms of social activity, including church-going as well as all other functions. To Puritanism, no religious freedom is permissible, and the State has the power to condemn the individual who thinks differently. The Puritans believed in the absolute sovereignty of God, and the leaders of the State were, of course, His representatives on earth and capable of deciding His exact will in the control of individuals in society. This, in essence, is the basic argument of the Mathers during 4 generations. Cotton, alone, produced over 500 books and pamphlets in his productive lifetime.

Jonathan Edwards (1703-1758)

The greatest American mind of the Colonial period was that of a rather quiet clergyman. Born in Connecticut, educated at Yale, Jonathan Edwards served as pastor of several churches and as missionary to the Indians. Shortly before his death, as a result of a smallpox inoculation, he was made president of Princeton College.

Edwards was, of all the divines of the period, the most susceptible to new ideas. His was an inquiring mind and he wrote voluminously throughout his life as he studied nature and read all the books he could procure on theology and metaphysics. He wrote some 36 books, all didactic* and scarcely belonging to the realm of aesthetic literature. He had a compact style and his sermons, as well as his philosophical argumentations, are clear and vivid and follow logical patterns of reasoning. His most famous book is *The Freedom of the Will* in which he argued profoundly that man does not act by virtue of a free choice but in accord with the will of God. A man can do what he wills, yes, but that will which decides his actions is not his own but that which the supreme being has planted in him.

Edwards was, of course, a strict Calvinist and he always operated, in his search for truth, within whatever limits Calvinist principles placed upon him. But Edwards did stand in a transition period between the old Puritan stand and the new and more liberal American thinking to come. He was far from being modern, as his ideas of an avenging and angry God show in his *Sinners in the Hands of an Angry God* (1741):

> The God that holds you over the pit of hell, much as one holds a spider or some loathsome insect over the fire, abhors you and dreadfully provoked. . . . If you cry to God to pity you, he will be so far from pitying you in your doleful case that he will only tread you under foot. . . . He will crush out your blood and make it fly, and it shall be sprinkled on all his garments so as to stain all his raiment.

Benjamin Franklin (1706-1790)

Despite the fact that New England and the Southern colonies had produced almost all of the writing in America during the period, it remained for Pennsylvania, a middle colony, to nurture the first true man of letters in the English portion of the New World.

Franklin was born in Boston but ran away to Philadelphia at the age of 17, where he found a liberal atmosphere more to his liking in the land of the Quakers. He devoted himself to the business of printing and engaged in politics, being elected to the Pennsylvania Assembly in 1736. Gradually Franklin added to his list of activities, becoming a true man of the world, a rare thing in a period noted for its provincialism and restricted views. He founded the American Philosophical Society, established the first subscription library in America, the first organized fire company, the second American magazine, and wrote extensively for his own press. He invented the Franklin stove and conducted valuable experiments with electricity and invented the lightening rod. All this time he was active in all phases of public life and held many positions, both in the Colonies and abroad, during his active life. He helped frame the *Declaration of Independence* and gained great prestige for the cause of independence through his scientific reputation and his simple diplomacy in France.

Franklin, the man

Franklin was a liberal, but he was not radical. He was a humanitarian who believed in thrift, hard work, and sobriety. His ideas were far from being flights of imagination. His mind was a veritable storehouse of cool common sense and his expression of his thoughts was clear, concise, and filled with simple logic and grace. Franklin stood solidly between Colonial and Revolutionary America, embodying the finest ideals of both periods. He retained the sobriety and sense of organization of the Puritans, without holding any of their narrow provincialism and their mad fiery form of worship. He had a simple frontier sense of individual worth, but he based his free ideas upon solid English law and not upon the romantic natural principles that were to tear France apart in its revolutionary period. Franklin represents for us the epitome of the American mind, with its practicality and its rationalism, that was to face into the future task of solidifying a new nation in the next century. Ben Franklin was one of the most versatile and well-balanced men that America had created in 2 centuries.

Franklin, the writer

One must not yield to a personal enthusiasm over this man to the extent of ranking him as a great writer. That he was not. He shows little creative originality. He was basically a journalist and had the clear, concise, and straightforward style of journalism. He could rework material and present it simply. His *Poor Richard's Almanac* (1732) is a rustic presentation of a miscellany of data, as well as the famous Franklin proverbs, none original but summations of similar expression from a multitude of world sources of the wisdom of the past.

Franklin wrote many papers on many varied subjects, some satirical and humorous, others purely expository. But one work (and that a relatively nonaesthetic one) will cause Franklin's name to endure forever in the history of literatures: his *Autobiography* (which carries his life to 1759). This work is a permanent classic and has become a model for autobiography on a world-wide basis to the present day. It has been intensely popular and no one has tried to calculate the number of editions which have been issued of this masterpiece of semiliterature, a treasure of pleasantly didactic prose. The work lacks elegance and imaginative richness of expression but it is clear and forceful and radiates a simple humorous charm. It embodies the secret of successful autobiography: it is the man himself, with his heart and genuine nature exposed in every line. It is the revelation of a fascinating personality, without literary garnish. It is the first "must" reading of American literature.

Young Ben, baptized Presbyterian in Boston, thus describes his first resting place in the Quaker capital:

> I have been the more particular in this Description of my Journey, and shall be so of my first entry into that City, that you may in your Mind compare such unlikely Beginnings with the Figure I have since made there. I was in my Working Dress, my best Cloaths being to come round by Sea. I was dirty from my Journey; my Pockets were stuff'd out with Shirts and Stockings; I knew no Soul, nor where to look for Lodging. I was fatigued with Travelling, Rowing and Want of Rest. I was very hungry, and my whole Stock of Cash consisted of a Dutch Dollar and about a Shilling in Copper. The latter I gave the People of the Boat for my Passage, who at first refus'd on Account of my Rowing; but I insisted on their taking it, a Man being sometimes more generous when he has but a little Money than when he has plenty, perhaps thro' Fear of being thought to have but little. . . . Then I walked up the Street, gazing about. . . . I walk'd again up the Street, which by this time had many clean dress'd People in it who were all walk-

ing the same Way; I join'd them, and thereby was led into the great Meeting House of the Quakers near the Market. I sat down among them, and after looking round awhile and hearing nothing said; being very drowsy thro' Labour and want of Rest the preceding Night, I fell fast asleep, and continu'd so till the Meeting broke up, when one was kind enough to rouse me. This was therefore the first House I was in or slept in, in Philadelphia.

Chapter II

REVOLUTION AND FOUNDATION
OF THE REPUBLIC (1765-1810)

By 1760 the Colonies had a population of about 1,600,000, two-thirds of which had been born in America. Into this new breed of men had gone many racial strains: English, French, Dutch, Swedish, Scotch, Irish, and German. More and more this new man thought of himself as an American, independent and liberty-loving, and less and less as a foreign individual or as a British subject.

HISTORICAL AND CULTURAL NOTES

The New American Ideals

During the Colonial period the elements which divided the colonies, one from the other, and contributed to the marked provincialism in the various societies were the outstanding features that served to identify the settlements and to keep them safely within the British influence. But the growing individualism and feeling for liberty that the frontier life engendered, combined with the dawdling and repressive colonial policies of George III and Parliament to give the American colonists a common cause upon which to join forces and to leave aside local prejudices and provincial shyness. The colonists, north, south, and middle, joined gradually into 2 common causes which succeeded in welding them into a common ideal for future greatness: independence from England and the founding of an American Republic "conceived in Liberty and dedicated" to the ideals of a new concept of freedom and democracy among the nations of the world. All the self-reliance, hardy endurance, and love of freedom of the 150-year struggle against a wilderness was now to be turned slowly to a common future. The American colonists had reached their Heroic Age* and it unrolled in 3 phases: the war itself, the establishment of national political unity, and the expansion into the West. American conversation, oratory, reading, and writing met on a common ground: politics.

The Historical Events

The period from 1765 to 1810, in our history, roughly divides itself into 2 parts: the Revolution (1765-1783) and the foundation of the Union (1783-1810). Although discontent and distinct rumblings of a revolutionary spirit were heard in the colonies as early as 1760, it was the Stamp Act of 1765 which brought the condemnation of British policy into open discussion and action in America. The battle cry of "taxation without representation" rose on every side and led to a series of events (including the Boston Massacre of 1770 and the Boston Tea Party of 1774) which culminated in actual fighting at Lexington and Concord in April of 1775.

Every American student is thoroughly familiar with the campaign from the famed Battle of Bunker Hill (June, 1775), through Trenton (1777), Burgoyne's surrender at Saratoga, and the hardships of the 1778 winter at Valley Forge, to the defeat of Cornwallis at Yorktown in 1781. In the political arena, our famed assemblages and documents are equally known: the first Continental Congress in 1774, leading to the second meeting in 1775 and the signing of a _Declaration of Independence_ on July 4, 1776. The Articles of Confederation in 1781 loosely held the colonies together after the fighting until, finally, the document was drawn which gave the world notice of American independence, the Treaty of Paris in 1783.

Then came the period of the painful and the slow series of compromises which led to the formation of a stable union of diverse elements, no longer united by the common desire to throw off the foreign bonds of colonial control. From 1783 to 1788 it was touch-and-go for the ideal of union, as provincial jealousies came again into the fore in many men's minds. But under the influence of the orators and writers and the strong political personalities like Washington, Hamilton, Franklin, and Samuel Adams, a federal constitutional convention was convened in 1787 at Philadelphia. By 1810, Washington was the capital of the new nation, all the original colonies had come under the federal Constitution, and new states were being admitted almost yearly. Exploration and scouting expeditions (such as that of Lewis and Clark) had penetrated deeply into the western territory. The United States of America was now prepared and eager to create a culture of its own that would be independent, yet would incorporate the best thought, forms, and imagination of the great world contributions of contemporary times and of the past. There was little of the backward look into the barren production and the narrowness of principles of the Colonial age. In 1810, the new nation had as yet produced little of aesthetic value, but the seeds of great cultural achievement were present, and more important, the spirit of an independent, hopeful people of vision and enthusiasm was present.

REVOLUTIONARY WRITING AND LITERARY BEGINNINGS

The writing of the turbulent years of the Revolution was an outpouring of deep conviction, filled with varied and rich coloring of the spirit of liberty and of the controversies of the various elements of political conviction in the times. Most of it is oratory or material suitable for propaganda. During a 25 year period, from 1765-1790, the presses of America were pouring forth a flood of patriotic pamphlets, essays on government and the rights of man. Poetry mainly took the forms of fiery satires* in the English neoclassic* manner and eulogistic-patriotic epics*, songs, and ballads* in praise of the new land and its blessings. The style of the prose was clear, laden with patriotic fervor and moral earnestness. Little of this mass of writing has survived because of its literary value, but it stands as an invaluable chapter in the formation of a national unity and a free atmosphere in which artistic literature could be produced.

Gradually, mid all this outpouring of patriotic fervor, appeared hopeful threads of aesthetic value. The dry theological argumentations of the Colonial period were gone from popular favor. The new writings (though still hovering just beyond the fringes of artistic production) did show a concern for the American scene and were building up a body of ideals for greatness in literature. The mass of patriotic verse produced in the last years of the century was read eagerly by increasing numbers of the public and there began to appear writers who lived mainly by the products of their pens.

And slowly, during the early years of the union, drama and

the novel, virtually proscribed throughout the period of Colonial settlement, began to appear in the major cities. Drama, in theme, was patriotic and American; in form, it followed closely the neoclassic English drama of Goldsmith and Sheridan. The novel began its career in American literature, based closely upon the models of the sentimental* and of the gothic* fads that had been so highly popular in English society for half a century. By the end of the 18th century some 35 American novels had been published. These works, highly sentimental and morally didactic, were written both by men and women and were devoured eagerly by the ladies of the age, despite the dire warnings of their evil effects upon the mind and the condemnations of them that were heard from the pulpits and from the more sober intellectual centers.

Until a decade of the 19th century had passed, little had yet appeared of permanent value in the new nation. But American writers were freed from the shackles of the past and their products were being consumed by growing numbers of readers, learning slowly to desire and to demand aesthetic satisfaction and intellectual stimulation from this new pastime of reading. Demand for literature was at last sufficient to call forth the literary geniuses who hovered just over the horizon in American letters. A genuine and an artistic American literature was about to begin.

TYPES OF REVOLUTIONARY WRITING

Political Prose

The first period of revolutionary fervor produced a great deal of oratory, fiery and enthusiastic. It was a period of pamphleteers and speech makers. A few names which every American remembers from this period of remonstrance and challenge (1760-1776) are: James Otis, whose _Speech Against Writs of Assistance (1761)_ set off a chain of denunciatory expression against British abuses; John Dickinson, a conservative who pleaded for conciliation in cautious, cultivated prose; Samuel Adams, an agitator who stirred the fires of revolt with his many pamphlets, finally acting as the leader in the Boston Tea Party; Francis Hopkinson, a scholar, who wrote many essays and satirical poems in the American cause.

Patrick Henry: master of fiery oratory

Certainly the best-known name today among these early orators is that of Patrick Henry, a gentleman of the Southern frontier, whose burning oratory did much to precipitate the active phases of the Revolution. Fearless and passionate, gifted with a natural power of projection of expression, Henry hurled his masterful and ardent phrases in speech after speech. The famed peroration to his _Speech on Liberty (1775)_ has provided the world with its most quoted phrase on the subject of liberty.

> It is vain, sir, to extenuate the matter. Gentlemen may cry, "peace, peace!"—but there is no peace. The war is actually begun! The next gale that sweeps from the north will bring to our ears the clash of resounding arms! Our brethren are already in the field! Why stand we idle? What is it that gentlemen wish? What would they have? Is life so dear, or peace so sweet, as to be purchased at the price of chains and slavery! Forbid it, Almighty God! I know not what course others may take, but _as for me, give me liberty or give me death!_

Thomas Paine (1737-1809)

During the war years no writings had a greater reading public than those of Thomas Paine who, until 1774, was an officer and a loyal subject of England. Paine had come into contact with the American cause through Franklin. Once in America he became editor of the _Pennsylvania Magazine,_ not yet in favor of independence. However, in January of 1776, he published _Common Sense,_ a stirring pamphlet in favor of a complete break with England. He continued throughout the war to issue his series of pamphlets, called _The Crisis,_ timely discussions of the issues of the day and valuable contributions toward keeping the morale of the American forces at a high level. The opening phrase of the first issue, "These are the times that try men's souls" has become symbolic in American minds of the epic beginnings of the American republic.

After the war, the remainder of Paine's career was a checkered one. His _The Rights of Man (1791)_ was written in England, in defense of the French revolutionary cause. In France, he proved too moderate in his views and was thrown in prison by the Republic. There he wrote _The Age of Reason (1794-1796),_ attacking Christianity. He returned to America during Jefferson's administration and lost public favor because of his supposed atheism and his attacks upon Washington. Acclaimed as a hero during earlier days, Paine died in poverty, shunned by his fellow men.

Thomas Paine was the best of the political writers of the period. His style was clear, simple, direct, and witty. He knew how to develop his arguments so as to appeal both to the emotions and the mental capacity of his readers. He was saturated with the belief that men are good and all their institutions are bad. He opposed both organized religion and organized government as being corrupt and evil. He advocated that man should live more in accordance with natural law and avoid pinning his faith too strongly upon artificially created institutional systems. Paine was our first great political writer who combined intelligent argumentation with a strong appeal to emotion. His writings influenced greatly the leaders of both the French Revolution and those of the Spanish American wars for independence from Spain.

Writers for national unification

As soon as the battles with Britain were over, the real internal struggle began for the national union. Union, as we know it today, was beyond the wildest dreams of the men who had joined together in the cause against England. Each returning soldier thought only in terms of his home colony. In the unsteady days from 1781 until the Union was a functioning organization (roughly 1809 when Jefferson came to the presidency) a new body of political writing came forward to strengthen men's convictions in favor of the Constitution and to argue that the revolutionary dream of independence could lead logically onward to the creation of a powerful republican union. Most of the names of these writers are well known as our early national leaders. They were not professional writers but, by and large, they were among the best-educated men of the times and are convincing. They all are valuable sources for the ideas and ideals upon which our republic is founded. The principal names and their main contributions in written expression are:

George Washington (1732-1799) contributed a mass of state papers, letters, and speeches during his career. Much of this writing has literary, as well as historical, value. His _Farewell Address_ to the people of the United States (1796) is generally regarded as the best summation of this leader's political and social ideas for the nation. It is interesting to view Washington's ideas in regard to isolationism and the avoidance of "entangling alliances" with foreign nations in the light of today's ideals for world unity and peace in an atomic age.

John Adams (1735-1826) is famed as a writer of tender and revealing letters to his wife during the stirring years of crisis.

Thomas Jefferson (1743-1826) was the most scholarly of our early presidents. He was deeply grounded in the theory and practice of statesmanship. He wrote the *Declaration of Independence,* a literary accomplishment of the first order, in addition to its importance as our best-known national document. Jefferson's *Notes on Virginia* (1784) contain his basic political principles as well as much practical wisdom and beautiful descriptive passages on the natural setting of his home state.

James Madison (1751-1836) was the most closely connected with the *Constitution* of the early writers on the theory underlying the principles embodied in the document. He, in fact, made the first draft of the instrument which was presented to the convention and continued with some 30 of *The Federalist* papers in support of ratification of the framework by which our nation is governed.

Alexander Hamilton (1757-1804) is best known to us for his many contributions to *The Federalist.* Hamilton knew political writings from Aristotle through the latest theories of the contemporary European political leaders and philosophers. He brought all of this wide knowledge to bear on his explanations and defense of the provisions of the Constitution.

Hamilton's ideas are aristocratic; he believed (with Hobbes) that people are motivated by self-interest. He believed in and visualized enormous future industrial development for the country, and though he advocated control by the rich, he favored strict checks and balances upon excessive power and repressive controls by this group.

Hamilton was an excellent political essayist and possessed a clear and concise style. His arguments are logically developed and he leads the reader by a series of simply reasoned steps, in orderly and dignified prose, directly to the writer's conclusions.

Of the total of 85 papers which comprise *The Federalist,* Madison contributed 29, Jay accounted for 5, and Hamilton wrote 51. *The Federalist* is our most complete explanation of the political theory underlying the *Constitution.*

The Poetry of the Revolution

We have noted that the majority of the verse during Colonial times was devoted to Puritan ideas. During the Revolutionary and early national periods American verse showed a marked increase in quantity, a radical departure in subject matter, but very little improvement in aesthetic quality. Today the verse of this period seems rather careless, heavy, and unrefined. It is highly artificial and didactic. The principal inspiration for American poets was the neoclassic verse of the English Pope. But the American versifiers were not the skilled practitioners of artificiality that England possessed; they were weak imitators.

As the prose, most poetry was closely associated with the Revolutionary cause and was political in content. The few poets who departed from this theme were too ambitious. They tried bulky epic eulogies of the new land and their ideals for it. Most of this artificial and flowered imitation of the epic genre is very flat and boring reading for later generations, but in those epic days these poets were proclaimed as rivals in greatness to Milton and Homer.

Some of the poets produced a few poems that show feeling and lyrical promise. But usually these same poets soon swung over, in most of their verse, to political satire* or to highly artificial language, didactic purposes, and overwhelmingly ambitious themes.

The war produced many songs and ballads that live to recall for us the battle scenes, the heroes and brave deeds, and the desires and feelings of the Revolutionary soldier. Of these little ditties, some by the most famed poets of the times, the most enduring little jingle was written by an obscure Harvard student, Edward Bangs. _Yankee Doodle_ lives in our folk literature today to give us the flavor of this grand age in our national lore.

> Father and I went down to camp
>   Along with Captain Gooding
> And there we see the men and boys
>   As thick as hasty pudding.
>   (Chorus)
> Yankee Doodle, keep it up,
>   Yankee Doodle, dandy
> Mind the music and the step,
>   And with the girls be handy.

The Connecticut wits

The first literary group, or school, in America is also known as _The Yale Poets_ or _The Hartford Wits._ The term simply refers to a group of young college men of the 18th century, most of them from Yale, who felt themselves linked by a common inspiration, that of establishing a classical standard for literature in America similar to that which prevailed among the followers of Pope and Samuel Butler in England. The group, further, took inspiration from the early-century residence in America (1729 to 1731) of one George Berkeley, an eminent English scholar and philosopher who had predicted a golden age for American poetry. He had stated that the poetic muse was weary in the Old World atmosphere and was eager to seek the freshness and innocence of this new land of exotic nature and human virtue. These young students determined to make Berkeley's dream come true. There were few formal meetings; it was no club. But Hartford, Connecticut, became the center of the most eminent of some ten or a dozen names which come to us through their popularity in Revolutionary times. From this Hartford group 3 poets deserve to live in our memory, not because they are truly great poets, but because they represent the first concentrated awakening in American intellectual life and the first true effort to establish literary standards for our aesthetic production. It is a pity that the standards which they adopted for their work were imitated and artificial ones and that their vision was so overly ambitious.

John Trumbull (1750-1831) became the most popular poet of the Hartford Wits. After graduation, he became a tutor at Yale and wrote his first long satiric poem in imitation of Pope and filled with classical allusions, by which the poet demonstrated his deep knowledge of Greek and Latin epic masterpieces. His _The Progress of Dulness_ is a satire on the shallow and impractical education being offered to young ministers and women. In its 3 cantos, the poem laboriously follows the misadventures of Tom Brainless, Dick Hairbrain, and Miss Harriet Simper.

Trumbull's most famous poem is _McFingal_ (1782), a burlesque epic about a windy Tory squire who fancies himself a great orator and a power in Colonial politics. He winds up in all sorts of ridiculous situations in his stubborn persistence in following the Tory cause in spite of the overwhelming defeats and disasters which the British cause is receiving at the hands of the Revolutionary patriots.

America's epic poets

Timothy Dwight (1752-1817) and Joel Barlow (1754-1812), both of the Hartford group, wrote the 2 most ambitious poems in our literature, book-length poems of epic sweep, aiming at the magnitude and the grandeur of the work of Milton, Vergil, and Homer. Both poems miss epic grandeur for the same reasons; they are unnatural and monotonous. Both poets attempted their long efforts in the rimed couplets* of Pope. The style of both epics resolves into bombastic and rhetorical effects; little about them seems inspired or natural.

Dwight's effort is a biblical epic called *The Conquest of Canaan* (1785), based on the wars of Joshua, from the bloodiest of the Old Testament books. His hero is made to assume superhuman powers for the destruction of his enemies. Dwight's Joshua mows down his foes with merely a glance from his fierce eyes.

> Like two red flames his vivid eye-balls glow,
> And shoot fierce lightenings on th' astonish'd foe;

Dwight's 9,672 lines contain poetic excellencies but they are hard to find for the modern reader.

Barlow's 11 long books of *The Columbiad* (1807) is an expansion of his earlier *The Vision of Columbus* (1787). Barlow has Hesper (definitely a Western spirit) conduct the aged Columbus from prison and shows him a vision of the glories of the New World and the promising future of the young republic. In Barlow's day he was acclaimed as a rival to the greatest poets of all time; today we look upon *The Columbiad* as one of the unique curiosities of our literary heritage.

Barlow is better known to modern readers for his charming mock-epic* piece, *Hasty Pudding* (1792). Here he treats in glowing humorous epic grandeur nothing more serious than cornmeal mush.

The century's greatest poet

Philip Freneau (1752-1832) is America's first poet of real promise. He was born of French Huguenot extraction in New York City. After graduating from Princeton in 1771, he spent some time as a sailor, being captured and held aboard a British prison ship for 2 months during one of his voyages. Off and on during his adventurous and stormy life he returned to the sea for peace of mind. When he was ashore in America he wrote poetry, edited *The Freeman's Journal* in Philadelphia, took part in bitter political discussions, and stirred up considerable dissension as a result of his extreme pro-French sympathies and his deism.

Freneau had the temperament of a poet but too often allowed his fiery nature and his intense hatred of everything British to lead him away from his poetic ideals into the popular and bitter satire of the day. His was a poetic temperament in an extremely unpoetic age, an age of wars and readers of newspapers and political discussion. He gradually grew to have a contempt for democracy and a people who did not appreciate his nature lyrics, but who went wild in praise of and paid well for his lampooning satire.

> Expect not in these times of rude renown
> That verse like yours will have the chance to please;
> No taste for plaintive elegy is known
> Nor lyric ode—none care for things like these.

When he could no longer endure residence with his satire-loving fellow citizens he would embark upon another voyage.

> No pleasure on earth can afford such delights
> As the heavenly view of these tropical nights:
> The glow of the stars, and the breeze of the sea,
> Are heaven—if heaven on ocean can be.

Freneau was an American preromantic poet and utterly alone in an age which could not appreciate his talent. His lyric bent was largely stifled in an unfriendly environment and the necessity to earn his living on its terms and, with his fiery temper, these things caused him to grow slowly more bitterly resentful and morose. But he was not of a type to suicide; he lived until 1832 and died in a blinding snowstorm.

Freneau's best verse

Few of Freneau's poems are polished masterpieces but in many of his lyrics of nature and his verse written under the influence of the sea and the tropical isles he visited on his voyages show clearly that Freneau wasted most of his talents in a long lifetime. He had the capabilities to become one of our great poets. The clash between his nature and his environment let his poetic genius show through his claptrap verse very seldom.

But the little that we see of his better efforts leads us to the conviction that Freneau was our first romantic poet. His *The Wild Honeysuckle* (1786) is a finished nature lyric*. Like the English Crabbe, Cowper, Burns, and Blake, he was an isolated romantic, years before a public was of a temper to appreciate poetic expression of a true individual feeling for the beauties of nature.

> Fair flower, that dost so comely grow,
> Hid in this silent, dull retreat,
> Untouched thy honied blossoms blow,
> Unseen thy little branches greet:
> > No roving foot shall crush thee here,
> > No busy hand provoke a tear.
>
> By Nature's self in white arrayed,
> She bade thee shun the vulgar eye,
> And planted here the guardian shade,
> And sent soft waters murmuring by;
> > Thus quietly thy summer goes,
> > Thy days declining to repose.
>
> Smit with those charms, that must decay,
> I grieve to see your future doom;
> They died—nor were those flowers more gay,
> The flowers that did in Eden bloom;
> > Unpitying frosts, and Autumn's power
> > Shall leave no vestige of this flower.
>
> From morning suns and evening dews
> At first thy little being came:
> If nothing once, you nothing lose,
> For when you die, you are the same;
> > The space between, is but an hour,
> > The frail duration of a flower.

The Beginning of Drama

The production of plays was virtually unknown throughout the Colonial period. In all the Puritan-controlled areas any tendency to represent ideas or fancy through pantomime was immediately taken to be the work of Satan and the consequences were harsh. In the more tolerant Southern colonies there were few cities or groups of sufficient concentration to warrant much production of drama*. There are reports of English plays being performed by professional companies in Williamsburg, Virginia, as early as 1715, in New York in 1732, in Charleston, South Carolina, in 1734, and in Philadelphia as early as 1749. The war years brought a renewed ban on theaters and no relaxation is known until 1787 in Philadelphia. In Boston, no play was produced officially until 1791.

When American drama did come, it was historical in theme and reflected the patriotic spirit of Revolutionary times. The early native drama was highly didactic and has little literary value. Some titles of early plays are sufficient to give an idea of their content: *Ponteach, or The Savages of America* (1766), *The Battle of Bunker Hill* (1776), *The Death of General Montgomery* (1777).

"The Contrast"

The first comedy by an American to be performed by a professional company was *The Contrast* (1787) by Royall Tyler (1757-1826). It was presented in New York and ran some 12 performances. The play was considered a success and was published some 4 years later.

The Contrast is a satire on manners and devotes its 5 acts (in prose) to a *contrast* between Colonel Manly, a handsome and devoted American officer, and Dimple, who is a highly affected and comic Englishman.

Early American Romance

America had no novel* of its own before 1789. The novel was classed with drama as one of the sure paths to perdition. There is much evidence, however, that English romances were bootlegged into various sectors of the colonial "female" society and were being devoured avidly as far north as Boston. The course of the souls of these undercover readers of the sentimental romances, which had been flooding English feminine society for half a century, has not been determined.

In the Southern colonies, and particularly in Philadelphia, certain English books were not considered novels. The criterion for the novel seems to have been largely whether the clergy liked to read the books. Richardson's *Pamela* (the first English novel, 1740) was considered a book of moral instruction and was reprinted by Franklin, the first novel published in America. Other early American reprints of English books included *Robinson Crusoe, Rasselas, The Vicar of Wakefield,* and the works of Sterne. All these had had wide circulation by 1775.

Early feminine novelists of America

The first American novel was published at Boston in 1789. It was called *The Power of Sympathy: or, the Triumph of Nature; Founded in Truth,* written in the form of letters, in imitation of the English Richardson's work. The author was Mrs. Sarah Wentworth Morton, who described herself as "A Lady of Boston." This tearful and highly exemplary-proclaiming tale of sex claimed to be founded on truth and apparently this was so. A Boston scandal of the day had involved a prominent husband who had seduced his wife's sister who had come to visit the family. The sister had suicided, following the birth of her illegitimate baby. Despite the novel's apparent revelation of "fact," the book was immediately suppressed officially.

The Power of Sympathy set the tone for other late 18th century romances. They were all of the sentimental or the Gothic types, so popular also among the ladies of London. They loudly proclaimed their purposes of giving moral instruction, particularly in regard to the dangers of "seduction." The heroine of Mrs. Morton's novel, in her death agony, loudly proclaims:

> "O SEDUCTION! how many and how miserable are the victims of thy unrelenting vengeance! Some crimes indeed cease to afflict when they cease to exist, but SEDUCTION opens the door to a dismal train of innumerable miseries."

All the early American novels were sad in their lurid revelation of the consequences of unwise love.

The second novel to have sensational popularity in America was *Charlotte Temple* (1790), written by an English lady, Mrs. Susannah Haswell Rowson, who had lived her early life in America as the daughter of a British officer. This new tale of seduction and horrible villainy and of a tearful and wronged heroine was a best seller for half a century. It is said to have sold 25,000 copies to the ladies of the new republic within a few months. Mrs. Rowson returned to America and conducted fashionable schools for the moral instruction of young ladies for the last 40 years of her life. She wrote 7 more novels.

Another well-read romance of the same type, which passed through 13 editions, was *The Coquette* (1797) of Mrs. Hannah Webster Foster.

These tales, always proclaiming their "truth" and "high moral" purposes, became a fad which could not be stemmed by the wave of indignation against them in the pulpits, schools, and presses of the states. The ladies of the new states devoured every new issue of the sentimental tale and impatiently awaited the next until well into the 19th century, hoping that it would be more luridly "truthful" and "morally" stimulating than the last. The failure of the attempts to discourage the craze is well illustrated by these words taken from the Boston *Monthly Anthology* (an issue of 1805), in which the editors felt the necessity to review a new novel just off the presses. The novel (about the thirty-fifth up to this time) was *The Gamsters; or Ruins of Innocence; An Original Novel Founded in Truth,* by Caroline Matilda Warren of Boston.

> Among the ephemerae of this species that continually flit from the press and expire, this is unquestionably the most puny. It appears to have been conceived by an intellect in a state of stagnation. . . . The avidity with which it was run after by the town the moment it was hatched reminded us of Sir Joseph Banks in the pursuit of a butterfly. . . . In what way the ladies have been infected by this vermin we confess ourselves unable to determine, for it appears on examination not only too inanimate to buzz but too insignificant to sting. . . . As we experience no particular exultation in swinging a club to dislocate a flea, we resign this minimus—to be empaled on a pin for the scrutiny of the curious.

The sentimental novel from England had conquered feminine America in the first years of independence.

Novelist of mystery and horror

The Gothic romance of wild and improbable incidents gained popularity in England about mid-century with such thrillers as Walpole's *The Castle of Otranto* (1764). This type of superficial tale of crowded incidents of horror and suspense usually had a grain of historical basis, but its chief claim to fame was its racing narrative, with weird and exaggerated happenings succeeding each other with astonishing rapidity. These thrilling tales achieved popularity in America at about the same time that the sentimental novels were flourishing in favor. The Gothic school in England greatly influenced our first serious novelist, *Charles Brockden Brown (1771-1810)*.

Brown was a frail youth from a Quaker family. He studied for the law but soon deserted this career to take up writing as a profession. His first writing, aside from some scattered poems, was a pamphlet entitled _The Dialogue of Alcuin_ (1797), which vigorously argued for women's rights.

"Wieland," Brown's major novel

Brown was very impressed with the English Gothic novels, and their influence is strongly present in the novels which constitute his major production.

In 1798 he wrote _Wieland,_ usually conceded to be his best effort in the novel. The story concerns a cultured family of Germans who settled near Philadelphia. The story is told years later by Clara Wieland, who relates that her father was a religious fanatic who died mysteriously, with his clothing in flames from, as it was believed, internal combustion from the inner fires that were searing his soul. The mother died very shortly after the father's death.

Young Wieland, married to a beautiful girl and with a growing family of lovely children, gradually grows more and more superstitious and seems to have inherited his father's religious zeal. For a while things seem to be going smoothly with the Wielands. They are strongly attached to a young stranger named Carwin. But soon Wieland becomes obsessed by the supernatural voices which he hears. Finally a voice calls to him to kill his beautiful wife and daughter. Thinking it is the voice of God, Wieland obeys. He is imprisoned in a madman's cell.

Clara also heard voices as she becomes more and more involved with Carwin, an inveterate prankster. Eventually it is revealed that he is a ventriloquist. His influence had been strong over both Wieland and his sister. About this time Wieland appears, having broken out of prison. He plans to kill Clara and their friend, Henry Pleyel. He learns that Carwin had provided him with his first experiences with the mysterious voices as a prank. Realizing that his superstitious fanaticism had led his weakened brain to project him into imagining the voices that had commanded him to kill his loved ones, Wieland plunges a knife into his throat and dies.

Years of tribulation pass for Clara before she at last knows peace. Eventually she is able to renew her association with Carwin. They marry and hope to find happiness in spite of their memories.

Brown's _Ormond_ (1799) and _Arthur Mervyn_ (1799-1800) are likewise filled with scenes of disease and horrible death.

Brown and the American setting

Edgar Huntley; or Memoirs of a Sleep-Walker (1799) is the novel in which Brown shows his descriptive powers to best advantage. The book has many excellent portrayals of a wild and exotic natural setting. Brown introduces the American Indian into this novel and gives many incidents from Indian life and warfare. His savages are ruthless and cruel but scarcely realistic. They are brave but, of course, no match for white fighters. His descriptions of animals and plant life are vivid and accurate. Brown, as a main theme for this rambling storehouse of early Americana, is concerned with a study of crimes which can be committed by a person while in a state of somnambulism.

Brown's *Clara Howard* (1801) and *Jane Talbot* (1801), in epistolary form, are rather weakly constructed love plots. They lack the sensationalism of his earlier novels and return to his early theme of feminism.

Estimate of Brown's novels

Brown is our best fiction writer until Poe, Cooper, Hawthorne, and Melville. He is certainly the best of the first 200 years of our literature. His descriptive passages are vivid and well managed. He was weak in structural technique and somewhat dull and stilted in his rather pompous style. He was greatly influenced by the Gothic romance in his scenes of horror and by Richardson in his seduction scenes and his treatment of feminine psychology, but he added something that made him definitely a true precursor of the greater novelists to come, a true appreciation for the American setting, the strongest element in his works. His descriptions of woodland scenery and life are as powerful as any to be found in Cooper.

Descriptive Prose of the Frontier

The mountain chains to the west had seemed insurmountable barriers to the American colonists for a century and a half. But, suddenly, about the close of the French and Indian War (1754-1760), hardy farmers had pushed westward to the foothills and migrations of wagons and foot-weary pioneer families poured through the gaps and passes of the Alleghenies to carve out a new life from the wilderness beyond the horizon. The populations of Tennessee, Kentucky, and Ohio grew by leaps and bounds. A new breed of American was being born.

Two European-born writers have left us most interesting accounts of the rural backland setting and of the new western frontier life and types: the scout, the hunter, the trapper, the farmer, the Indian fighter, the frontier mothers and their children. One was a Frenchman, *St. John de Crèvecoeur* (1735-1813) and the other was a Scotsman, *Hugh Henry Brackenridge* (1748-1816).

Crèvecoeur, in a very delightful and refined prose, gave a Frenchman's view of upper New York and the backlands of Pennsylvania in his series of charming letters, known as *Letters from an American Farmer* (1782).

The far western frontier is equally well described for us by Brackenridge in his *Modern Chivalry* (1792-1815), a very witty and satirical account in which a fictional Captain Farrago and his servant, Teague O'Regan, go wandering through the American countryside and over the mountains into the wild west. There is much truth and much fiction in this account.

As preparation for a proper enjoyment of much of the great body of Western frontier literature to come in the 19th century, a reading of these two accounts of life among the self-reliant and hardy back country folk is highly desirable. Both men possessed charming prose styles and one captures what the other misses in the colorful realities of the western fringes of early America. Crèvecoeur is aristocratic and sentimental; Brackenridge approaches his subject with tongue in cheek and presents his human comedy with all the exaggeration and gusto that Mark Twain was to perfect in his treatments of western and midwestern life. Both men were interested in manners, and the combination of the two accounts gives the reader both the uncolored realistic view and a broadly tinted, semifictional study of early life on the frontiers of an expanding America.

1607-1810: The Best Writing

As has been stated earlier, the first 200 years of our literary history produced little that is great as artistic literature. The values of the writing of that long formative period are present for Americans but they must be sought in other than the sphere of purely aesthetic considerations.

The literary cream of this mass of early writings seems to consist of 3 elements discussed in our first 2 preliminary chapters: the charm and unaffected qualities of the *Autobiography* of Benjamin Franklin and the artistic promise present in the works of the two greatest literary figures of the 2 centuries: Philip Freneau, the poet, and Charles Brockden Brown, the novelist.

Chapter III

RISE OF AMERICAN
ROMANTICISM (1810 to 1865)

In 1810 the United States census showed a population of approximately 7,240,000. By 1815 there were 18 States and four Territories; New York City now had 100,000 inhabitants. The purchase of the vast Louisiana Territory from France in 1803 had pushed the horizon for expansion far to the west. The Lewis and Clark Expedition of 1804-1806 had shown the feasibility of settlement of the north and the west. Already, by 1810, close to a million of the population of the new nation had poured through the southern gaps of the Alleghenies, and the central and southern areas of the country were being tamed for civilization.

HISTORICAL AND CULTURAL NOTES

The final major step in assuring doubters that the Constitution was working and that a new independent nation had risen to take its place beside the old and seasoned powers of Europe was the second war with England in 1812. By its end in 1815, the new United States stood on its own feet at last, freed from fear of foreign domination. Time now to turn attention wholeheartedly to growth and consolidation of its parts. Time now to expand and to look to a development of a culture of its own, to join the world stream but not to give up its native self-reliance and individuality, so recently tested and found strong in the stresses and strains of the post-Revolutionary quarter of a century.

The Historical Parade of Events

Events important to the internal prosperity and security of the new nation and leading to a solid basis for foreign respect for the American flag succeeded each other rapidly in the years following the election of James Monroe to the presidency in 1817. The 8 years of his tenure he, himself, called "the era of good feeling." And it was the beginning of a period of stirring national pride and patriotism.

This was a period of rapid expansion, both in population and in territory settled. Seven of our states were admitted to the Union in the 9 years from 1812 to 1821. Immigrants from all over the world poured into the new land and pushed the frontier rapidly westward.

It was a period of taking advantage of the opportunities to secure for the United States ample room to expand and freedom from fear that powerful European nations might become dominant forces in the Western Hemisphere. The Monroe Doctrine of 1823 warned Europe against the seizure of territory in the Americas, North or South. The annexation of Texas in 1845 and the War with Mexico in 1846-1847 paved the way for our present national boundaries. In 1847 the discovery of gold at Sutter's Mill sent a wave of settlers all the way to the west coast and California was admitted as a State in 1850.

It was an age of invention and preparation for industrial expansion. The growth of industry was slow except in a few of the eastern cities. Even by 1810 only 5 per cent of the population lived in cities of 8,000 or more. Throughout this first great national period most necessities were still grown or made at home. The move to take industry from a domestic plane to factory production began as early as 1790 with the establishment of a large cotton factory at Pawtucket, Rhode Island, but even as late as 1810, 90 per cent of clothing was still made at home. Luxuries, of course, all came from abroad. The major surge forward in industry was to wait until after the Civil War.

But invention was paving the way during this period.

    1794 Whitney's cotton gin.
    1807 Fulton's steam boat passes through the new Erie canal.
    1830 America's first passenger train.
    1834 McCormick reaper.
    1835 Morse invents the telegraph.
    1844 First telegraph line—Washington to Baltimore.

The Age's Major Hurdle to Progress

It was a period, also, of the building of future internal conflict, which finally brought civil war among the states. In 1815, 1,200,000 of the near 8 million population were Negro slaves. The importation of slaves had been forbidden in 1808, but the problem was already present and grew in importance as the balance of political power shifted with the admission of slave or nonslave states. The cause for abolition of slavery grew with increasing bitterness. The publication of Stowe's *Uncle Tom's Cabin* in 1852 fanned the fires. Incident followed incident until the Civil War broke out in 1861. With the end of the bitter conflict and Lincoln's assassination in 1865, the painful process of reconstruction occupied the years to 1870. By this time America's face was ready for another major change; a great era of industrial expansion took the place of the prior drive toward territorial expansion and the settlement of internal political and social conflicts.

Intellectual and Cultural Development

Aside from literature, other agencies for a distinct American civilization were taking shape in the first national period of our history.

Education

Prior to the Revolution, education was very largely a privilege for the upper-class rich. In Colonial times, especially in New England, public education was hardly "public"; it was church dominated, and instruction was almost exclusively confined to the imparting of dogma. In 1791, in Philadelphia, the Lancastrian system of public instruction was introduced, and in 1809 New York instituted public schools. All the new state constitutions were encouraged to provide for a system of public schools. By 1830 New York was giving public support to more than 1,000 schools.

On the higher levels, academies and colleges multiplied rapidly and the curriculum was expanded radically from the colonial emphasis on law and the ministry to cover sciences and liberal arts. By 1815 there were more than a dozen major colleges in the east, and by 1840 the western states had established numerous institutions, there being 48 in the Mississippi valley alone.

Newspapers, magazines, and books

The revolution and the interest in the political issues of the first years of the government had caused newspapers and magazines to flourish. The public consumption of reading material of this level was great by 1800. By 1820 there were 578 active newspapers in the country and the quality of political journalism was generally high.

Periodicals and magazines on a cultural plane were slower in acquiring sufficient circulations to warrant more than initial issues. Many were established and expired after only a few issues before 1825. But by this date the new magazines were enjoying stable circulations and they spread westward rapidly with the advance of transportation facilities and the governmental encouragement in the form of reduced rates for carrying them. Subscriber groups supporting literary publications sprang up even in the western hamlets. By 1857, when the *Atlantic Monthly* was first published, the literary periodicals were beginning to prosper financially without subsidies.

The lack of copyright protection of an international nature discouraged our national literature during the period. American publishers were reprinting English books in cheap editions at will and the public was reluctant to buy works of American authors whose books were priced well above the English reprints in order to insure some small return for their efforts. Our first copyright law was passed in 1790 but there were no mutual agreements on an international basis until late in the 19th century which would limit the free reprinting of English books in this country.

Limited Development in the Arts

Notable native developments in the arts generally were confined almost entirely to the large cities of the east and to a very small group of the rich in this period. Architecture tended to remain on a very "classical" English pattern for homes of the rich and public buildings. Duncan Phyfe had become a famous name in early furniture but customers for his creations, of course, were hardly representative of the general population. Native painting was largely restricted to portraits of the wealthy or of public figures. Charles Wilson Peale was a famous early portrait painter. Native composition of music during the period lagged far behind European developments. There were early attempts at opera but none have survived as other than curiosities.

Public Demand for an American Literature

In the *Edinburgh Review,* issue of January, 1820, appeared an article by one Sydney Smith which echoed down through the century in America. Not many Americans were looking back into the Colonial period, but many now were being sharply critical of the low state of letters in America, always in comparison, of course, with England. Many Englishmen had previously expressed contempt of what one called American savagery, another named "the turbulent spirit of democracy," and still another qualified as "the spitting, gouging, drinking, duelling, dirking, swearing, strutting republicans." But now Smith launched a bombshell that was to show the futility of further words.

> In the four quarters of the globe, who reads an American book? or goes to an American play? or looks at an American picture or statue? . . . Literature the Americans have none . . . it is all imported. . . . Why would the Americans write books when a six weeks' passage brings them, in their own tongue, our sense, science, and genius, in bales and hogsheads. Prairies, steamboats, gristmills, are their natural objects for centuries to come. . . .

Rather than having the effect of setting off a storm of retaliatory remarks and angry protest, these and other bitter verbal pills from abroad were swallowed by American intellectuals. They knew that there was much truth in these statements and were prepared to admit it even to themselves. In the decade from 1820-1830 there began a searching analysis of the situation in America's literary magazines, college groups, and other gatherings of the best minds. A school of American literary criticism was forming and became active throughout the major population centers of the east, with writers for the *North American Review* leading the discussion. The growing American reading public joined these writers in the conclusion that the nation could not be said to achieve a true independence until a literature could be established which would command respect abroad. The fact that so many Americans sought their intellectual and aesthetic stimulation, as a matter of course, in cheap pirated editions of English books brought a sense of shame to many patriotic young students, among them boys of wealthy families such as Emerson, Lowell, Parkman, Ticknor, Longfellow, and Hawthorne. Young Hawthorne expressed a desire "to write books that would be read in England." (He was to produce books that would be read also in Siberia.) Within 20 years from Sydney Smith's famed denunciation of America's literary barrenness, England was reading the production of such American writers as Holmes, Prescott, Longfellow, Poe, Hawthorne, Cooper, Bryant, Whittier, Bancroft, and Emerson.

AMERICAN ROMANTICISM

When our first great period of national literature began, in the times somewhat vaguely linked with the era of shame and self-searching criticism that surrounded the remarks of Sydney Smith, the form and atmosphere for our first great artistic writings had already permeated our intellectual structure. It was but natural that American literary men should be allied with European romanticism*. In Europe the romantic revolt in literatures was a reaction against the rigidity in form and the unimaginative and unfeeling reason in treatment of themes that had prevailed during the previous period of neoclassicism* during all of the 18th century, and extending back into the 17th.

In America, our first great literary movements begin as the romantic revolt is at its height of productivity in England. In America our romantic movement is no revolt; it is our first genuine literature. Some anthologists and historians prefer to call this period an American renaissance for this reason (since the term "romantic" implies in European literatures a revolt against something "classical"). A further reason for using the term "renaissance"* in America is the argument that our upsurge of literary activity about this time follows a short period of barrenness since the efforts of Freneau and Brown. But "renaissance," in its generally accepted meaning, implies a revival or rebirth of something really great from the past. While the beginning of our national literature has greatness, it is to be admitted, it revives little that is great from our literary past to achieve it, nor does it have deep classical roots from an ancient Greek and Roman past.

This writer merely calls attention to this tendency to refer to this period (vaguely from 1825-1860) as an "American renaissance" in many school histories and anthologies of our literature. A survey of the more scholarly and profound studies of our literary heritage fails to show that the term is common among them. The disparity in the use of terms does not in the slightest affect the quality of the productions of the period; nor does it lessen or increase the aesthetic profit to be derived by a reading of them. It is of a quibbling unimportance. This writer will refer to the period as one of "romanticism," corresponding generally to the characteristics of the movement prevailing at the time in the older and established literatures and will attempt to introduce the elements which make our romantic movement (minus the idea of literary revolt) a particularly American form of the world attitude toward artistic material.

Neoclassicism and Romanticism Contrasted

Neither the terms *romanticism* nor *classicism* can ever be satisfactorily defined by rule-of-thumb characteristics nor by general terms since they are abstractions just as the terms *right* and *wrong*. Brief discussions in general terms cannot be precise; the best understanding of the terms can be derived from a wide and varied reading and study of the products which are considered the best resulting works written under the influence of the qualities present in these two contrasting attitudes of the human mind toward ideas and their expression. Moreover, the specific application of the terms in different literatures and different areas produces widely differing results in literary works because of local environments and circumstances.

Romanticism in literature is a tendency to seek an ideal aesthetic world in fancy and imagination and to express it in an individualized and sentimental form, appealing to the needs of the emotions more than to the reason. Romanticism therefore is a tendency toward inspiration and away from discipline (classicism) in the writer's approach to his materials. It is, further, a rebellion against whatever is orthodox and regulated; it is a rebellion against the past. Romanticism is a sum of qualities found in all literatures, in all epochs or places. It only varies in intensity, when contrasted with classicism present in writing at the same time. Both romanticism and classicism are simply abstract terms, used to measure the degrees of opposing tendencies in literary production. In general, the degree of inspiration (romanticism) or discipline (classicism) present in any particular epoch or literature may be determined on the basis of the presence of the following specific qualities:

ROMANTICISM	*versus*	CLASSICISM
1. emotional appeal	*instead of*	appeal to reason
2. the subjective point of view	*instead of*	the objective point of view
3. an individual approach	*instead of*	a normal and typical approach
4. dissatisfaction with the known	*instead of*	suspicion and horror of the unconventional and unknown
5. experimentation with musicality and color in expression	*instead of*	clear and ordered expression and form, a belief in beauty of measured precision
6. emphasis on feelings and emotional reactions	*instead of*	emphasis on content and idea
7. emphasis on the immeasurable and undetermined	*instead of*	emphasis on the measurable and the determined
8. importance of particular and individual thought	*instead of*	importance of universal thoughts and ideas
9. love of external nature in its wild and primitive state	*instead of*	love of man's accomplishments in taming and controlling the wild and rebellious in nature
10. rejection of tradition (except from earlier romantic periods—in particular primitive folk cultures, Renaissance developments or idealized historical associations)	*instead of*	acceptance of tradition (of earlier classical periods—particularly those of ancient Greek and Roman cultures)

This list of contrasting qualities might be continued indefinitely, but a list of any length would show the same general desire of the romantic to escape from reality which seems to oppress his aesthetic expression, and to experiment with an ideal more satisfying to the individual, and the contrasting fear of the classic to depart from known and tried norms of form and theme established by settled and prosperous aristocratic groups.

The 18th century had been one of enlightenment and classical thought throughout Europe. The social and political upheavals of the century's end resulted from the failure of classical thought to provide solutions for the inequalities and rifts in society brought on by industrialization and commercial prosperity and the increasing inequality in the distribution of their benefits. The romantic tendency spread like wildfire and resulted in revolutions and radical social reforms; in literatures it resulted in a dominant romantic tendency in the expression of thought. The romantic influence that swept into control of literature around 1800, with its insistence on individual viewpoints, has never died in world literatures. No literature has again been controlled by a new classic literary dictator of the power of a Pope, a Dryden, or a Johnson (in English literature). The accomplishment of the romantic groups is still with us in literature to an important degree.

The romantic revival in world literatures

The romantic movement (revival or revolt) was common to all world literatures in the period after 1800. England and Germany had isolated romantic developments during the 18th century, and in both countries the movement burst into full bloom shortly before the end of that century. Although France and Italy showed some signs of romantic spirit in their literatures prior to the turn of the 19th century, they participated wholeheartedly in the movement only well after the first years of the 19th century. They were both highly influenced by English and German romanticism. Spain reacted very late, largely due to the invasion of Napoleon and the tyrannical rule of Fernando VII. The liberals, who became Spain's romantic writers, were in exile until Fernando died in 1833. Both the new United States and the equally new Spanish American republics joined the world flow of romantic literature, but tardily. And it is to be noted that the height of the movement passed much sooner in Germany and England than it did in France and Italy. In Spain and the Americas romantic production continued unabated until well after mid-19th century. In Spanish America, major romantic writings were produced until very late in the century. And in the United States, romantic idealism in literature declined very slowly until realism became the dominant tendency after 1870. And although other tendencies came into world literatures during the 19th century, the freshness, the vigor, the color, the originality and spirit, that came with the new wave of individualism in literature during the romantic period, have not gone out of writing to the present day.

Distinctions in American Romanticism

In the light of the above discussion of romanticism and the classical tendency it replaced in Europe it is easily seen that, prior to the post-Revolutionary period, America had had some meager influence from English neoclassicism in the scant and imperfect literature that was produced. It is also seen that the English preromantic tendencies of *sentimentalism* and the *Gothic* were widely spread throughout the early states by the importation of English novels and the production of imitations in the period around 1800. Philip Freneau, again, was an isolated romantic spirit before 1800, but he neither caused a movement nor did he fulfill his own promise because of the hostile environment in which he found himself. But in the few poems of his that we have, he shows all the individualism and lyric concern for nature of the early English romantic poets.

But, in America another 20 years were to pass before the demand for an independent literature would produce results in a generation of young writers, many of whom were not born when Brown died (1810) and Freneau had become morose and bitter and had turned his lyricism to invective and satire. The birth dates of our great writers to be discussed below bear this out.

> 1783 Washington Irving
> 1789 James Fenimore Cooper
> 1794 William Cullen Bryant
> 1796 William H. Prescott
> 1800 George Bancroft
> 1803 Ralph Waldo Emerson
> 1804 Nathaniel Hawthorne
> 1807 Henry Wadsworth Longfellow
> 1807 James Greenleaf Whittier
> 1809 Oliver Wendell Holmes
> 1809 Edgar Allen Poe
> 1812 Harriet Beecher Stowe
> 1817 Henry David Thoreau
> 1819 Herman Melville
> 1819 James Russell Lowell
> 1819 Walt Whitman

The first period of American romanticism represents the beginning of a national literature, the attempt to create a distinctive American literature, and its writers were highly influenced by English romanticism. Our literature began its first great cycle of important production with writers who lived and wrote in New York and Pennsylvania.

The second period of American romanticism (from about 1830 to the outbreak of the Civil War) centered in a New England school of writers.

Specific distinctions in American romanticism

While American romanticism followed, in general, the tendencies of the European movement, there are distinctions worthy of being observed, which give to our literature of the period a definite American flavor.

1. Here the movement had little evidence of being a surge of revolt against a neoclassic literary standard. The American writers wished to establish our national literature upon the basis of American self-reliance and independence with which the colonists had carved a civilization out of a virgin wilderness, had freed themselves from foreign domination, had founded a Union from diverse creeds and peoples, and had pushed expansion into a new primitive area to the West.

2. A major portion of American romantic writings directed the characteristic romantic surge of powerful emotion and passion toward the expression of individual pride and patriotism, thus making our writing highly national, full of local color and the folkloric elements of the times.

3. In England, many of the romantic passions were crystallized into expression directed toward the social injustices which followed in the wake of industrialization and the rise of factories. American romanticism found many of those characteristic romantic passions (mainly in Massachusetts) directed toward the cause for the abolition of slavery. Thus in America the political radicalism of English romanticism was largely absent, being replaced by an attack on a more fundamental human injustice.

4. American romantics found little in their country's past history to idealize and there was naturally no thought of directing attention toward the historical past of England (so thoroughly developed by Scott and other English novelists). Here the tendency toward idealization turned toward more contempo-

rary elements of American life: the Indian, the frontiersman, and the wilderness setting. When the mind of the American romantic did turn toward a more remote historical idealization, it turned toward continental Europe, and not England. The historical past of Spain was chosen by several leading romantics as a fit subject for development (notably Irving, Ticknor, Prescott, and Longfellow). In this aspect of the American movement, it is obvious that our writers were following the influence of German romanticism, among whose writers the historical and folk past of Spain was a favorite theme.

5. Perhaps the most distinctly unusual direction which American romanticism took was the development of our literature of transcendentalism* in New England (after 1830). This form of philosophical idealism reached America from Europe, having developed from the philosophies of Kant in Germany. Its influences, direct from German sources, and through English writers such as Coleridge and Carlyle, had a profound influence in New England. Transcendentalism, in essence, developed in the ideals of an intense individual freedom of belief. It taught an unwavering faith in the worth of individual man and reliance on the goodness of his nature to guide him, intuitively, into the paths of right behavior and into the development of the transcending values of his personality. The wholehearted acceptance of this idealistic way of life in many of the writings of the second romantic period gave the American movement its most distinctive element of revolt against restrictive influences of the past. Here the revolt was against a repressive, pessimistic, and mind-enslaving Puritanism. Characteristically, it was a New England movement, and its writings almost entirely came from the authors of that area, but in the broader sense, it was an expression of the new American mind as it was developing throughout the nation. The self-reliance in action that was pushing the American pioneers to the Pacific coast was the same type of self-reliance which was being expressed in our romantic literature of such men as Emerson, Thoreau, Parker, and Whitman.

DIVISIONS OF AMERICAN ROMANTICISM

Sectional Literatures with Common Ideals

Despite the common and unifying tendencies toward a world swing to romanticism and toward a native nationalism, American writers in the period ending with the Civil War tended to fall into sectional groups with marked distinctions as to attitudes and the development of themes. We shall treat the period to 1865 in accordance with these sectional groupings, realizing that such arbitrary groupings are never hard-and-fast ones and with the understanding that, after 1810, the conscious attempt among all American writers was in the direction of the creation of a national literature worthy of the new Union.

While hardly a "renaissance," the literature of the period is a national one in its creative stage with few ties to a Colonial past except occasionally in subject matter. The chief literary ties during the whole period are in Europe, and especially in England. American literature of this period was not, and could hardly be, a thing in itself. It was yet an infant, struggling to cast off parental ties, but not yet capable of standing alone. The rebellious struggle is evident throughout the period. The early writers of the period had to depend very largely upon England for a larger reading public than they found in America. They imitated English models and tried, and occasionally succeeded, in being different. This violently pursued attempt to be different often, however, resulted in as much bad writing as did the opposing tendency to imitate blindly the English masters.

American literature was aiming toward maturity but it was, until late in the century, still an adolescent with occasional flashes of independent genius. This writer cannot, as have some overly enthusiastic and hyperpatriotic literary historians, avoid facts and state that an American literary miracle took place overnight. Young American literature was ready to grow up and it has done so in recent years, but, as in each of the new Spanish American republics to the south, it was a slow and normal separation from the mother literature and showed little real artistic greatness until the last years of the 19th century.

ROMANTICISM: THE NEW YORK GROUP

The New York group, known also by the name *Knicker-bocker**, from the use of the term by Washington Irving in his kindly historical satire of the Dutch in 1809, included the first names in American romanticism to achieve world notice. Thus New York City, from this early date in our national culture until the present, has enjoyed the distinction of being our chief center of artistic accomplishment. New York City also, from that time to the present, has been a cosmopolitan center in which many diverse artistic tendencies from the nation and from abroad met and mingled or pursued their separate ways side by side. The early romantic group, also, was hardly a literary "school" in that they brought to their creations diverse and scattered tendencies. New York City was simply the common center about which their activities revolved.

Washington Irving (1783-1859)

Many call Irving the first American romantic. This is, of course, a position to be disputed by the names of Philip Freneau and Charles Brockden Brown, who certainly should receive our designation as preromantics. They were romantics whose labors went almost unnoticed in their time, much as the works of Cowper, Burns, Crabbe, and Blake were redolent of romantic tendencies prior to the first acknowledged group of Wordsworth, Coleridge, Southey, and Scott.

Irving was from a wealthy merchant family. He was frail in health and spent most of his early years traveling and reading. He received a classical education and was directed toward a career in law. His delicate health caused his brothers to send him to the south of Europe for an extended tour. He spent 2 years, drinking in the varied aspects of the German and Spanish landscape. Upon his return, literature competed with his reading of law and his desire to pursue a literary career. He began to express himself in *Salmagundi,* a little literary periodical which was maintained by an inner family group, Washington and his brother William, and James Paulding, their brother-in-law. The periodical was abandoned after 20 issues. Irving, an indolent and spoiled young man of 23, had developed an imaginative and sensitive mind that would never be content with a legal career. He determined to pursue literature as a career, and his only struggle was with his own classical education. He remained a bachelor, a state in keeping with his indolence and his desire to pursue a leisurely and unfettered existence.

Irving's literary life

Irving's first major work was *A History of New York . . . by Diedrich Knickerbocker* (1809). The author had spent much of his youth in solitary wandering about the New York countryside and gathering data about the early Dutch settlers of the area. All his findings are fictionalized in this humorous extravaganza which is not to be taken seriously as history. This first book presents the delicately whimsical and satirical manner that was to characterize all of Irving's production. The "Knickerbocker History," purportedly by a "small elderly gentleman, dressed in an old black coat and cocked hat," was read with delight by everyone but the descendants of the Dutch settlers. who were offended by Irving's mocking parody.

Irving did little more writing until the family hardware business failed and he was forced to supplement his meager funds. He found himself in London when the sad news arrived. He immediately began writing feverishly and produced the first issue of his acknowledged literary masterpiece, _The Sketch Book_ (1819-1820). His whimsically comic tales and sketches enjoyed a tremendous popularity both in America and in England. His folk tales of the Dutch colonial settlers of upper New York have remained as American classics, particularly such tales as _Rip Van Winkle_ and _The Legend of Sleepy Hollow_ (193).

Irving continued to produce a book every two or three years to the end of his life. His biographies of Columbus, Goldsmith, and Washington, with his charming and carefully wrought style, were considered masterpieces in his day but are seldom read any more. His _Bracebridge Hall_ (1822) and _Tales of a Traveller_ (1824) are collections of humorous and fanciful miscellany, only slightly inferior to his earlier sketches and tales.

Irving's second most popular book of sketches and tales is _The Alhambra_ (1832), containing romantic legends of the past glories of the Moorish palaces of Granada, in Spain. In 1829 he had treated Spain also in his semihistorical _Chronicle of the Conquest of Granada_. His interest in Spain and her legendary past continued throughout his life. He was minister to Spain from 1842 until 1845, when he resigned to return to America and a quiet life at Sunnyside, his estate on the upper Hudson.

Irving's place in American letters

Irving worked with spurts of activity and long periods of inactivity. He had little creative imagination. He did not try for emotional depth in his writing but succeeded in skimming the surface of his subjects with a light, natural, and charming prose. His blend of the sentimental and the humorous is his saving grace as a writer. His production is fragmentary and his best work is to be found in the little sketches and tales scattered among his mass of writing. Particularly those pertaining to American legends will endure as foundation stones of a genuine American literature. Irving is the first notable writer of the short fictional tale with an American background. He was the first American writer to win European approval.

James Fenimore Cooper (1789-1851)

Cooper, like Irving, was as much at home in Europe as in America. In his personal life and varied literary career he was a man of many contradictions. His personality was a curious mixture of the aristocratic and the democratic. Before his life had ended, he succeeded in antagonizing both Europeans and Americans with his caustic writing. He experimented with every form of prose and produced pioneer American novels of at least 6 different varieties. There is little to be found that is really great in any of the some 40 books which he produced, but his 5 romances of the American frontier, _The Leatherstocking Tales,_ will live as foremost landmarks in the developement of our fiction.

The young Cooper

Cooper's father was a successful country squire and the aristocratic lord of countless acres of land in upper New York. He was a law unto himself and dominated everyone about him with the iron hand of a feudal baron. James inherited from him a massive physical frame and much of his irritable and determined disposition. Cooper entered Yale at the age of 13 and was dismissed in the third year. The self-willed and adventurous youth then found a way of life entirely to his liking. He joined the navy and for 3 years roamed the seas of the world. Home in 1810, he married Miss Susan De Lancey, the frail and beautiful daughter of an old loyalist family of New York.

Suddenly the Cooper adventurous spirit seemed completely domesticated, for he spent the next 10 years in the quiet occupation of a farmer and country gentleman. While reading a novel of English social life aloud to his wife one night he hurled the book from him in disgust, swearing that he could write better. With the encouragement of his wife, he produced his first novel, _Precaution,_ a cross section of English genteel society.| This stilted sentimental claptrap was a literary failure but it succeeded in arousing the Cooper persistence in the young author and he plunged himself into the writing of a second book. _The Spy_ (1821) was an immediate success in America and in England. Cooper's novel of the Revolution involved the romantic exploits of a secret agent of Washington who posed as a British partisan to gather information. *The Spy* was translated into every major world language. Cooper had written the first widely successful American novel. He started a whole chain of Revolutionary novels which were eagerly read in the capitals of the world. None equaled the original, which still can be read as a thrilling romance, despite its pompous and overdrawn style.

Cooper's varied literary career

During the next 30 years of his life, Cooper, the accidental author, had as varied a literary career as any American writer has experienced. He is one of our most voluminous writers. But very little of this mass of writing is still read today. Cooper was careless to the end and never developed a finished technique. He was sensitive to criticism and gradually his early immense popularity waned, both in America and in England. He criticized the English for being aristocratic and the Americans for being democratic. Much of his writing, including several of his novels, is highly propagandistic. During the later years of his life, he usually had several libel suits pending at the same time. He fought them all and won most of them. He remained stubborn and obstinate to the end and became gradually more embittered. Cooper was a loyal patriot, honest and gentle in his personal relations, but unrelenting in his castigation of what he considered dishonest and unjust in peoples.

His sea tales are scattered throughout his career, beginning with *The Pilot* (1824) and ending with *The Two Admirals* (1842). These tales are still interesting, but contain little depth of character development or a real feeling for the life of the sea, which was to be so admirably developed by the English Conrad late in the century. Cooper's tales are fast moving, but contain many improbable situations.

Cooper's miscellaneous novels cover a wide range of subject matter. Some are historical: *Lionel Lincoln* (1825) concerns Lexington and Bunker Hill and *The Wept of Wish-ton-Wish* (1829) concerns Massachusetts in the time of King Philip's War. *The Bravo, The Heidenmauer,* and *The Headsman,* written in Europe, praise American democracy as contrasted to a decadent European feudal aristocracy. *The Monikers,* written shortly after his return from his trip, is a bitter satire on the very American institutions he had praised in his previous novels written in Europe. At least 5 of Cooper's novels are attacks on phases of American democracy.

Cooper's frontier novels

Cooper's enduring position in American literature depends mainly upon 5 novels, written at various periods of his career, collectively called *The Leatherstocking Tales,* from the frontiersman, Natty Bumppo, known as "Leatherstocking" among other names, one of the world's most famous fictional characters. These 5 novels are best considered in the sequence which follows the life of Natty Bumppo: *The Deerslayer* (1841) shows the frontier scout as a youth; *The Last of the Mohicans* (1826) and *The Pathfinder* (1840) show him at the height of his manly powers; in *The Pioneers* (1823) he is an old man; *The Prairie* (1827) brings death and glory to the famous scout. This series gives us, in a sense, a prose epic of an American type of a bygone era of our colorful early history. Whatever the faults of Cooper's style and plot construction, the career of Natty Bumppo will always represent for American readers an idealized concept of the epitome among hardy and self-reliant frontiersmen who carved a modern United States out of a virgin wilderness filled with lurking dangers. Natty Bumppo is the only real epic hero of an American "heroic" age.

The plots of these frontier novels are all quite simple. There are rousing battles, pursuits, rescues, and all manner of suspense. That the characters are wooden, that Cooper never really lived the life of the frontier about which he writes, that sentiment overflows occasionally, that the style is stilted and the conversation is artificial—all these defects can be forgotten by the modern reader who wishes to follow the action and thrill to the best literary depiction of the American frontier (false as it may be) in existence. Cooper was not the careful student of his material as was Scott; he was, by far, not an equal of Scott as a romantic novelist. But his Natty Bumppo will outlive all of Scott's characters, and his blood-curdling adventures and his Indians are of the most colorful and romantic past which America possesses.

The Deerslayer finds Natty Bumppo as a young hunter, growing up among the Delaware Indians. He rescues the family of Tom Hutter and his noble-born foster daughter, Judith, from an Indian attack. Judith loves Natty, but he refuses her advances and dedicates himself to life in the wilds. In *The Last of the Mohicans* (197), the strongest of the 5 plots, Natty is a scout, known as Hawkeye, in Fort William Henry, under attack by the French and the Indians. Hawkeye rescues Cora and Alice

Munro, daughters of the commander. Later when the fort is surrendered to the French, the girls are again seized by the Indians. Cora and Uncas, last of the Mohican aristocracy, are killed in another dramatic rescue. *The Pathfinder* opens as Natty is 40. His thrilling adventures continue unabated through this novel and *The Pioneers*. *The Prairie* finds Bumppo nearly 90 but still active in his contributions toward pushing civilization westward. He guides an emigrant train across the plains, finding himself once again called upon to rescue the "tenderfeet" from attacks by the Sioux, a prairie fire, and a buffalo stampede. Old Natty Bumppo finally dies by the trail, surrounded in his last hours by both peoples whom he befriended when they were good and fought when they were evil, the whites and the Indians.

Cooper did not die listening to echoes of his praise from many of his fellow Americans, but every generation, including his own, of Americans has thrilled to the first genuine novels to come upon our literary scene. Cooper was a bungler of literary style, an overenthusiastic crusader for perfection in his fellow men's moral conduct, a careless depicter of reality, but he will continue to live and thrill readers the world over with his tales of the wild American frontier.

William Cullen Bryant (1794-1878)

Hardly a true "Knickerbocker," our first great romantic poet was born in Massachusetts. The son of a scholarly physician of old *Mayflower* stock, young Bryant spent his boyhood and youth among the Berkshire Hills. He was educated for the law and spent 9 years at this career in Plainfield and Great Barrington. He hated the pettiness attached to his profession and grieved that he could not afford to write poetry as a full-time occupation. Finally, he could endure his inner conflict no longer and went to New York, where he took a job as journalist on the *New York Evening Post*. He rose finally to editor-in-chief and spent 50 years with this popular newspaper. He was praised throughout his life for his liberal views in the many articles and editorials he wrote for the *Post*.

Bryant the poet

Young Bryant had written <u>*Thanatopsis*</u> at the age of 17. This has proved to be his most popular poem. Bryant began life as a Calvinist, a Federalist, and a classic; he gradually shifted to become a Unitarian, a deist, a Democrat, and a romantic. *Thanatopsis* (as revised two or three times after it was first written) is a rather fatalistic blank verse* meditation on death in the best tradition of the English "graveyard school"* of poets. Bryant shows his Puritan preoccupation with his somber theme, but his approach is stoical and shows his early concern with man's relation to Nature. In the poem he bids man live with dignity and grace so that he can join "the innumerable caravan which moves, to that mysterious realm" with an unfaltering trust. He does not speak of man's soul, nor of his resurrection, but takes his cue from Wordsworth, that the earth eventually reclaims all her living things. He predicts that a proper life will lead man to "pleasant dreams" after death.

Bryant wrote few great poems and repeated himself often. His *To a Waterfowl* (1815), also an early poem, usually disputes first place in reader interest with *Thanatopsis*. Here the flight of the bird leads the poet to associate the Power that guides its wings with his own plodding course through life.

> He who, from zone to zone,
> Guides through the boundless sky thy certain flight,
> In the long way that I must tread alone,
> Will lead my steps aright.

Most of Bryant's best poetry takes a moral turn; he cannot resist didacticism. He is occupied with Nature but cannot quite free himself from lesson-teaching sufficiently to revel in its beauties with a carefree lyricism. He tends to be dully lyric and lacks emotional fire. He has technical command of verse forms and a grandeur of expression, seemingly more suited to classic than to romantic verse. His blank verse translations of *The Iliad* and *The Odyssey,* late in life, give free rein to his lofty nobility of style. He also did some excellent translations from the early Cuban romantic (the first of the romantic poets in the Spanish language), José María Heredia. Bryant's translations of Heredia's *A Niágara* is still considered the best poem written upon the famous American scenic wonder.

Bryant lived a noble and exemplary life. He was highly respected and wrote nothing designed to antagonize his fellow men. His poetry is likewise exemplary and will continue to command a steady respect among readers for its stately nobility of form and thought. His is not a blithe, light verse, but few have stated moral ideals so excellently.

> Truth, crushed to earth, shall rise again;
> Th' eternal years of God are hers;
> But Error, wounded, writhes in pain,
> And dies among his worshipers; . . .
> (from *The Battlefield*)

Minor figures of the early period

James Kirke Paulding (1778-1860). The brother-in-law of Washington Irving and coeditor of the Irving family literary venture, *Salmagundi*, was a leading poet and novelist. He was the chief interpreter of the New York Dutch among the "Knickerbocker" group. His *Koningsmarke* is a satire on the policy of the Whigs, written also as a burlesque of Scott's novels. His *The Lay of the Scottish Fiddle* (1813) is a poetic parody of Scott. He wrote a number of novels, of which *Westward Ho!* treats the frontiersmen. His books are almost entirely neglected today, but Paulding exercised great influence in the first years of our national literature and produced work which is on a par with that of any of the early satirists and novelists.

The names of *Nathaniel Parker Willis (1806-1867)*, *Fitz-Greene Halleck (1790-1867)*, and *Joseph Rodman Drake (1795-1820)* would deserve more space in a more extensive discussion of the early writers of romanticism in New York. All these men were well known in this early 19th century as poets and journalists.

The "one-poem" poets

Every American is familiar with certain poems and songs of the early romantic period, little pieces which have become fixed items of Americana. Two of these poems have become our national songs. Few people today, who are familiar with these verses, could identify their authors. These writers, whose other production is forgotten, will live on in American hearts in one poem or song: Francis Scott Key (1779-1843), "The Star-Spangled Banner" (1814); Samuel Francis Smith (1808-1895), "America" (1832); Samuel Woodworth (1785-1842), "The Old Oaken Bucket"; John Howard Payne (1791-1852), "Home, Sweet Home"; George Pope Morris (1802-1864), "Woodman, Spare that Tree!"

Two Great Figures of the Second Period

We have noted that the rise of American romanticism corresponds with the rise of our national literature, which tends to remain in a formative stage until after 1830. In the earlier period our first writers of literary importance begin to attract a world-wide audience, though their work is short of being really great. But after 1830, in the various sectional areas into which our writers tended to group themselves, a decided improvement in literary quality can be noted. American literature had reached its first really "creative" stage. The new writers are decidedly romantic, but the days of imitation and concern about specific European models are gone. Now an occasional individual writer develops distinctively native themes, and does so in a distinctive and robust American fashion. In this later romantic period writers appear who are, in every respect, our greatest writers to date. Two such figures in the New York area during the period are Herman Melville, the novelist, and Walt Whitman, the poet.

Melville: novelist of exotic themes

Herman Melville (1819-1891) was born in New York City, of a rather poor, but aristocratic, Scottish family. The family moved to Albany where Herman attended the local Academy. The death of the father left the mother destitute with 6 children. Herman worked as a clerk until 1836 when he joined the crew of a merchant ship bound for the South Seas. Upon his return he wandered about doing odd jobs until 1841, when he shipped aboard a whaler. After enduring the harsh treatment the sailors received aboard the *Acushnet,* Melville and a young companion deserted the ship in the Marquesas Islands. The boys fell in with the Typees, a wild tribe of supposed cannibals. His companion escaped and Melville remained in captivity. He won the tribesmen's confidence, however, and lived 4 months in a tropical paradise with them. Finally he was picked up by an Australian whaler and eventually made his way back home aboard a U.S. warship.

Melville married in 1847 and settled for a while in New York City. He did some newspaper work while he was writing his first novels of these sea experiences. In 1850 he moved to a small farm in Massachusetts where he became a friend of Hawthorne. By 1863 he had made several more ocean voyages. He finally took a job as customs inspector in New York City, after failing to secure more desirable posts. He worked at this ill-paying job from 1866 to 1885, producing hardly any writing of value.

Melville and society

To appreciate Melville's books, one must understand something of the personality of the man who wrote them. Almost all his great works were written by the time he was 33 years of age. The man who produced what many critics term America's greatest novel wrote practically nothing of value during the last 40 years of his life.

Melville was embittered and antisocial from an early age and showed traits of a strange form of mysticism*. The dark inner conflicts of the man reached the surface many times in his writings. In his first books, *Typee* and *Omoo*, written before he was 26, he had already revealed his pessimistic and acrid views on man and society. He seemed obsessed with the idea of the evil surrounding him in civilized society and with the best methods for a purer man to combat it. More and more, as he wrote, he revealed his bitterness and rage against civilization. The public eagerly seized upon his first novels, but their popularity soon faded as fewer buyers appeared to take his successive books. When his masterpiece, *Moby Dick*, was issued in 1852, it found few readers. The author became more pessimistic and his efforts to analyze the problem of evil reached the point where his last books became abstruse and hard to understand. At last he virtually abandoned writing and took a confining and ill-paying job as customs' inspector to provide his family with sufficient funds to subsist. The plates for his best works were burned in a publishing house fire in 1853 and they were not reproduced. During the last two decades of the writer's life he was almost completely unknown and his books were forgotten.

Around the beginning of this century many literary historians did not bother to mention Melville in connection with our literature. But in the past 30 to 40 years, with a lessening of prejudice and a better critical perspective, Melville's reputation has grown until today he is considered one of our few great novelists and one of the best the world has produced. Modern criticism places _Moby Dick_ among the best books ever written.

Melville's mind could not find peace; he was constantly reminded that he hated the civilization about him. He constantly longed for the purer atmosphere of the tropical paradise he visited and described in his early books. But he could not come to a decision to abandon life in civilized society; he continued to probe and to become more misanthropic. Hawthorne did not agree with his views but he appreciated fully the inner struggle that racked his friend's soul. "He can neither believe nor be comfortable in his unbelief, and he is too honest and courageous not to try to do one or the other."

The major novels

Melville's first novels were _Typee_ (1846) and _Omoo_ (1847). Both are autobiographical. The first deals with the author's experiences after abandoning the _Acushnet_ in mid-Pacific. The novel is filled with magnificent descriptions of Polynesian life and of the tropical splendor in which he spent 4 months as a semicaptive of the cannibalistic tribes of the Marquesas. His pictures of primitive island life are voluptuous and detailed. Even in this first book Melville rails more than once against the evils that civilization has brought to the unspoiled natives of the Pacific islands.

Omoo deals with the author's escape aboard the Australian whaler. He left the ship at Tahiti. He describes vividly his adventures among the friendly natives and his impressions of this tropical paradise. He is particularly strong in his portrayal of the character of Dr. Long Ghost. _Omoo_ (meaning "rover") again deplores the harmful effects which the interbreeding of natives with foreigners has brought to the purity of island character.

Melville's 2 books brought the South Seas into literature. This field has had very distinguished (and less apt) cultivators in world literature since Melville's day but none have surpassed the freshness and creative imagination, the accuracy of detail, of the originals. Melville's dialogue is lively and his descriptions are vivid. These two novels will live long in the exotic literature of the sea and of its primitive island charms.

In _Redburn_ (1849) and _White Jacket_ (1850), Melville sticks closer to shipboard experiences and mingles fact and fiction to provide us with unforgettable sea stories. In _Redburn_ he deals with his first voyage and presents vivid character studies of various members of the crew. _White Jacket_ records the author's life aboard the U.S. frigate on his return from Australia. It is a powerful novel, although laden with propaganda for correction of naval practices, such as flogging.

In _Mardi_ (1849) Melville gives us a sample of the type of symbolic allegory* that is to form the framework of _Moby Dick_. The fancy induced by his mental turmoil and his obsession with the problem of evil is introduced into this story. The book contains some of Melville's best lyrical passages but tends toward rather cold intellectual and philosophical fantasy in many of its sections. It is a rather ill-constructed book and is not light fictional fare. One must penetrate beneath the story and follow the allegory, which concerns man's fruitless search for beauty and happiness, in order to appreciate its power. A later book, _Pierre_ (1852), takes Melville's fantastic philosophical pessimism almost into the realm of the incomprehensible. Here he gives unrestrained vent to his pent-up anger at the failure of his efforts in the face of the blasé public contempt that was being shown his masterpiece, _Moby Dick,_ which had appeared earlier in the year and which was attracting little notice. _Pierre_ went almost unread until well into this century. The edition of 1929 was the first in 70 years.

"Moby Dick, or The Whale"

Moby Dick (199) is a book that needs to be read in its entirety for more than a superficial understanding of the many currents of symbolism* that run beneath the surface of its story. It is a book about the obsession of Captain Ahab to kill the great white whale. To the captain, Moby Dick stands, in a most direct way, for evil. The ocean is life within which the evil force has free sway. The captain, at least to Melville, seems to be an avenging force of good that must struggle to the end in order to resolve the problem of evil.

Captain Ahab had lost a leg in his first struggle with the monster and he returns with a monomaniacal determination to find the great mammal and exterminate it and bring its enormous supply of oil back to port. The book concerns this mad search into the seven seas, both captain and crew becoming almost equally crazed. Before the final struggle with the whale begins, the reader knows the complete biography and significance of whales and the intimate lives of the human beings who sail the seas in their search.

Moby Dick is a great novel in all respects. It is a good story and a superb study in character, normal and abnormal, and the thin line that separates them. It is an epic of the sea and of its power in the scheme of nature. Its language is majestic, yet as delicate as the finest lyricism. It ebbs and flows as the very ocean it portrays. _Moby Dick,_ one of the world's greatest books, almost perished during 2 generations of Americans. But it was not a dated book; its values were timeless when Melville wrote it.

Whitman: America's bard of optimistic individualism

<u>Walt Whitman (1819-1892)</u> laid to rest any doubts that American literature was capable of seeking its own paths into the future. With Whitman, American poetry received its strongest injection of robust vigor. Indeed, the Whitman hypodermic was so laden with robust and optimistic individualism, with frank and outspoken idea, with radical departures from classic form, that readers and critics alike, even today, are unable to agree as to whether Whitman's outpouring of verse is America's greatest poetic production or simply an eruption of magnificent and lusty expression that fashions will decree are noteworthy, but without the realm of pure aesthetic literary art. Whatever critical tides may roll over Whitman's powerful verse, it will still tower as a huge monument to American literary independence. The force and booming power of Whitman's voice will stir readers of English for many generations to come.

> Poets to come! orators, singers, musicians to come!
> Not today is to justify me and answer what I am for,
> But you, a new brood, athletic, continental, greater than
> before known,
> Arouse! Arouse—for you must justify me—you must answer.

Whitman's life

This "best loved and most hated" of our writers was born on Long Island of ancestry which had little claim to either culture or to aristocracy. The mother was Quaker and had a great influence on Whitman's development of a quiet mind and the calm optimism that prevailed in his buoyant spirit in the last years of his life, when he was a hopeless invalid.

The poet's ancestors were farmers and seafaring men. Whitman, far from feeling inferior, accepted the tenets of democracy at their face value and early had a fierce pride in his humble origin, in his sturdy roots in the soil, and in his healthy American stock.

> Starting from fish-shape Paumanok where I was born,
> well-begotten, and raised by a perfect mother, . . .

> My tongue, every atom of my blood, form'd from this soil,
> this air,
> Born here of parents born here, from parents the same, and
> their parents the same.

Young Whitman was forced to leave the public schools of Brooklyn at the age of 13 to earn his living as errand boy for a firm of lawyers. Following this job, he successively was employed in various capacities in print shops and finally became a country schoolteacher. Eventually he opened a print shop of his own and edited a weekly paper. He contributed stories and sketches to various New York papers and leisurely studied American life and the ideals of democracy.

After a period as editor of *The Brooklyn Eagle,* in 1848 he went to New Orleans in an editorial capacity on *The Crescent.* He traveled at his ease through the middle states to reach his post and soon was wandering northward again. More and more he spent his time in solitude, in observing life and in reading the classics. He finally felt sufficiently grounded in knowledge and inspired by the stirring ideas with which he might begin his major career. Whitman's first edition of his many-times revised *Leaves of Grass* appeared in 1855. This collection grew through the years, and with its revisions and augmentations, contained at last the major production of the poet. From the first edition (1855) to the seventh (1881) it follows an expanding America, portrayed in its joy and its sorrow by the American poet who was closest to its soil and to its rude vibrating life.

Whitman suffered a stroke in 1873 and spent his next years traveling, giving lectures on Lincoln, or living quietly on his brother's farm in New Jersey. In 1888 he had a second stroke and remained an invalid from this time until his death in 1892.

The Whitman verse

That Whitman's violation of all classic traditions of verse form would have aroused a storm of protest from critics, still steeped to a remarkable degree in the stilted and flowery style of the 18th century, was a foregone conclusion. But that apparently he trampled upon all the taboos against open discussion of the functions of nature and the bodily relations of the sexes, was too much. Many persons, perhaps, still shudder and pass over hastily his more robust expression. Needless to say, many voices in his day, and afterward, grew hoarse in denunciation of this upstart barbarian who was to become known as "The Good Gray Poet" and the "Prophet of Democracy." Whitman covered life as a central theme for his major verse, in all its aspects and gloried in all its functions. He was proud, egotistic, open, and

kind, an independent soul who had no shame of his love of life
and his fellow man.

Most of his verse is in a sort of unrimed free verse*, with lines
of extremely differing lengths. The world had seen no verse
like it. Whitman's aim was to express himself and in a rhythmical
manner. That he does this, is admitted. Whether to call his
expression poetry or prose is still a moot question. Much of this
poet's expression lies, unquestionably, somewhere in the in-
determinate area between prose and poetry, as these terms are
conventionally understood. That he could maneuver the traditional verse forms and make them vibrate with metrical life is
proved by much of his short lyric stanzas. His elegy* on the
death of Lincoln, *Oh Captain! My Captain!*, is Whitman at his
best in mingling the traditional metrical arrangement with tender
and poignant lyricism.

> ... Here Captain! dear father!
> This arm beneath your head!
> It is some dream that on the deck,
> You've fallen cold and dead.

> My Captain does not answer, his lips are pale and still,
> My father does not feel my arm, he had no pulse nor will,
> The ship is anchor'd safe and sound, its voyage is closed and
>   done,
> From fearful trip the victor ship comes in with object won:

> Exult O shores, and ring O bells!
> But I with mournful tread,
> Walk the deck my Captain lies,
> Fallen cold and dead.

"Leaves of Grass" and the Whitman theme

Whitman's 1855 edition of his poems went through 11 revisions
during the poet's lifetime. Many editions have appeared in this
century. This collection absorbed each new poem of Whitman
and much of his work underwent revision in successive editions.
Today the Whitman verse can be procured in its totality, much
as the poet himself arranged it. Whitman's prose, discussing the
problems of democracy, war memoranda, and personal views is
often included in present-day editions of *Leaves of Grass*. The
most interesting of this prose matter is the preface to the 1855
edition in which the poet defends his work and his style.

Whitman's theme in *Leaves of Grass* is in reality a single one—

America in all its expanding aspects and the expansive ego of the poet as he follows with his expression the decades from 1850 to 1880. He reacts to all the issues of the country, foreign and domestic. He wrote of the city and of the wild frontier. He wrote of people, individually and collectively. He wrote best, perhaps, of himself, his thoughts, his reactions, his teeming pride in his individuality and his part in the natural and the social setting about him. Pages could be filled with individual titles, illustrating Whitman's varied reactions to specific themes, his attitude toward nature, the slave issue, and myriad other topics. His _Song of Myself_ (202), his longest poem (covering some 70 pages) is his most representative and personal revelation of his life plan. It is loosely constructed, filled with characteristic Whitmanesque egoism, of diverse and vivid details of American life. It is robust and lusty in certain passages and tenderly lyric in others. It is the most important single selection to lead the reader to his appreciation of America's most unique poet. Whitman became an American legend and, in the sense he understood the word, an American institution.

> I hear it charged against me that I sought to destroy
>   institutions;
> But really I am neither for nor against institutions;
> (What indeed have I in common with them?—Or what with
>   the destruction of them?)
> Only I will establish in the Mannahatta, and in every city of
>   These States, inland and seaboard,
> And in the fields and woods, and above every keel,
>   little or large, that dents the water,
> Without edifices, or rules, or trustees, or any argument,
> The institution of the dear love of comrades.

> (1860)

ROMANTICISM: THE SOUTHERN WRITERS

As one looks southward from New York during the early 19th century, he finds that Philadelphia, a leader in all aspects, political and cultural, of the late Colonial and Revolutionary periods, has begun a slow decline from its earlier position of leadership. In 1800, the national capital was moved to Washington, and the commerce that once filtered through Philadelphia into the central regions of the Ohio and the Mississippi now moved either north through New York or south through New Orleans. The Erie Canal, far to the north, had done much to destroy Philadelphia as a developing literary center for the country. By 1825, the city that had produced Franklin, and Charles Brockden Brown had ceased to attract men of letters.

Two southern centers, however, maintained and nurtured a literary tradition during the rise of American romanticism and gave us notable writers, and one great one (Edgar Allen Poe), during the period: Richmond, in Virginia, and Charleston, in South Carolina.

The Virginia Writers

In Virginia the plantation system, with its distances and lack of contact between families, had tended to discourage literary endeavor. However, after the war, life became more leisurely on the plantations, transportation was better, the wilderness was conquered, the slaves and their overseers managed the farming, and the owners and their ladies had time to develop cultural interests and to compare their ideal lot with that of English manorial aristocracy. During the period between 1800 and 1825 the Virginia aristocracy seems very self-satisfied if one reaches that conclusion from the many writings which come from the area, tending to idealize plantation life. Thus romanticism in Virginia, during the formative period of our literature, took the direction of an idealization of reality.

Kennedy and the "plantation tradition"

John Pendleton Kennedy (1795-1870) was a novelist who presented for us our best view of a section of our early nation which took on many of the characteristics of feudal England, with its lords and ladies living a leisurely life in the castle while the vassals did the work and reaped little of the profits. Kennedy presented an idyllic view of plantation life, painting it in soft tints. His view of American life in the early period of our national history gives little of the democratic vision.

Swallow Barn (1832) is a book of sketches, similar in tone to Irving's Bracebridge Hall, given the change of setting from English country life to that of the plantation of the southland. The book is a series of charming views of the manners and interests of plantation aristocracy. Kennedy's books have had a great influence in the development of a so-called "plantation tradition" in our writing.

Kennedy also wrote Horseshoe Robinson, a romantic novel of the Revolution, Rob of the Bowl, an idealized historical novel of colonial Maryland, and *Quodibet* (1840), a witty satire on Jacksonian democracy.

William Alexander Caruthers (c. 1800-c. 1846) continued the aristocratic tradition of the southern writers in the imitation of Scott in the historical romance and Irving in the sketch of the manners of the gentry. His collection of sketches is *The Kentuckian in New York* (1834), very much in the pattern of *Swallow Barn* and *Bracebridge Hall*. His best historical romance is *The Cavaliers of Virginia* (1835).

John Esten Cooke (1830-1886), of a later generation, attempted to introduce the frontier into his novels and to soften the aristocratic tradition with a bit of Jeffersonian humanitarianism. But his novels crackle with the courtly manner and everything but a frontier sociability. Some of his titles indicate his attempted departure from the plantation tradition: *Leatherstockings and Silk, Henry St. John, Gentleman, The Virginia Comedians* (1854), his best book.

Poe: poet and master of tales of fear

Edgar Allen Poe (1809-1849) was the exception to the southern writers who treated the "plantation tradition" in the rosy haze of historical romances and sketches. He was born in Boston of actor parents, both of whom died in Poe's infancy. The boy was adopted by a wealthy tobacco merchant of Richmond and grew up to consider himself a southerner in all respects. He received an excellent preparatory education in England and entered the University of Virginia in 1826. Young Poe drank and gambled through the first year and was removed by his foster father. The youth, in a peevish rage, left home and joined the army under an assumed name. He served 2 years and returned home and secured an appointment to West Point through his foster parent, Mr. Allen. He succeeded in being dismissed in 1 year by accumulation of demerits.

Poe had published a small volume of poems in 1827. In 1831, he published a second and augmented edition. He attempted a reconciliation with his foster father, and failing this, sought employment. In 1833 he won a $50 prize for his story *MS. Found in a Bottle*. He won other prizes for stories and poems, which led him to an editorship of *The Southern Literary Messenger* of Richmond. Shortly afterward, he married his 14-year-old cousin. He continued to drink, write poems and stories, and to try one editorial job after another. By 1845, when he published *The Raven,* he was gaining a considerable reputation with his writings.

Poe and his wife took up residence in a cottage near Fordham, near New York City, where he tried to earn his living by contributions to magazines and newspapers. Here Poe increased his drinking and began to take opium. His wife fell ill and Poe's own health began to fail as a result of his excesses. In 1847, his wife died. Poe, now penniless and brokenhearted, settled into a period of gloom that he never shook off. He wrote some of his best work as he slowly disintegrated physically and spiritually. *The Bells* and *Annabel Lee* come from these last days.

Poe as a critic

Poe was our first genuine literary critic. American criticism, until Poe, had been largely an emotional and biased matter in our early literary history. Excess praise or utter condemnation were the standards usually followed in judging works, depending upon personal reactions and prejudices of the particular critics involved. Poe introduced an analytical approach to criticism based upon a wide knowledge of literature and a sure sense of weighing values. Poe's unbiased and cool opinions were little imitated by critics of his day or later, but he was a pioneer in pointing the way to the more impartial criticism to come in the late 19th century.

Poe's literary virtues and faults

Poe produced more than 60 stories and is known to have authored 48 poems. Poe was a true artist and approached his material with the sole thought of creating beauty of expression and of conveying to the reader his idea and his mood while forming it. His prose is direct, energetic, clear, and calculated to focus reader attention sharply on one particular idea at a time. He was a world master of the short story. His narrative skill and his unique handling of plot structure has received worldwide imitation in this highly developed literary genre in modern literatures. Poe ranks among the best of world writers of the short story*.

As a poet he was not so versatile as in his narrative prose. His subject matter was of narrow range. He was, however, a master in the musicality of his lines and in the creation of moods by use of both internal and external rhyme*. His poetry breathes a delicate melancholy, beauty, and sadness. It is among the most melodic of verse in English. Poe was much admired in France and his poetic musicality was of great influence in the late-century French symbolist school of poets. His short stories were an inspiration to the great French master of the genre, Guy de Maupassant.

Poe's subject matter was unique. He showed little concern for the American scene and still less for the aristocratic traditions of the writers of his time. His themes are mostly characterized by their horror, strangeness, and melancholy. He deliberately developed the weird, the abnormal, and the grotesque. Both in his poetry and in his tales, Poe gives us unforgettable experiences in the imaginative realm of fear and shuddering suspense, in the haunted world of sadness and terror. He had all the elements of the Gothic writers, plus creative skill and a delicate balance of aesthetic value.

Poe had literary, as well as personal, faults, and perhaps the latter contributed considerably to the former. Poe was his own greatest enemy in personal life and perhaps the same could be said of his literary production. He was a sensitive intellectual. He was an introverted personality and perhaps early failed to understand the workaday world about him and withdrew into his own sensitive inner world. His outward manifestations of this inner gloom were his drinking and taking of dope. Poverty only increased these outward signs of inner rebellion and despair.

His work shows neither mirth nor humor. He shows little sentiment in his prose and often the reader feels that Poe is merely leading him through calculated paths of experience in horror and fear. He is thus to be accused by many of being artificial, of being inhumane, unfeeling, and without concern for the introduction of moral principles into his works.

These criticisms detract little from the fact that Poe was a master of his particular literary material, and therein lies his genius and influence. Poe is a great writer in the scope of world literatures and unsurpassed in his chosen thematic area. He is, at the same time, a consummate literary artist.

Representative poems and tales

The sentiment, lacking in Poe's tales, is present in every stanza of his verse. It is always the feeling of an anguished soul, crying out for hope and for union with joy and happiness, but always with a tone of hopelessness and fear that it will continue to wander in the "ghoul-haunted" shadows of unrest.

Some of Poe's best poetic efforts are to be found among his early poems. _To Helen,_ an expression of the poet's grief at the death of a Richmond lady who had befriended him, was supposedly written when Poe was a mere 15. It is a gem of elegiac beauty and reveals the boy's precocity which, unfortunately, was never properly directed. This early poem is one of Poe's best and reveals Poe's deep poetic sense as well as his intellectual yearning for a world of beauty, which he conceived the ancient splendors of Rome and Greece to have been.

> Helen thy beauty is to me
> Like those Nicean barks of yore,
> That gently, o'er a perfumed sea,
> The weary, way-worn wanderer bore
> To his own native shore . . .

The Raven (1845), the most known of Poe's verse, shows the poor student, sitting wearily at midnight over his books, mourning the death of a beautiful woman.

> Once upon a midnight dreary, while I pondered weak and weary,
> Over many a quaint and curious volume of forgotten lore—
> While I nodded, nearly napping, suddenly there came a tapping,
> As if someone gently rapping, rapping at my chamber door.
> " 'Tis some visitor," I muttered, "tapping at my chamber door—
> Only this and nothing more."

When the tapping again came at the window, he threw open the shutters and the raven entered, perched above the door, and monotonously croaked, "Nevermore." The student pours out his grief to the bird, imploring him to give up the answer of life and death.

> And the Raven never flitting, still is sitting, _still_ is sitting
> On the pallid bust of Pallas just above my chamber door;
> And his eyes have all the seeming of a demon's that is dreaming,
> And the lamp-light o'er him streaming throws his shadow on the floor;
> And my soul from out that shadow that lies floating on the floor
> Shall be lifted—nevermore!

Poe, in such poems as *Ulalume* and *Eldorado,* continues to show the eternal search of a tortured soul, wandering through "the misty mid-region of Weir" for peace and happiness and finding that the quest is a vain one.

In *Annabel Lee (1849)*, written only days before his death, Poe sounds his last melodic notes in a tone of triumph, asserting that no force can sever his soul from that of his wife, for whom he has grieved during the last 2 years of his life without her.

> And neither the angels in Heaven above
>   Nor the demons down under the sea,
> Can ever dissever my soul from the soul
>   Of the beautiful Annabel Lee:——
>
> For the moon never beams without bringing me dreams
>   Of the beautiful Annabel Lee;
> And the stars never rise but I see the bright eyes
>   Of the beautiful Annabel Lee;
> And so, all the night-tide, I lie down by the side
> Of my darling, my darling, my life and my bride,
>   In her sepulchre there by the sea—
>   In her tomb by the side of the sea.

Poe did not invent the short story but he gave it definitive form and became the idol of those who followed him as this literary form gained world-wide popularity in the late 19th century and in contemporary writing. Poe stressed brevity and the elimination of all moralizing, philosophizing, and other material which detracts from the shortest direct approach to the single effect for which the writer should strive. His *The Fall of the House of Usher* (204) is a famous example among his tales of the supernatural, of the application of Poe's concepts of what a perfect short story should be.

Poe, in many of his tales, had as his chief purpose the creation of an atmosphere of the grotesque and the terrible. His *The Cask of Amontillado, The Tell-Tale Heart, The Black Cat, The Masque of the Red Death,* and *The Pit and the Pendulum* (206), are superb examples of the masterful creation of a mood of fear and suspense.

Poe created the modern mystery tale. His *The Murders in the Rue Morgue* (206), *The Purloined Letter,* and *The Mystery of Marie Roget* established the technique for the modern detective story which has become the most popular semiliterary reading in this century.

Poe excelled in other types of tales. One of his most notable, and least terrifying, types is well represented by _The Gold Bug_, a tale of cryptology and its use in locating a buried treasure, showing admirably Poe's employment of ratiocination in his plots, a sharp and logical process of exact reasoning. However skilled Poe was at other types, however, his chief importance lies in the tales in which he sought to convey impressions of fear, horror, and melancholy. At this he has been excelled by no other short story writer in world literatures.

The Charleston Group

Further to the south, Charleston, in South Carolina, was the center of an attempt among southern leaders to carry their state of culture into a slightly different, but no less aristocratic, sphere than did their Virginia neighbors of the "plantation tradition." Here the leaders dreamed of a brilliant era of southern classical learning, patterned on the Greek models of ancient Athens in the glorious days of Pericles, in the 5th century before Christ.

Before 1830, the deep south had contributed little to the new national literature. But from 1830 to 1860 the southern leaders (chief among whom was John C. Calhoun) dreamed of a southern aristocracy, the basis of which was to be wealth in land and a system of slavery which would give to the upper class the leisure to develop a refined and cultured life—democratic, to be sure—in the ancient Greek sense.

The romanticism of this group, then, lies in that idealized dream. Charleston was the ideal intellectual center _(Athens)_ of this aristocratic culture. In literature the idealized dream of Greek democracy produced writers who dwelt upon a colorful past in the feudal sense. The resulting writings are less romantic than those produced in Virginia, with many of the tints of a coming realism in American literature. In Virginia, the literary explorers of a romantic past aped Scott, while in the deep south, the past was more closely linked to the contemporary scene. The best of these southern writers receive less attention today than they should. Some were equally as good as were writers in the north, but the centers of population were there and the focus of attention of the majority of critics and readers was on the particular writers who lived in New York and New England.

Simms, leader of the Charleston group

William Gilmore Simms (1806-1870) was the most talented of the Charleston writers. Born in the southern gentry, he was its strongest literary advocate of Greek democracy. Trained for the law, his first literary effort was a fairy-tale type of poetry, *Atalantis; A Story of the Sea,* in which a sea fairy is pursued by a sea demon. This effort aroused little enthusiasm either in the North or in the South.

In 1833, Simms wrote a prose romance, *Martin Faber,* the first of some 40. novels he was to write. Simms became one of our most prolific writers, turning out close to 100 books in his lifetime. At his best, Simms is the equal of any novelist of his age. He has been little read, however.

Guy Rivers, a tale of a Georgia highwayman, is his first notable novel. His best is perhaps *The Yemasse, A Romance of Carolina* (1835), in which he centers attention upon early Indian life. Simms' Indians are far more realistic than those of Cooper, whose concept of the savage was of the "noble" variety, symbolized best by Uncas in *The Last of the Mohicans.* Simms portrays the more debauched Indians that he had seen in frontier towns.

Simms wrote many romances of the Revolution, involving melodramatic situations and love affairs between partisans and royalists. He also treated the southern frontier extensively, always in a rather sentimental manner, giving his aristocratic characters a highly unreal and idealized treatment and his rough frontiersmen and Indians an opposite tint of rowdyism and debauchery.

Henry Timrod (1829-1867) and Paul Hamilton Hayne (1830-1886) were the outstanding poets of the southern group. Timrod's poetry was overly ornamented and highly sentimental, but he had true lyric notes. The harsh reality of the Civil War, which enveloped his life, was fatal to his sensitive nature. He died at 38, disillusioned and broken. But his early nature poems, such as *Spring* and *The Cotton Boll,* should be included in the best lyric expression of the age.

> . . . Small sphere!
> (By dusky fingers brought this morning here
> And shown with boastful smiles),
> I turn thy cloven sheath,
> Through which the soft white fibres peer,
> That, with their gossamer bands,
> Unite, like love, the sea-divided lands,
> And slowly, thread by thread,
> Draw forth the folded strands, . . .
>   (from *The Cotton Boll*—1861)

Hayne, like both Simms and Timrod, was caught in the meshes of the Civil War. He lost his property, his chance for fame, and his health was broken by the time he was 30. Hayne had all the attributes of greatness as a nature poet, and even in his early verse, shows many of the best effects achieved by Wordsworth. Unfortunately, his talents never had a chance to reach fruition. After the war he lived the rest of his life in bitter poverty and recurring illness in Georgia.

ROMANTICISM: THE WESTERN WRITERS

The South had come into the stream of the American surge toward a national literature at a late date and then under great handicaps. Both in Virginia and in Charleston the literary movements which had gathered force between 1830 and 1860 were crushed by the war and the slow and painful period of reconstruction.

The West was only coming into a state of civilization conducive to literary production by the war period. Eastern writing was read eagerly on the frontier, but little was produced there. The westerners, of course, were living romanticism and paused little to write of the process. When some of them did, their products tended to reflect the rude and direct speech of their authors. One does not look here for finished literary pieces; but one finds all the qualities of a living romanticism in them. A period of great western writers was due to await a new generation, whose authors began to write about the end of the great conflict between the states in 1865. Some writers, however, are worthy of note even in a review as brief as this:

Timothy Flint gives us chronicles and tales of the early settlement of the Mississippi valley in his _Recollections of the Last Ten Years_ (1826). He also wrote several novels in the romantic pattern, full of melodramatic and harrowing episodes.

David Crockett, a true frontiersman, in his _A Narrative of the Life of David Crockett of the State of Tennessee_ (1834) is a sterling example of what western democracy was like. The book is rough and crude, as the man who wrote it, and filled with the type of ignorant braggadocio that characterized our western leaders of the era.

Augustus Longstreet wrote an excellent and very realistic book of sketches of the Georgia frontier, _Georgia Scenes_ (18 pieces dating between 1833 and 1835). Longstreet was a lawyer, relatively uneducated, and his sketches are sometimes crude and the humor is broad, but they present an invaluable and interesting insight into frontier life in the area which was then our southwest.

Alexander Ross presents the Oregon frontier in _Fur Hunters of the Far West_ (1855).

Abraham Lincoln gives us our best writings of the political side of the westerners and their ideological concepts. Lincoln's prose is simple and his arguments are examples of direct logic, spiced with his inimitable wit. His many letters, his debates, his inaugural address, and above all, his Gettysburg speech, insure this great American figure a place in our literature.

ROMANTICISM: THE NEW ENGLAND WRITERS

The two chief elements of a literary romanticism are stronger in New England than in the other sections of America—a gospel of individualism and a search into nature for man's enduring values of peace and happiness. From the outbreak of the Revolution until 1830, there is little more to be found of literary value in this area than there had been for more than 150 years of Puritan domination of its intellectual life. A true American literature did not begin in New England; it began in New York and Pennsylvania. But in the second and third decades of the 19th century, both intellectual and aesthetic revolt is evident here as in no other section of America. In the South, a past was idealized and glorified. Here the tendency is to condemn the past and try to substitute something for it, conducive to the rise of the free interchange of ideas.

The Intellectual Side of New England Romanticism

Many critics have come to refer to this upsurge of New England intellectual life as a "renaissance." Be that as it may, the new intellectual atmosphere was one of 3 facets: (1) a revolt against Calvinistic theology, resulting in the rise of Unitarianism; (2) an idealistic philosophy, the primary ideas of which were imported from Europe, and in true romantic tradition, adapted to the local American impasse, by liberal minds among descendants of the New England hierarchy: _transcendentalism;_ (3) an antislavery or abolitionist element. However important it may be to American life and thought, this writer intends to treat this intellectual revolt as briefly as possible. Most of its writing is highly didactic and enters the realm of artistic literature only at the points where writers who treat it are masters of language and style. Its content belongs properly in the fields of philosophy, theology, and political science. Actually, these revolts against a past of intellectual and cultural sterility only opened a free path for artistic literature to develop; they are not really a part of it. They succeed only in giving it an atmosphere in which it could develop at all.

Briefly, these intellectual undercurrents, which help to free the way in New England for the development of literature, in the face of an iron curtain of Puritan prohibitions against imaginative inspiration, are:

The rise of Unitarianism

Unitarianism was a revolt against Calvinism, within the Church itself; Calvinism was gradually replaced by Unitarianism. In New England, in this period of revolt against the old and the established, there was a veritable swarm of new "isms," some of which grew strong and influenced large sectors of American life and thought to this day: Milleriteism, Dunkers, Groaners, Seventh-Day Baptists, Transcendentalism, Unitarianism, Agrarians, Muggletonianism, etc. All these currents of philosophy and theology sprang from desire to protest the New England past and to introduce new and broader views. It was a period of orgy in intoxicating ideas.

There had been many rumblings of liberal forces of discontent with New England orthodoxy before 1800. But when, in 1805, a Unitarian minister was elected Professor of Divinity at Harvard over the protests of Calvinist leaders, a full-scale break with the past was under way. Liberalism arose everywhere in the pulpits of New England.

By common consent, this new romantic liberalization of religion in the region is called Unitarianism. At least, that is the branch of the new "isms" that includes the literary figures of the age, our only concern here. Basically, as a religious belief, the Unitarian doctrine was not new to this group. Many had held, in ages past, against the idea of the Trinity and for the free will of man to follow the teachings of Christ and his own conscience. This belief in the doctrine of one God is the element that gives Unitarianism its name. Actually, in New England, in this period, there was little unifying doctrine except this in the group calling themselves Unitarians. They were individual ministers who were interpreting the gospel for their congregations in accordance with their own consciences and intelligences. The common emphasis among them all was that of the worth of the individual, that man's will is free and that salvation depends upon individual character. They preached that man is essentially good and that he is capable of unlimited progress, as an individual or in society, with dependence upon the element of the divine that is in him. These, in essence, were the elements of romanticism in the new New England religion, without which a romantic literature would never have sprung up.

The early great leader of Unitarianism in New England was William Ellery Channing (1780-1842). Channing, more than any other single church figure, helped pave the way for an intellectual awakening in New England.

A brief idea of transcendentalism

This unwieldy name represents neither a religion nor a philosophy. The group of intellectuals in early New England who called themselves "transcendentalists" were interested in the individual and his goodness. They developed their high ideals somewhat from the liberal philosophy of the German philosopher Kant and the writer Goethe, somewhat from the ideals of the natural man of Rousseau and from the ideas of liberty, equality, and fraternity of the French Revolution, somewhat from the idealized concepts of man and his place in nature of the English romantics, Wordsworth, Coleridge, and Carlyle, somewhat from the Oriental teachings of the Hindus, and a great deal from their own interpretations of these ideals for the living of the good life.

All one needs to know of the very complicated network of ideas that can be built up around the term *transcendentalism,* in order to appreciate the body of literature it gave rise to in New England, is that the doctrine was the lay intellectual counterpart of the Unitarian doctrine that was being preached in the pulpits. It was the doctrine that put total faith in the individual and his worth and goodness, that was a supreme romantic protest against the doctrines of damnation, doubt, and pessimism of the Puritans. The belief endowed the individual man with a sense of ennobling divinity within himself.

Ralph Waldo Emerson, the chief figure of the transcendentalist clubs and organs for spreading the propaganda for the new thought, defines the new American thought in his essay*, *The Transcendentalist.*

What is popularly called Transcendentalism among us, is Idealism: Idealism as it appears in 1842. As thinkers, mankind have ever been divided into two sects, Materialists and Idealists; the first class founding on experience, the second on consciousness; the first class beginning to think from the data of the senses, the second class perceive that the senses are not final, and say, The senses give us representations of things, but what are the things themselves, they cannot tell. The materialist insists on facts, on history, on the force of circumstances and the animal wants of man; the idealist on the power of Thought and Will, on inspiration, on miracle, on individual culture.

The abolitionist doctrine

Growing up side by side with Unitarianism and transcendentalism in New England was the demand to free the negro slaves, for those doctrines held that the worth of the individual did not except individuals of color. It was in New England that this political and social issue reached into literature and produced a great mass of antislavery works. In poetry, Longfellow, Whittier, and Lowell are the chief contributors to this branch of a particular romanticism in our literature. In the novel Harriet Beecher Stowe contributed a work that not only had vast influence in bringing about the abolition of slavery, but has contributed, for better or worse, the most widely known characters and plot in American fiction: *Uncle Tom's Cabin*. On the more didactic side, the issue produced a mass of orations, tracts, essays, and argumentative speeches.

Emerson and the intellectual writers

Ralph Waldo Emerson (1803-1882) was descended from a long line of New England ministers. Graduated from Harvard at the age of 18, he was ordained in the ministry in 1829, when he became pastor of the Second Unitarian Church of Boston. Restless in spirit and subject to recurring attacks of consumption, he resigned his post in 1832.

It was then that Emerson began his lecturing and writing. After an extended trip to Europe, he took up his residence in the "Old Manse" in Concord in 1834. During his stay in Europe, he had met all the intellectual and literary figures in England and his already liberal ideas were beginning to crystallize for expression in masterful essays. From this point on, Emerson's writings contain not only the major expression of transcendentalism, but also the outpourings of the greatest formal essayist (see *essay* in Appendix B) in our literature.

Emerson's literary importance

Emerson, in his writing, was an expounder of ideas. He was a clear thinker and delivered his speeches and lectures with a clear and sweet voice. There is little of this sweetness in his written prose. He had a brilliance of diction, however, in his lectures which does show through in his unique presentation of his ideas. His written works show his remarkable facility to string together his arguments in concise and epigrammatic prose. His transition between ideas is often rough, but once he is launched into an idea, his treatment of it is majestic and clear. Occasionally, he becomes abstruse and hard to follow, but not often.

As a poet Emerson was too philosophic and lacked a great lyric gift. He was, however, intensely personal. His poetry reflects the optimistic viewpoints of his beliefs, his feeling for nature, his humanitarianism, and his keen sense of duty to God and to self.

Emerson's greatest contribution to literature lies in his essays. These treatments of varied subjects of interest were usually delivered originally as lectures and then revised and polished for publication. His major collections are simply known as *Essays* (First Series 1842; Second Series 1844). The First Series is the most widely read and contains his great treatments of *Self-Reliance* (emphasizing his beliefs in individual worth), *Compensation* (his belief in a moral order within the universe), and *The Over-Soul* (a search into the spiritual nature of man to discover a hidden source of truth).

Emerson's most famed speeches and the invaluable sources for his entire system of beliefs are: *Nature* (a source for his most abstract ideas on Man's spiritual ties with Nature), *The American Scholar* (a plea for more American independence from European domination in ideas and creative endeavor), and *The Divinity School Address* (in which Christ is assigned definitely human characteristics and Emerson denies belief in certain miracles and ritual). This speech roused a great deal of protest even within the liberal Unitarian ranks. Emerson himself described the voices that rose up against his utterances as "a storm in our washbowl."

Emerson is our major serious, or formal, essayist. His importance lies first in his ideas and second in the epigrammatic style in which he presents them. His essays are, in essence, lectures on serious topics. They are not informal, or intimate, essays. They hover on the borderline separating aesthetic from didactic writing. But the essays of Emerson represent a high-water mark in American romanticism, the most extreme reaction against the dogmatic Calvinism of the first 230 years of New England history.

Henry David Thoreau (1817-1862)

His is the second greatest literary name among the followers of the transcendental doctrines. Thoreau, more than any other member that belonged to the Transcendental Club and contributed to *The Dial** (the quarterly periodical of the group), actually lived the nonconformist life for a time in his wilderness retreat on Walden Pond.

Thoreau repudiated all institutions of civilization and resolved to reduce his wants to an absolute minimum. He refused to work for others and to exploit the labor of others for his own gain. He was closely associated with the transcendentalists and the antislavery groups, but along with Emerson, refused to join the famed transcendental cooperative project at Brook Farm.*

Thoreau wrote a great number of antislavery articles and some poetry, but his writings as a close student of nature assure him a place in literature beside our best prose stylists. One of his 2 main literary works is a volume on various of the excursions he made into the Maine woods, around Cape Cod, and into Canada. But his most famous writing is *Walden; or, Life in the Woods* (1845). Thoreau, to test his theories about a life of solitude, built a hut on Walden Pond and lived alone in it for slightly over 2 years. The book, then, is a narrative account of his actual life close to nature, his walks and his nature studies, his labors and efforts to provide for his needs in a primitive environment, only a few short miles from Concord and civilization. Also, the book is a record of Thoreau's meditations and the development of his theories and beliefs.

Thoreau wrote in a crystal-clear prose. His smooth flowing, unaffected, and uncomplicated language is both imaginative and witty. Thoreau was a supreme individualist and his account is an excellently written and unique record of a man, alone in nature and in perfect harmony with his own optimistic spirit. Thoreau was undoubtedly antisocial and nonconformist. He lived in solitude, but he was neither a recluse, nor a hermit. He fled to the wilderness, not to escape life but to experiment with a full life for the individual. His "antisocial" and "nonconformist" account of the quest is perhaps the least bitter and most pleasantly interesting book of its kind ever written and one of the most beautifully phrased. *Walden* is pre-eminently an American classic.

Below Emerson and Thoreau, the transcendentalists, the Unitarian, and the other reform groups of the period produced many other writers, all of them didactic in their approach to the various problems and beliefs to which they were attached. Famed among them were *Amos Bronson Alcott, Theodore Parker, Margaret Fuller, William Ellery Channing, James Freeman Clarke,* and many others.

"Uncle Tom's Cabin" of Harriet Beecher Stowe

Practically all the Unitarian and the transcendental writers occasionally delivered sermons, lectures, or wrote abolitionist propaganda. The writer of abolitionist literature's most famous book, however, was a woman of stern Calvinist upbringing, who had little sympathy with any of the followers of "isms" bent upon reforming New England intellectual life. She had simply become convinced that the institution of slavery was morally wrong and she was determined to make herself heard on the issue. Her novel, *Uncle Tom's Cabin; or, Life Among the Lowly* (1852) (207) became better known than any 19th century book. Its sale in many editions of the original novel, and in many translations, abridgements, children's versions, dramatic forms, and parodies is estimated in many millions of copies. The names of Uncle Tom, Little Eva, Topsy, Eliza, and Simon Legree are symbols of their particular types in popular speech the world over. But the novel is not a great one; nor is it in any sense a well-written or even moderately balanced novel.

The faults of the book are quickly obvious. It is carelessly written and dripping from cover to cover with sentiment. The characters are types, rather than individuals. The situations are melodramatic and exaggerated. The very faults of the book account for much of its appeal. Its major virtue was that it was timely and that the author had poured into it but a single aim, to arouse a moral indignation. This, plus the effects of strong emotional treatment, the use of types to heighten virtue and vice, and the exaggerated situations all combined to give the book a human appeal that immediately struck a common responsive chord in readers of every clime.

Uncle Tom's Cabin was our first sociological novel, and

Stowe, by accident perhaps, rather than skillful intent, gave her message the treatment that caught the fancy of people the world over. Mrs. Stowe treated a major social problem of our country effectively some 50 years before the social novel came into vogue in America around 1900. Whether we arch our brows or no at the crudities of this book, it has been a major force in our literature and an American book that immediately reached into the remote corners of civilization in 37 foreign languages.

Harriet Beecher Stowe wrote 2 more antislavery works: *A Key to Uncle Tom's Cabin* (1853), in which she defended her novel and attested to the authenticity of its situations, and *Dred, A Tale of the Great Dismal Swamp* (1856). She then turned to popular romances dealing nostalgically with the past glories of the 18th century Puritan New England. The best (all better-constructed novels than her famed effort) are: *The Minister's Wooing* (1859), *The Pearl of Orr's Island* (1862), and *Oldtown Folks* (1869).

The Major Mid-Century Romantics

By 1840, the new order was established in New England. Slowly but surely, the old Calvinist dogma and tradition died under the onslaught of Unitarianism, transcendental doctrines, and an all-enveloping romanticism. As intellectual sterility vanished, an aesthetic literature began to rise. The chief figures of the aesthetic side of New England romanticism are not all found in a group, or "school." Two figures, Whittier and Hawthorne, are isolated romantics, belonging to no tradition or school. They are not of the Cambridge aristocratic traditions; they are simply individual writers, both middle-class Yankees. Longfellow, Lowell, and Holmes, however, belong to the New England Brahmins,* the name applied to the aristocratic society of the area, and follow the elegant taste and manners of Boston society. They belong to what has been called the "genteel tradition," the tradition of gentlemen, the rich, the Harvard-trained, and the blue-blooded, the self-styled arbiters of an elegant society which inherited and passed on its standards of respectability, of "good" and "bad" taste, the determination to admit within its circle no forces to detract from its aura of self-satisfaction in its own artificial and impregnable appearance of well-being and success. In no corner of America did an upper-class society, with its inviolable code of custom and prejudices, its family ties and frigid culture, hold sway with such an iron hand as in Boston. But with romanticism and the new intellectual movements, this group simply contributed their own, but very important, production to the total of romantic writings of the period. Nowhere in America did the group of the "genteel tradition" find a counterpart which more resembled the Victorians* of England of the same time.

But romanticism was no respecter of genteel tradition. It was an all-pervading spirit that touched both the traditionally literary Brahmins and the poor but gifted sons of tradesmen. The greatest writers of the period in New England have little in common. Equally romantic, Emerson's group had no other common tie with Longfellow and the Cambridge group. They both showed an equal spirit of creativeness. Whittier was a lone Quaker, fired with abolitionist zeal, who ignored both the transcendentalist-Unitarian groups, the members of the genteel tradition, and was ignored by them. Hawthorne had no zeal for any of the reform movements, little scholarship, and little desire to travel any path except that of a solitary and poor recluse. But all these writers come together in American literature as our major and most varied flowering of literature at the height of the romantic period, near the mid-years of the 19th century.

John Greenleaf Whittier (1807-1892)

Whittier's early life was largely devoted to his antislavery writings, although in this period he did write a few poems depicting the New England rural setting. However, the poems for which we know him best were written after 1865 and show distinct tinges of realistic description in their "local color" slant.

The prewar Whittier

Whittier came from a family tradition of Quaker faith. He received a meager education, his health was poor, and he faced a lifetime of poverty. Whittier grew up to be a frail man, intensely devoted to his religion of tolerance, kindness, and personal serenity. He withdrew from contact with all the violent intellectual controversy that was raging about him. His one intense hatred was slavery and he became abolitionism's chief poet. Of course, after the Emancipation Proclamation, this early verse of Whittier was ignored.

Before 1865, no voice in America rang louder against slavery than that of the frail, partially deaf, color blind, Whittier, in his many short abolitionist poems. His was a moral warfare.

> A hate of tyranny intense
> And hearty in its vehemence.

The postwar poet

After 1865, the ailing New England Quaker wrote his best-loved poems, all in a quiet vein, exploring the themes of his rural surroundings. Mingled with his poems of "local color" are many pieces of childhood reminiscences and expositions of the principles of his gentle and peaceful Quaker philosophy.

Whittier's intimate little descriptive poems of New England rural settings are still perennial favorites. He explored the Colonial period with many ballads*, of which *Moll Pitcher* is perhaps the best. He tramped the countryside, describing the natural settings in quiet, colorful, word-pictures, as in *Among the Hills, The Last Walk in Autumn, Hampton Beach*. He was interested in the people he met and many of his poems portray realistic personages, given his mellow tones of idealization. One such person was a country girl, who, when he approached her, grew embarrassed at her scanty attire and covered her bare feet with hay. He immortalized her in his imaginative ballad *Maud Muller,* having her long for the city and one day meet her ideal, the city Judge. She falls in love with him but he rides away. Later he marries a fine city lady but always holds dearly the picture of the pretty country girl. Maud works in the fields and continues to dream of how fine it would have been to have become the bride of such a fine man.

> God pity them both! and pity us all,
> Who vainly the dreams of youth recall.

> For of all sad words of tongue or pen,
> The saddest are these: "It might have been!"

In *Skipper Ireson's Ride* the poet weaves one of his best ballads with the rich dialect of Marblehead.

Whittier's longest and most famed poem is *Snow-Bound* (208), one of America's most-loved poems. Here the poet is at his descriptive best in recording the memories of his birthplace and his recollections of early childhood.

Whittier wrote a great deal of prose, the best of which is a little volume called *Margaret Smith's Journal (1848)*, in which he gives a very detailed and accurate account of the Quaker spirit and hardships in Massachusetts Bay in 1678.

As a poet, Whittier is not great. His rhyme is uneven and his viewpoint is limited to a narrow world. But he is perhaps our best local-color poet and his word pictures of rural New England and his quietly tender reminiscences will be popular for a long time to come. He is a thoroughly American product, showing little of the influence of European romanticism. He is simple, tender and serene; no deep melancholy or violent passions mark his verse which is remembered. He is limited in scope but, within those limits, he can reach American hearts with many of his poems.

> Blessings on thee, little man,
> Barefoot boy, with cheek of tan!
> With thy turned-up pantaloons,
> And thy merry whistled tunes;
> With thy red lip, redder still
> Kissed by strawberries on the hill;
> With the sunshine on thy face,
> Through thy torn brim's jaunty grace,
> From my heart I give thee joy,—
> I was once a barefoot boy! . . .

Nathaniel Hawthorne (1804-1864)

Hawthorne was a strange member of a strange family. His ancestors were shipbuilders of Salem. His father, a ship captain, died while on a voyage in the Caribbean. The mother became a psychopathic recluse for the rest of her life. The 2 daughters seemed to have acquired the same malady.

Nathaniel lived with an uncle for a while and then entered Bowdoin College. During the 4 years there he lived a very solitary existence. He either read alone in his room or associated briefly with companions at the local tavern. When he left college, he could not decide upon a profession and returned to his mother's old home in Salem. His own words portray vividly the sort of life he lived during his twenties.

> . . . I had always a tendency towards seclusion, and this I now indulged to the uttermost, so that for months together I scarcely held human intercourse outside of my own family, seldom going out except at twilight, or only to take the nearest way to the most convenient solitude, which was oftenest the seashore. . . . I had very few acquaintances in Salem, and during the nine or ten years that I spent there in this solitary way, I doubt whether so much as twenty people in the town were aware of my existence.

Even in college Hawthorne was trying to write sketches in the manner of Irving. At last he attempted a novel. He seemed obsessed throughout his life with a guilt complex, as though he had committed an unpardonable sin and was damned to solitary confinement. At last he wrote some legendary sketches of Salem history which were published in the *Salem Gazette*. No recognition came from these.

Finally, a friend secretly financed publication of a collection of 19 of Hawthorne's sketches under the title *Twice Told Tales (1837)*. There is an eerie atmosphere about his *Sights from a Steeple, The Minister's Black Veil, The Toll-Gatherer's Day*, and the rest of this odd assortment of allegory and parables. It would almost seem that much of it could be jottings in the notebook of a Puritan preacher. But the reviewers were favorable and for a while Hawthorne's spirits soared. He even took a job in the Boston customs house. After 2 years he was back in the bleak house at Salem. He married and again seemed to be happy for a time.

Hawthorne's masterpieces

In 1850, at the age of 46, Hawthorne published *The Scarlet Letter* (209). It was hailed as the "American novel." Here Hawthorne was on familiar ground, the dark and foreboding shadows of the Puritan past. The book is a poetic treatment of sin and its consequences. The atmosphere is one of despair and gloom. Hawthorne succeeds adequately in keeping his authentic atmosphere throughout. *The Scarlet Letter* is not a bright book but it is an enduring masterpiece in our literature for its skillful blending of mood, character development, and poetic prose.

Little actually happens: it is the story of Hester Prynne who is doomed by her Puritan neighbors to wear the scarlet letter "A" for adultery. The book is mainly a vivid set of sketches of the darker side of the Puritan conscience. Hawthorne is more concerned with the effects of concealed sin than with the sin itself. Hawthorne lets each character struggle with his own conscience. There is never a doubt in the reader's mind that each, in his own way, will be punished for whatever type of sin of which he is guilty. It is no surprise to the reader when the minister, Arthur Dimmesdale confesses publicly that he is the father of Hester's child, instead of fleeing with Hester, as was previously planned.

The treatment of adultery in a book scandalized many in Hawthorne's day. The resulting uproar and the fact that many libraries refused to put the book on their shelves undoubtedly resulted in the greater popularity of the novel.

The House of Seven Gables (1851) is again a joyless narrative with a Salem Puritan setting. It seems that a curse had been laid on the Pyncheon house when old Colonel Pyncheon had first acquired it by laying a charge of witchcraft against its rightful owner, Wizard Maule. The present occupants, Hepzibah Pyncheon and her simple brother Clifford, live in the gloomy old seven-gabled house with their cousin Phoebe and a lodger, Holgrave. Hepzibah runs a little shop in front to eke out their living. The villain is old Judge Pyncheon, who constantly hounds his relatives, believing that they are concealing the family fortune. Phoebe and Holgrave fall in love despite the circumstances which surround them. After many pages of stress on the evils of inbreeding and the sins of heredity, Hawthorne has Phoebe and Holgrave marry. Holgrave, a descendant of old Maule, is thus responsible for bringing joy back into the old house and for lifting the curse.

This novel is again an artistic treatment of the gloom and the shadows of a Puritan spirit which envelops the characters and the house. Hawthorne, as in _The Scarlet Letter,_ ends with the ray of promise that good deeds and pure heart can do much to expiate the sins of the past. In this book, also, are many digressions from the plot to develop customs and character of a Puritan background.

Other novels and the short stories

Hawthorne's _Blithedale Romance_ (1852) deals with the surroundings of Brook Farm, the transcendental retreat, where he lived a year, but with little sympathy for the doctrines of its inhabitants. This book is light and airy, in comparison to Hawthorne's two main works. The plot is poor, however, and neither this novel nor _The Marble Faun,_ laid in Italy, approaches the classic artistry that the author imparts to his two major works.

Hawthorne was an artist, and like Poe, his major virtue is his uncanny ability to impart a mood with his prose. In his two masterpieces he succeeds admirably. In many of his short sketches and stories, concerned with sin, fantasy, pseudo science, and history, he also succeeds. Notable short pieces in which he blends his atmosphere to harmonize with well integrated plots are: _Dr. Heidegger's Experiment, The Birthmark, The Ambi-_

tious Guest, The Maypole of Merry Mount (see page 7), *Rappaccini's Daughter, Lady Eleanore's Mantle,* and others.

From 1853 to 1856 Hawthorne was U.S. consul in Liverpool, England. After another year in Rome, he returned home and seemed to break both physically and mentally. He continued to write but produced nothing of merit during the rest of his life. In his last writings he was plagued with a technical fault that also mars his novels. He always seemed to begin with a short story plot and would then try to expand that into a novel. Only in *The Scarlet Letter* and *The House of Seven Gables* did his artistry succeed in overcoming this obvious shortcoming in all his long fiction.

The Brahmin Poets
Henry Wadsworth Longfellow (1807-1882)

Longfellow was born in Portland, Maine, into a wealthy Puritan family. At Bowdoin he showed great aptitude for foreign languages and was later made a Professor of Modern Languages there. He spent 3 years in France, Spain, Italy, and Germany between 1826 and 1829. His wife, a childhood sweetheart, died in Rotterdam on his second trip through Europe. In 1843 he married again, this time to a daughter of wealthy Boston society, and settled into the chair of Modern Languages at Harvard.

Longfellow's first writing was an undistinguished prose. It was inspired by his European travels and his reading of the German romantics, particularly the idealistically mystic Novalis. His *Outre-Mer* (1833) are sketches of his travels in the manner of Irving and his *Hyperion* (1839) is light prose romance in which the narrative becomes lost in the author's airy creation of an elaborate sentimentalized atmosphere, a "mingling of daylight and starlight." But from his collection of verse, *Voices in the Night,* the same year, until his retirement from his Harvard chair in 1854, Longfellow wrote most of the poems for which he became America's most widely read poet.

Longfellow's poetic talent

Longfellow was no great poet. He was a charmingly simple stringer of rhymes with little depth and scant originality. But he became the most popular American poet and is, perhaps, still the most read and best known of our poets. School children the world over have received their earliest impressions of poetry from this simple rhyme of Longfellow. He bids fair to continue in popularity in school anthologies and popular general anthologies for years to come. And as such, he is an important figure in the history of our writings.

Longfellow had learning and talent and is best when he deals in simple narrative verse with smooth and easy rhyme or when he is pointing up a lesson or an obvious virtue.

> Lives of great men all remind us
> We can make our lives sublime,
> And, departing, leave behind us
> Footprints on the sands of time;
> (from *The Psalm of Life*)

Though Longfellow wrote most of his verse for adult readers, most of his poetry is delightful adolescent fare. Occasionally, he pointed his patriotic or homily-type rhyme toward children.

> Listen, my children, and you shall hear,
> Of the midnight ride of Paul Revere . . .

But he contemplated genteel readers among his own class and apparently his verse found adult and genteel readers on both sides of the Atlantic. By 1857 his volumes of verse had sold 300,000 copies; in London his *The Courtship of Miles Standish* sold 10,000 copies the first day it was issued. When he visited England in 1868 he received honors from every side, degrees from Oxford and Cambridge, and was received by the Queen. Longfellow was well representative of his Brahmin society in Boston, as Tennyson was of a comparable Victorian England. Longfellow could not plumb the soul nor the deeper emotional depths of nature or of humans. His romanticism was typical of mid-century Bostonians of the upper-class genteel tradition. They were romantic as long as it was an obedient romanticism; they would never allow their pet literary experimentation to get out of hand and ruffle unduly the placid surface of emotional respectability and the genteel calm of the Brahmin spirit. Longfellow, at times, assumed in life a Byronic countenance and sighed deeply, but his romanticism was skin deep, bookish, and deliberate.

Longfellow's rhymed narratives (211)

With exception of oft-quoted lines from short poems, the most widely known production of Longfellow consists of 3 long narrative poems: _Evangeline (1847), The Song of Hiawatha (1855)_, and _The Courtship of Miles Standish (1858)_. A fourth long narrative, _The Building of the Ship_ (1850) deals with national issues and has not enjoyed popularity since the Fugitive Slave Law, the Free Soil Party, and other issues of the day were being debated. The 3 major poems, however, have become a part of the democratic culture of America and, for better or worse, reflect much of its nature.

All 3 poems are sentimentalized love romances. _Evangeline_ is the sad account of the displacement of Nova Scotia farmers during the French and Indian Wars. Evangeline is separated from her lover and the epic-type poem is largely the relation of her search for him. When she finally becomes a nun, she finds him, dying from an epidemic. The poem ends as both lovers die and are buried together. _Hiawatha_ is the Indian epic of America. Longfellow's jingling meter is an imitation of that of _"Kalevala,"_ the Finnish national epic. This sentimental romance deals with the love of the wise chief, Hiawatha, and his lovely Indian wife, Minnehaha. Again, as in _Evangeline,_ the ending is delicately sad as Minnehaha dies and Hiawatha departs from his people to rule over the land of the Northwest wind. _Miles Standish_ transports the reader to the Plymouth Colony where John Alden, beloved of Priscilla, nobly offers to woo the maiden in the name of the bashful, but brave, Captain Standish. The "speak for yourself, John" of the lovely Priscilla is engraved upon the memory of every literate American.

During the last 20 years of his life, Longfellow turned his main efforts to long narrative and translations. These, including a translation of _The Divine Comedy_ of Dante, are not particularly distinguished.

Longfellow's work also includes a number of ballads, both adaptations and translations, from European folk sources. He did much to bring this unknown ballad literature of the Continent to Americans who were aware only of English balladry. His most popular use of the ballad form, however, is an original piece called _The Wreck of the Hesperus_ (1840), based upon an actual shipwreck off the Gloucester coast. The skipper had taken along his little daughter to bear him company and Longfellow, in his characteristic sentimentality, records the naïve conversation between the captain and his daughter as the boat dashes itself to pieces against the reef of Norman's Woe. The following lines illustrate well this poet's simple, sentimentalized manner.

> At daybreak, on the bleak sea-beach,
>   A fisherman stood aghast,
> To see the form of a maiden fair,
>   Lashed close to a drifting mast.
>
> The salt sea was frozen on her breast,
>   The salt tears in her eyes;
> And he saw her hair, like the brown seaweed,
>   On the billows fall and rise.

Longfellow will long retain popularity in a democratic literature. His simple rhyme and uncomplicated treatment of his
themes will continue to please generations of schoolchildren,
and even adult sophisticates who, occasionally, like to relax
their minds mid the jingling movement of adolescent rhyme.

> Under a spreading chestnut-tree
>   The village smithy stands;
> The smith, a mighty man is he,
>   With large and sinewy hands;
> And the muscles of his brawny arms
>   Are strong as iron bands. . . .

James Russell Lowell (1819-1891)

Lowell was from a prominent Cambridge family. He took a
law degree from Harvard in 1840, but soon wearied of law
practice. Though of the most distinguished of Brahmin families,
he soon became known among the members of his social class
as a "radical." In 1844 he married a girl who was an ardent
abolitionist; at this time he was also lending a sympathetic ear
to the transcendental arguments. He wrote most of the poems for
which he is best known during this early period when he temporarily had deserted the calm dignity of his social group and
was associating with the reformers and romantic idealists of the
period.

Lowell and Longfellow compared

There are many parallels between Lowell's life and that of
Longfellow. The basic difference is the fact that Longfellow
never bent from his Brahmin upbringing, except to indulge
superficially into the European romantic spirit of the times. His
poetry was a pale American imitation of that spirit on a level
of surface sentimentality and light moralizing. Lowell who, like
Longfellow, wrote his best verse early in life, mingled into his

romantic writing a good deal of the rationalism and reform ideas of his age. He was more in contact with American life and its problems than Longfellow, at least during his most productive decade, between 1840 and 1850.

From 1850 on, Lowell's life ran remarkably in the path of that of Longfellow. His wife was an invalid. He took her to Europe in 1851, where she died 2 years later. By this time Lowell had tired of his earlier leanings toward reform and for the rest of his life maintained the placid indifference of his ancestral group toward social problems and their solution.

In 1855 he took over the chair of Modern Languages at Harvard from Longfellow. He held this position until 1875. Following his resignation, he was American Minister to Spain for 8 years. When Lowell died, the genteel tradition in American literature was already dead.

"The Biglow Papers"

Most of Lowell's early writing is collected in the two series of *The Biglow Papers* (1848; 1867). Lowell adopted the pen name "Mr. Ezekiel Biglow of Jaalam" for his many letters, Yankee-dialect poems, and satirical matter which he published in the *Boston Courier* and the *National Anti-Slavery Standard*. This diverse matter contains much of Lowell's humor and punning wit. An especially amusing example of the poet's early dialect verse is *The Courtin'* (1848), in which the bashful Zekle pops the question to the anxious Huldy:

> "You want to see my Pa, I s'pose?"
>   "Wal . . . no . . . I come dasignin' "—
> "To see my Ma? She's sprinklin' clo'es
>   Agin to-morrer's i'nin'."
>
> To say why gals act so or so,
>   Or don't, 'ould be presumin';
> Mebby to mean *yes* an' say *no*
>   Comes nateral to women.
>
> He stood a spell on one foot fust,
>   Then stood a spell on t'other,
> An' on which one he felt the wust
>   He couldn't ha' told ye nuther.
>
> Says he. "I'd better call agin";
>   Says she, "Think likely, Mister":
> That last word pricked him like a pin,
>   An' . . . Wal, he up an' kist her . . .

The portions of *The Biglow Papers* which are most serious in tone show Lowell attacking slavery, opposing the war with Mexico and the annexation of Texas. Taken together, these two volumes of miscellaneous content represent Lowell's most enduring writing.

Lowell as a critic

During Lowell's 20 years at Harvard, after 1855, his major attention was directed toward critical essays, both on literary and on public issues. In 1848 he had published a long verse *Fable for Critics,* in which he combined his wit and common sense to comment upon the writers of his times, including Poe, Cooper, Thoreau, and others. His criticism is severe, but fair; his poetry is crude and irregular. He became more addicted to classic writers in his later period. His criticisms of the writers of his day, Thoreau and the French Taine, are considered today to be highly unfair.

Miscellaneous verse

An outstanding early poem of Lowell, and his most purely romantic production, is *The Vision of Sir Launfal* (1848), in which the poet deals with the Holy Grail legend. The poem is quite mystical* and drives home the message of brotherly love and service to mankind. Aside from the use of the legendary subject matter, Lowell's descriptions of nature and the effects he achieves by changing his meters during the poem are strong evidence that he is capable of more power and depth in romance than Longfellow.

Lowell's short lyric verse is didactic and moral and only occasionally does he give way to what might be called any unrestrained emotionalism. Lowell seems to feel that he must be either witty or didactic, or that, at least, he must be profound and dignified. Lowell had the ability to laugh at his own self-admitted shortcomings; he does so a number of times in his critical notes. In his poem, *The Origin of Didactic Poetry* (1875), he has the goddess Minerva take to verse writing. When she has penned a sufficient number of highly moral rhymes, she proposes to read them before the gods. After hearing the first lines, one by one the gods excuse themselves and leave. Poor Minerva tears up her rhymes and throws them to the winds. Some of the pieces of parchment kill fish, others are used by famous physicians to distill powerful drugs.

Years after, when a poet asked
  The Goddess's opinion,
As one whose soul its wings had tasked
  In Art's clear-aired dominion,
"Discriminate," she said, "betimes;
  The Muse is unforgiving;
Put all your beauty in your rhymes,
  Your morals in your living."

Oliver Wendell Holmes (1809-1894)

Holmes was an essayist and a writer of poetry, mainly a short, light, sentimental, or playful verse of a sophisticated nature (known as *vers de societé* or society verse). He was descended from a long line of aristocratic New England stock. His father was a prominent Cambridge clergyman. Holmes studied medicine in Paris and took his M.D. at Harvard in 1836. He was Professor of Anatomy at Dartmouth for 2 years, moving to an equal position in Harvard, from which he retired in 1882.

Holmes had no part in the violent intellectual turmoil that was going on around him. He lived a quiet and serene life. The only subject which ever seemed to irritate him was orthodox Calvinism. The only bitterness in his writing is directed against that stern code. Though he was fanned by the breezes of romanticism, they affected him little except to provoke his laughter.

Holmes wrote many serious articles on themes pertaining to his specialties and some serious moral verse expressing his simple faith and humanistic point of view.

Build thee more stately mansions, O my soul,
  As the swift seasons roll!
  Leave thy low-vaulted past!
Let each new temple, nobler than the last,
Shut thee from heaven with a dome more vast,
  Till thou at length art free,
Leaving thine outgrown shell by life's restless sea!
          (from *The Chambered Nautilus*—1858)

His best-known series of books comprises *The Autocrat of the Breakfast Table* (1831-1832; 1858), a collection of essays and poems previously published in various magazines. Actually this volume and his later *The Professor at the Breakfast Table* (1860), *The Poet at the Breakfast Table* (1872), and *Over the Teacups* (1891) are rambling conversations on varied and sundry subjects. Much of the Holmes verse is scattered about in these intimate and informal essays. Holmes reveals every side of his genial and self-satisfied nature in these volumes. His treatment is varied, sometimes serious, mostly lightly humorous or satirical. He introduces many elements of contrast and his style is intimate and personal. He was widely read and gives the reader many sharply pointed comments on various fields of knowledge. These books of Holmes miscellany make pleasant reading today—especially the first book of the series.

Holmes the humorist

The most famed of the individual poems of Holmes are his light and humorous pieces. He is the first major humorist of our literature. His humor can be both broad and subtle, but seldom carries more than a mild satirical sting. His purpose was mainly to make his reader smile, not frown too deeply in anger or in indignation. Famed pieces of this nature have roused chuckles in every generation since Holmes wrote them and their exaggerations are still as timely today as when they were written. *The Deacon's Masterpiece, or the Wonderful "One-Hoss Shay,"* presents us with a vehicle so perfectly constructed that no part wore out faster than another. One day, 100 years after it was built, the deacon was riding in it when the inevitable happened and he found himself sitting alone upon a rock.

> The poor old chaise in a heap or mound,
> As if it had been to the mill and ground!
> You see, of course, if you're not a dunce,
> How it went to pieces all at once,—
> All at once, and nothing first,—
> Just as bubbles do when they burst.
>
> End of the wonderful one-hoss shay.
> Logic is logic. That's all I say.

This is a light satire on the collapse of Calvinism.

The Ballad of the Oysterman is one of his most popular pieces, a satire on the fad during the romantic period for poets to write ballads. *How the Old Horse Won the Bet* reveals the Holmes fancy for race horses. *My Aunt* shows the poet, blending his lighter and more kindly humor with deep human sympathy for the woman who was protected from harm by her father and given the most refined training for life—with the consequence that life never stopped at her door when she was finally prepared to welcome it.

My aunt! my dear unmarried aunt!
  Long years have o'er her flown;
Yet still she strains the aching clasp
  That binds her virgin zone;
I know it hurts her,—though she looks
  As cheerful as she can;
Her waist is ampler than her life,
  For life is but a span . . .

Minor Figures of the Mid-Century

Many figures of the period made major contributions to our fund of literary culture. There were literally hundreds of novelists and poets, journalists and essay writers, some only known for one book or for their efforts in nonaesthetic fields, but all producing works which are read and studied today. A few of these most notable minor writers are the following.

Richard Henry Dana, Jr. (1815-1882) sailed around Cape Horn as an ordinary seaman to provide himself with material for _Two Years Before the Mast_ (1840), a classic for its exciting record of actual adventure and hardship aboard the sailing ships of the day. Dana directed his book toward elimination of the cruel abuses prevalent aboard U.S. ships. It succeeded in arousing public indignation to the extent that the practice of flogging was banned immediately on ships of the United States.

William H. Prescott (1796-1859) was our first major historian. His favorite field was Spain and her conquests in America. Many of his conclusions have received new interpretation, but his detailed and interesting accounts are still a basic wealth of authority in those areas of historical studies. _George Tickner_ also pioneered in the history of Spanish literature at the same time, producing 3 volumes in 1849 which are still among the best coverage of the history of the field.

Francis Parkman (1823-1893) is most famous for his _The Oregon Trail_ (1849). Parkman was an early interpreter of many other phases of our western expansion, as well as the part the French played in the early history of the settlement of the continent.

John James Audubon (1785-1851) was our most famed naturalist of the period for his _The Birds of America,_ and especially for his huge set of remarkable and colorful pictures of the bird life in America.

TOWARD A NEW AGE

With the end of the Civil War, anything approaching the aspect of revolt or revolution in American romanticism was gone. A romanticism from Europe had served as a primer for the beginnings of a true national literature in the United States. A body of national literature had not yet been created, but romanticism was the prevailing influence that inspired writers in various sections of the nation to produce their own particular types of writing. There was never a true romantic movement or school in the nation, only isolated sectional groups and individual writers who aped Europe or timidly attempted to create some type of artistic interpretation of the American scene in imitation of European models.

A great deal of writing and a few notable works in our store of literary accomplishment stand out from this formative period in which there was little more than sectional interest in writings. Poe was unknown in New England. Hawthorne's novels did not penetrate into the South. Melville had scant influence even in his own New York. Walt Whitman was the only writer who spanned the Civil War years and continued to shout and expand his paeans of pride in the land, its peoples, and its achievements. His was the only truly national voice that made itself heard in both the prewar and the postwar periods.

Romanticism in American literature did not die with this mid-century period but became a major characteristic of our literature in the next period, along with the new elements of "local color" in a frontier literature and realism, which were to stand alongside it as the other major characteristics in our first truly national body of writings—writings which had immediate influence and an audience in all parts of the nation.

Chapter IV

THE GILDED AGE—LOCAL COLOR, ROMANTICISM, REALISM (1865 to 1890)

The Civil War marked the transition to a new age for the United States, equally as revolutionary as had been the transition from the Colonial age to the early years of the constitutional republic. The Revolution had welded the spirit of self-reliance and individualism in the colonies into a single purpose: to defeat England and to throw off foreign domination of their affairs. The following period had brought a nation into being and had expanded greatly the pre-Revolutionary frontiers to the West. But this period had brought no real feeling of nationalism to the various sections of America. Our nation was still provincial, and each area was little aware of what was happening beyond its sectional borders.

The literature of the period was imitative and largely adolescent. Writers functioned as individuals and their products vaguely came under the romantic banner only because all the individual writers looked to the same sources for their inspiration —romantic Germany, France, and England. With rare exceptions, the writers of the period ignored the course of national development and American thought, and maintained themselves aloof from the pulse beat of the expanding frontier.

After the period of reconstruction from 1865 to 1870, sectional interests became, for the first time, *national* interests, and each sector of the country looked upon the development of each other sector as a part of its own affairs. Interest came to be focused now upon the nation, rather than merely the state. Provincialism was vanishing. Genteel tradition and plantation tradition no longer commanded even sectional attention. The intellectual life of the nation was no longer to be the decree of the aristocratic and scholarly few.

A European romanticism in America was dead, and its writers, with the sole exception of the booming pride of Walt Whitman, were silent. But Whitman had spoken with the new voice before the war. A new and truly national literature was taking shape, an American romanticism, tempered progressively more and more with tones of realism and the colorful realities of the country, particularly the West where history was being made, that was eagerly being followed by the nation as a whole. New England, New York, and the South not only looked toward the West now; the descendants of their most established families migrated there in great numbers, while their Brahmin parents looked over their spectacles and raised their brows at the vulgarity of the new generation and muttered over their teacups, with Holmes, of "the great multitude" and "the homespun classes" that were shaking their cherished traditions to their very foundations. The traditional and the aristocratic were singing their swan song and a new American expression was about to drown out the last stanzas.

> All the past we leave behind;
> We debouch upon a newer, mightier world, varied
>   world,
> Fresh and strong the world we seize, world of labor and
>   the march,
>   Pioneers! O pioneers!
>
> All the pulses of the world,
> Falling in, they beat for us, with the western movement
>   beat;
> Holding single or together, steady moving, to the front,
>   all for us,
>   Pioneers! O pioneers!
>   (from Whitman's *Pioneers! O Pioneers!*—1865)

HISTORICAL NOTES—THE GILDED AGE

More and more, as perspective broadens with time, we are coming to look back upon the quarter of a century between 1865 and 1890 as a gilded age. It was an age of an intense nationalism and of the phenomenal rise of American big business. It was an age of scandal, of greed, and of self-seeking individuals and groups. It was an age of science, of pseudo-science, of technology, invention, commerce, and finance. It was an age of few standards to judge the real from the false, the good from the bad, the right from the wrong. Ideals of the past suddenly were swept aside and expediency leaped into a position of first importance in the determination of action. It was an age that brought the high idealism and the individuality of romanticism to a low ebb by the end of the century. It was an age of industry, of trial and error, of monetary gain, and of material progress. It was an age that brought realism into the forefront of American life and thought by the last decade of the century. It was an age that divided our thinking sharply upon the major values of life.

By the Civil War the sweep westward had reached the Pacific coast and our boundaries had become defined very much as they are today, both north and south. The Civil War focused our thinking upon the whole nation and upon provision for large groups of people. The individual, the domestic craftsman, the trail breaker, and the tight provincial group suddenly lost importance. The population had leaped from 7 million in 1810 to 38 million in 1870 and to 75 million by 1900.

At the War's end the southern aristocracy had lost its political power, and a New England genteel tradition had no message that would serve the widened national horizons. A struggle for power and control began between agricultural and industrial interests. At times it was a bitter one and at first that bitterness was reflected little in the new literatures. It was only in the period nearing 1890 that voices began to make themselves heard in our writing, protesting the evils that came in the wake of the quarter century of mad scramble in which few holds were barred.

The end results of the era reflected themselves in a rapidly rising standard of living for the majority of the people, a rapid exploitation of the great new areas to the west, a concentration of capital on an industrial, rather than an aristocratic, basis. The frontier vanished rapidly during the period and it was the activities of that vanishing frontier that most commanded interest throughout the nation. Population began to concentrate itself rapidly into the urban centers of manufacturing and commercial interests. Chicago leaped from a population of 44,000 in 1840 to become a city of 1,500,000 by 1900. Over 4 million immigrants from Europe poured into the country to settle the new lands in the quarter century.

The gilded age was a period of mad scramble for wealth and power. Gold was the symbol of the age; its possession guided the actions of individuals and groups throughout the land with rare exception. Economic progress and power among nations was the gain; the dethronement of high ideals of the spirit and of artistic accomplishment and the sharp divisions of our society on the basis of wealth and the power that it brought was the loss.

LITERATURE IN THE GILDED AGE

In literature, the aristocratic ideals for artistic achievement were largely gone. A genteel romanticism had no place in the new order of interests. The spirit of the new America was realistic. Sentimentality, idle dreams, idealization of past ages, polished phrases and ornate figures of speech, a softness of tone, mystery and moonlight, and idle wandering among the Gothic ruins of Europe—all these things had suddenly become history.

Demand for Democratization of Literature

People read newspapers and magazines in the decade between 1860 and 1870. By 1870, the young writers for these mediums had begun to produce books and these were eagerly read as books had never been read before in America. But these new books were written, not in accordance with European standards or with the desire and whims of scholarly intellectuals, books written for the consumption of a small aristocratic class of readers. These writings were designed and written for the mass consumption of large groups of the people. And the people demanded writings which would give them colorful and entertaining views of life as it was happening about them in the nation. Characters must be people who actually lived in some section of the United States. Incidents must be probable in life in the U.S.A. at the time. People in fictional settings must talk, think, and dress as they actually did. The demand in one section was for literature that portrayed realistically and colorfully the life in other sections. Provincialism was dead. People were interested in what was foreign to them within the nation, and what was exotic in their own surroundings. Thus far romanticism could go and no further. They were not interested in false views, nor idealized views, nor deeply philosophic views, nor overly ornamented and artistic treatment of their material. Literature had suddenly become democratic and real and tinged with local colorful people and events.

A New Combination of Romanticism and Realism

The gilded age brought literature to the common man, and by 1890, little evidence of opposition to that trend had yet shown itself in our writing. The writers of the prewar period were silent for the most part and few of the new generation followed their footsteps into a romantic idealism. But after the 25-year interim of the gilded age, a new generation, born in the period from 1860 to 1875, was building up a resentment that would appear in print only after 1890. That generation is the business of the next chapter of our history.

The major writings of the gilded age, then, are a blend of a colorful and exotic aspect of romanticism and of a reproduction of reality within that rose-colored romantic glow. Around 1880, this new literary fad dominated our literature. It has received the name of "literature of local color." Its major emphasis is on a particular geographical setting. Local-color writing capitalizes on the speech, manners, dress, habits, thought, and topography of a particular sector of the country. The major writers of the period accepted as their literary aim the "discovery" of sectors of American life which would provide interesting reading for all the people of the nation. Their revelations must be authentic and real, and their manner of treatment must be colorful and exciting.

A more conservative group of writers mingled their production with that of the local colorists in the period. They sought to tone down the colorful and sensational elements in their writings and to concentrate attention upon the significance of the actual events that were transpiring in the age. This group was composed of the individuals who wandered in their creative spirit, who doubted and could not settle upon a determined road in their writings. Hence their work runs from pure romantic idealism, through local color, and all the way to realism. These were individuals who felt themselves being swallowed up in a collective environment that was very real in its repudiation of the individual who disagreed with it. This group sought to color their realistic treatment of life with a mild revolt against the evils that the gilded age was bringing into American life. But this group did not forsake the exoticism of local color; they would not have been read in their age had they done so.

The age was one that would brook no attitude but one of a hearty optimism and these middle-of-the-road writers, despite the introduction of a mildly satirical tone into their works, maintained an over-all effect of outward optimism. They began to search for facts, but the search, when expressed for the reader, must continue to be a pleasant one. This group sought only to chip and crack false idols where they could, and this gently. They were cautious and gave reality only a glance here and there in their writings. America would not accept a literary realism in this age, and these writers were reluctant to remain unread. The writings of this group present a second curious mixture of romanticism and realism to complement that of the local colorists. The local colorists placed emphasis upon the romantic aspects of sensationalism and sentiment as they sought reality; these more conservative and iconoclastic writers sought to bring a weak realism to the front against a glaringly colorful backdrop of optimistic romanticism.

An Approaching Era of Realism and Disillusion

It was only after 1890, when an American public had become aroused and indignant at the revelation of the social inequalities present in the nation, at the public exposure of the greed, the graft, and the corruption in industrial groups, political groups, and self-seeking speculators in the natural resources of the country, that a new generation of writers could burst forth with a true literary realism—a realism produced by writers who faced the facts and presented them in the gray tones of the pessimism that came from disillusionment and a sense of individual helplessness.

After 1890, American literature became an instrument of sociology and psychology for a while. Romantic idealism was utterly dead in our best literature during this period. The products do not make particularly pleasant reading but they are a faithful reflection of the low state to which the gilded age had brought American morals. It is the final step in the slowly developing realism beginning around 1870, and one which produced its own series of masterpieces to record an age in American literary history.

THE WRITERS OF THE GILDED AGE

Local-Color Literature

Local color is not new to American writing in 1870. We have noted outstanding examples of the "tall" story and of witty and colorful delineation of frontier types as early as 1728 when the very staid and aristocratic Virginian, William Byrd, reported his impressions of the indolent North Carolina frontiersmen (page 7). The back country accounts of Crèvecoeur (1782) and Brackenridge (1792) are other notable literary treatments of colorful American scenes and peoples, presented with sympathetic humor or with witty exaggeration (pages 31-32).

The humorists

A broad and native brand of humor, based largely on exaggeration, dialect, and violent contrast, redolent of homespun philosophy and folk wisdom, had produced an entire school of writers by the end of the Civil War. Seba Smith, a Maine Yankee, produced the first of a long series of minor classics of American wit and humor with his *Life and Writings of Major Jack Downing of Downingsville, Away down East in the State of Maine, Written by Himself* (1833). The western frontier produced a mass of wildly exaggerated yarns with genuine frontier settings. Among the best practitioners of this semi-literary school were those mentioned here.

David Ross Locke (1833-1888) brought politics into humor during the Civil War days with the antics of his corrupt and ignorant preacher, Petroleum V. Nasby. His second book, *Divers Opinions of Yours Trooly, Petroleum V. Nasby* (1865), went to a seventh edition within a year.

Henry Wheeler Shaw (1818-1885) is better known as *Josh Billings*. Cracker-barrel philosophy is his specialty in *Josh Billings, His Sayings* (1865) and *Josh Billings, Farmers Allminax*, a series of annuals (1870-1880).

Charles Farrar Brown (1834-1867), known as *Artemus Ward*, produced a mass of broadly humorous and grossly illiterate matter to keep America laughing during the period of provincialism and serious conflict that attended the Civil War and reconstruction period.

The list of writers of the "tall" tale during this period is a long one. Both fictional and living performers of deeds of comic or mock-epic proportions have become American legends. Paul Bunyan is perhaps the most famous of the fictional "epic" heroes, and Davy Crockett is the outstanding living example of a self-styled "Hercules" of the frontier (page 70).

Ballads and folk songs

Also on the cruder and more popular fringe of the local-color lore of the age is the wealth of ballads and songs produced in the various regions of the nation which live today to remind us of isolated events and themes which received folk development during the period. These pieces, usually anonymous, catchy, and tuneful, with little artistic style or loftiness of theme, are a valuable store of folk culture and local color. Among the many favorites, representing varied aspects of the American scene in the period are: *Casey Jones; Hallelujah, I'm a Bum; Git Along, Little Dogies; Swing Low, Sweet Chariot; Frankie and Johnny.*

Local colorists of the West

Francis Bret Harte (1836-1902), generally known as *Bret Harte,* was the founder (or at least, the popularizer) of the school of writers we have come to know as the local colorists of the gilded age. Harte set the pace and defined the type of production which became a literary fad that swept the country during the period from 1870 to 1890 and is still found in semi-literary works to the present day. As practiced by Harte, and a multitude of others the country round, local color was a pleasant and sentimental presentation of typical life in a particular geographical setting. The local-color work delved little beneath the surface of manners and customs that distinguished the particular locale involved. There was little penetration into character and practically no analysis of causes and effects. In short, local-color literature was only a pleasant surface realism, colored heavily by romantically sentimentalized detail.

Harte was born in New York but was settled in San Francisco by 1853. He was variously a miner, a druggist, a teacher, and a journalist. He wrote novels, verse, and short stories. His novels are in reality short parodies of the styles used by famed 19th century novelists such as Dickens, Cooper, Dumas, Hugo, and others. His verse is of the frontier ballad type, as the following titles attest: *The Stage Driver's Story, What the Bullet Sang, In the Tunnel, The Society upon the Stanislaus.* His most popular ballad, *Plain Language from Truthful James* (better known as *The Heathen Chinee*) was written in 1870. It concerns the game of euchre into which Truthful James (who relates the happening) and Bill Nye enticed the innocent Chinese "with the smile that was childlike and bland." And, cheat as the two sharpers might, the Chinese won all the stakes, even to the extent of laying down cards which had been dealt to others about the table.

> In his sleeves which were long,
>   He had twenty-four jacks,—
> Which was coming it strong,
>   Yet I state but the facts;

Harte and the short story

Bret Harte is best known for his short stories and sketches which were published in book form in 2 collections, *The Luck of Roaring Camp and Other Sketches* (1870) and *Mrs. Skaggs's Husbands and Other Sketches* (1873). *M'liss,* from the first collection, had been published in 1867, the first of the local-color stories.

In his famed stories, such as *Tennessee's Partner, The Outcasts of Poker Flat, Miggles, The Luck of Roaring Camp,* and many others, Harte was interested in the dramatic and the picturesque and in varied and interesting western types. He manipulated this material into fast-moving narratives filled with humor and pathos. He moved easily and rapidly from dramatic tenseness to sentiment and laughter in his compact narratives. Mood was secondary in importance to action and color. He never varied his basic formula. He was criticized for his stark realism, for his rude language, for the immoral character of some stories, and for his flippant attitude toward religion. But in spite of the additional weaknesses of flimsy plots, melodramatic situations, and cardboard characters, Harte popularized a form of writing that occupies a considerable bulk of the mass of our literature. And he has been widely read and dramatized to the present day. (See Appendix A, page 214, for digests of representative tales of Bret Harte and Joel Chandler Harris.)

John Hay (1838-1905) is another early practitioner of local-color literature. Born in Indiana, he grew up in Pike County, Illinois. Hay is famed in this particular branch of American writing for his *The Pike County Ballads and Other Pieces* (1871), in which he employed the particular ungrammatical dialect prevalent in the unlettered sectors of the Midwest. Hay's comic poems and ballads, and the use of this dialect by Bret Harte and others, caused the "Pike" to be known widely. In California, where many midwesterners had flocked in the era, he was usually identified with any unlettered native from Missouri, Arkansas, Texas, or Illinois. Hay, a secretary to President Lincoln and a diplomat during several administrations, also wrote a 10-volume work on Lincoln, a book of travel sketches on Spain, called *Castilian Days* (1871) and a novel, *The Bread-*

Winners (1883). Hay illustrates the fact that the local-color writers often came from the most refined sectors of America. He was a highly educated and prosperous statesman who deliberately cultivated the genre and became one of its best-known writers.

<u>*Joaquin Miller (1841-1913)*</u> lived perhaps the most colorful personal life of all the local colorists. His life was one long series of stirring adventures. He roamed the entire West and sailed most of the oceans of the world. He wrote many books of verse, prose fiction, and drama. His local-color literature covers the entire West as a locale. His voice was loud and his style was bombastically rhetorical. His *Songs of the Sierras* (1871) is only one of many collections of his strident verse, shouting his pride in everything virile and lusty in the western scene.

> O bearded, stalwart, westmost men,
>   So tower-like, so Gothic built,
> A kingdom won without the guilt
>   Of studied battle, that hath been
> Your blood's inheritance . . .

Local colorists of the South

The South provided 2 highly interesting groups for local-color seekers with an active pen. The Creoles and the Negroes attracted many writers during the literary craze.

<u>*George Washington Cable (1844-1925),*</u> a native of New Orleans, had fought with the Confederate armies in the War. But his liberal ideas on the Negro question had caused him to be unpopular with his southern neighbors. He moved to Massachusetts in 1884 and began to write the books about the region he had just left which have placed him in the first ranks of the local colorists.

Cable wrote of New Orleans and its Old World atmosphere, its blend of colorful Spanish, French, and Negro elements. All his tales and sketches are exotically romantic and deal with Creole life on an artistic level uncommon to the average local colorist production. Cable, unlike most of his contemporaries, was capable of creating a mood of brooding melancholy. *Old Creole Days* (1879), *Madame Delphine* (1881), are collections of short stories and sketches, and *The Grandissmes: A Story of Creole Life* (1880) is his best novel for a study of Creole types.

<u>*Joel Chandler Harris (1848-1908).*</u> With the Civil War and the reconstruction period, the Negro suddenly came to the at-

tention of writers as a rich source for the local color type of treatment. Many writers appeared to treat the Negro, his manners, speech, and spiritual lore, romantically and sympathetically.

Joel Harris, a Georgia journalist, wrote many essays and stories of the reconstruction days in his state. He dealt with the Georgia "cracker" (poor white) dialect. But his great success came in his "Uncle Remus" stories. From 1880 to 1918, 8 volumes of the tales and sayings of this gentle, cotton-headed, old Negro were collected and published. "Uncle Remus" was full to the brim with tales of Brer Rabbit and his animal friends and enemies and of the varied pleasant aspects of plantation life. "Uncle Remus" became a national institution with his Afro-American dialect and good-natured wisdom.

The "Uncle Remus" stories and sketches have found an appreciative audience both among children and adults on an international plane. No American in the last 3 generations has failed to come into contact with the "Uncle Remus" lore. Regrettable as it may be that a world concept of the southern Negro should be based upon the dialect and the childlike simplicity of "Uncle Remus," it seems likely that the lovable fictional creation of Joel Chandler Harris will continue to carry his message for some time to come. Harris and Bret Harte seem to have survived, for better or worse, as the two most read and dramatized of the local-colorist contributors.

Local colorists here and there

The local-color literature produced writers throughout the breadth of the land, but the depicters of the South, with the Negro and the Creole people, and the West, with its motley assemblage of miners, cowboys, gamblers, Indians, rowdies, and frontiersmen, seem to have survived better with readers today than have all the others.

James Whitcomb Riley (1849-1916) treated the farm folks of the Midwest in his simple rhymes. He was, as no other among our poets, a "people's" bard. He idealized country life and made no attempt to introduce deep feeling or seriousness in any of his verse. For decades Riley has provided rich material for recitations in churches, grange meetings, and all manner of country gatherings. The titles of such simple jingles as *The Old Swimmin' Hole, Little Orphant Annie, The Raggedy Man, When the Frost is on the Punkin,* and others of the Riley reper-

toire cause lines to come back to the minds of many adults today who have long since forgotten the name of this unaffected
Indiana rhymer who brought the simple American farm life of
the 1880's into competition with the more exotic local-color
themes.

Sarah Orne Jewett (1849-1909), in her collections, Deephaven
(1877), Tales of New England (1890), and The Country of
the Pointed Firs (1896), gives us a very light and airy view of
the Maine landscape. Mary Eleanor Wilkins Freeman (1852-
1930) contributes to New England's local-color literature with
A Humble Romance (1887), A New England Nun (1891),
Edgewater People (1918), and other books. Both women penetrate very lightly into New England life and seek only the
pleasant and the sentimental aspects of reality. They possess
a facile style, however, and make light reading for one interested in the particular areas which they treat.

James Lane Allen (1849-1929), like the ladies mentioned
above, lightly treats the pleasanter aspects of life. The locale
is his native Kentucky, which he treats with a poetic and rather
ornate prose.

The most exotic of color in the age was hardly local. Lafcadio
Hearn (1850-1904) introduced Japan to America in a series
of accounts, combining poetic nature descriptions with an idealized treatment of the Japanese customs and philosophy.

Influence of the local colorists

The local-color school contributed a great deal toward un-
covering valuable sources of American themes for literature.
Their ground-breaking efforts have undoubtedly had great influence upon the more penetrating and infinitely greater realists
of this century who give the same areas a more authentic and
enduring treatment in many fine novels and short stories.

For the most part, the writings of the local colorists of the
late 19th century are shallow and sentimentally romantic. They
approached true realism only here and there. Much of their
"color" is simply that, a gaudy tinsel, an exaggerated and an
idealized view of both character and setting. Rarely did a local
colorist notice the drab and harsh realities about him. Hence
their view of reality is extremely one-sided, presenting only the
acceptable and pleasant aspects of the environments about which
they wrote. Their public would have been interested in no
other view.

VARIED DIRECTIONS IN GILDED AGE LITERATURE

We have noted that the local colorists of the gilded age were directing their material to popular taste, and taste in that age was little conducive to the encouragement of fine writing. Culturally, the age was shallow and the spirit of the times was one of sneering hostility toward artistic creation. Critics have variously referred to the period by the name we have chosen to employ in this discussion, or as "the wasted generation," "the brown decades," "the frontier age," "the dreadful decade" (1870-1880).

The attention given to the settling of the West, the progress of science and invention, the rapid industrialization and concentration of power in big business, the political corruption and wild financial speculation that attended the period—all these things gave to literature the same indecisive development that attended all our agencies for moral, artistic, and social advance. The same hurried temper of expediency hovered over literature as it did over every phase of American life. For a while literature wavered toward the same bright gilt that glittered on the surface of all the daily affairs of Americans. It was an era of conflict in ideologies, in moral attitudes, and in artistic standards. The 2 extreme attitudes that the spirit of the literary artist could bring to bear upon his material—the romantic and the realistic—struggled for domination in his literary interpretations of life.

Some romantic spirits held to their concepts of artistic expression, despite the hostile and distasteful attitude that surrounded them. Some turned to realism and tried to discover a way to report material that they found in life artistically, objectively, or subjectively, but what they found there, nonetheless. The most popular writers were the local colorists, which we have already observed. The lone individual, from an older age, whose booming verse commanded equally the attention of friend and enemy, whose unbounded and self-centered and almost pagan enjoyment of everything he saw about him, was Walt Whitman. And some few continued the genteel tradition of unruffled calm in their interpretation of a select culture for a select few aristocratic readers. These writers were oblivious of the life of America which was developing to the west of them. Some are even said to have had only windows with eastern views in their houses, views toward Europe and Old World culture.

Giants of Gilded-Age Literature

The best literary artists of the age and those whose writings are most likely to endure were individuals who belonged to no school or group. Some, like Lanier, were outright romantics— disillusioned romantics in an alien environment. One giant of the age, Mark Twain, shows a complete work that includes both extremes of romanticism and realism and all of the devices of the local colorist. Howells and James were realists, but followers of no creed except their own interpretations. Whitman and Emily Dickinson were simply themselves—distinctive and personal—impossible to classify.

The best writers of the period must be discussed as individuals and the traits of each noted. They belong to no artistic creed wholly or, if they did, they belonged to a creed of the pure romantic that was dying out of our literature. The best writers are either those or they are pathfinders toward a new artistic concept of American life—a concept that has dominated our literature to the present day. For the over-all emphasis in these transition writers is toward the realistic view and each had an individualized interpretation of reality.

Lanier and a dying romanticism

Philip Freneau, our first poet of true promise as a romantic, had lived in an unromantic age. His poetic genius became stunted, the man became disillusioned and bitter in an unfriendly environment, and only glimpses can be seen here and there in his production of the great lyricist that he might have become.

Another potentially great romantic (and perhaps the greatest we have anyway) was born too late to develop in the only period of a dominantly romantic view of life and art in America, between 1830 and 1860. Sidney Lanier (1842-1881) was a worshiper of beauty and a man with the spark of lyric genius who came to maturity with the triumph of materialism and the gilded age. Like Freneau, he was to feel the loneliness of a true romantic spirit, born into an age which was appreciative only of tinsel and glitter that accompanied a sentimentalized romanticism that was devoted to a local-color presentation of surface reality.

Sidney Lanier was born in Georgia. He served in the Confederate army and came out of the war broken in health. He moved to Baltimore where he became a flutist in the Peabody Symphony Orchestra. He was appointed Lecturer in English at Johns Hopkins University in 1879. Two years later he died of the consumption he had contracted during the war years.

Lanier's art

Lanier was one of our few true poets. He lived for music and art. His one aim was to create beautiful melody with his instrument and with his pen. He hated the crass materialism and the ugliness of the age in which he lived.

> O Trade! O Trade! would thou wert dead!
> The time needs heart—'tis tired of head.

The above lines open his long poem *The Symphony* (1875), dedicated in theme to the expression of Lanier's antipathy for the age in which he lived. But in form and expression, the poem is a symphony, with each instrument, by dint of imagery and changing cadence, performing its solo part. Lanier ends with his concept of the greatest need of his age.

> And yet shall Love himself be heard,
> Though long deferred, though long deferred:
> O'er the modern waste a dove hath whirred:
> Music is Love in search of a word.

Lanier refused to turn from his art, as disillusioned as he was with the lack of sympathy he found in Americans for his refined lyricism.

Lanier was endowed with a true poetic impulse. He had a gift of melody and cadence that the older poets had attained rarely. His response to nature was spontaneous and deeply religious. His faults were an overemphasis on moralizing, a tendency toward a bookish and mechanical utterance at times, and a limited scope of theme.

His best work has a Georgia setting. *Hymns of the Marshes* (1880-1882) is his major collection. *The Marshes of Glynn,* Lanier's best-known single poem, brings his melodic touch to a description of the marshes near Brunswick, Georgia, and the feelings and the mood they cause to rise in the poet.

Glooms of the live-oaks, beautiful-braided and woven
With intricate shades of the vines that myriad-cloven
    Clamber the forks of the multiform boughs,—
            Emerald twilights,—
            Virginal shy lights,
Wrought of the leaves to allure to the whisper of vows,
When lovers pace timidly down through the green colonnades
Of the dim sweet woods, of the dear dark woods,
    Of the heavenly woods and glades,
That run to the radiant marginal sand-beach within
    The wide sea-marshes of Glynn;—

The twilight of romanticisim included other poets, but none of the stature of Lanier. He was the supreme poetic artist of the gilded age.

Emily Dickinson: poetess in seclusion

Aside from Lanier, the romantic, Whitman, the unclassifiable poet who best spanned the gulf that separated the America of the past from the machine-age America that was emerging, and the local-color poets, the most notable verse of the gilded age was written by a woman who was unknown during her lifetime and who wrote her verse in solitude, with no intention that any of it ever should be published.

Emily Dickinson (1830-1886) lived a secluded life. She was the daughter of a lawyer in Amherst, Massachusetts. She received a genteel education and lived a Puritanical and Victorian existence. Her father, a trustee at Amherst College, was elected to Congress in 1854. About this time, it seems, Emily fell in love with a married minister from Philadelphia. Upon her father's return to Amherst, Emily had apparently decided to withdraw from society and live a solitary life. From this time until her death she recorded her ideas and inner feelings in poetry and in letters to her friends. Except for three or four poems, all of Miss Dickinson's writings were read only by intimate members of the family. She asked that everything be burned at her death. However, the family did not follow her instructions and a first volume of her writing was issued in 1890. More of Emily Dickinson's voluminous writing appeared from time to time until 1945.

The "artless" poetry of Emily Dickinson

Emily Dickinson, unknown in her own lifetime, became a

leading figure among the poets of the turn of the century and her popularity has continued to the present. She wrote a verse that, in its spirit and technique, belongs more to the 20th than to the 19th century. She wrote entirely from her own personal experiences and considered no theme too intimate or too trivial to record. Her verse has nothing in common with poetic schools or with any regional theme. She wrote from her heart and with unaffected emotional sincerity. Her phrasing is unconventional and impromptu. She is, at times, careless and naïve in her flights of childlike imagination. But her very faults contribute to the lasting qualities of her poetry. Emily Dickinson was a poetess, far in advance of her times. She contributed to American literature a verse that was unbounded by time or by fashion, a verse that was totally "free," before the new generations of poets were to declare themselves in revolt against poetic standards of the past. She became an idol of these poets of the "new" or "free" verse. The artlessness and simplicity of these verses of love, life, and eternity of Emily Dickinson will likely live long in the literature of a democracy.

> A word is dead when it is said,
> Some say.
> I say it just begins to live
> That day.
>
> (1872)

Samuel Langhorne Clemens (Mark Twain) (1835-1910)

Mark Twain, the name under which Clemens is best known, was born in Missouri and became, during his life, a citizen of the entire world and the best-loved American writer of the entire period. Mark Twain represents the entire national scene and the fluctuating impressions of optimism and pessimism that American life left upon the talented and impressionable individual. Mark Twain has retained his greatness for his individuality and for his sympathetic, if critical and often bitter, presentation of democratic life.

Twain's life and shifting attitudes

Mark Twain was born in the Midwest and was molded by the American frontier. In his youth he worked as a printer in a number of our eastern cities. He became a Mississippi river boat pilot in 1856. He then tried his luck in the fabulous silver camps of Nevada. While working as a reporter on the *Enterprise* of Virginia City, Nevada, Clemens adopted his pen name of "Mark Twain" (a Mississippi river phrase signifying a 12-foot depth of the river). Throughout his life Twain worked for newspapers, made world tours as a reporter, and lectured on his impressions and experiences. His one major business venture as a publisher ended in financial failure.

Mark Twain began his writing career as a western humorist, hoping that his permanent success as a writer would lie in the direction of social satire. A penetrating and sensitive observer of the realities about him, Twain became gradually disillusioned with the materialism of his age. Mark Twain's nature was eternally in conflict; he craved material success and felt that the individual artist could not perform his task honestly and retain a large body of readers. Twain, the man, become more bitter as he grew older. His optimism gradually faded and his late writings reflect a profound pessimism toward the human race and what he considered individual integrity.

Twain's personality in his writing

The literary production of Samuel Clemens is highly diversified. He remained first and foremost a humorist. He wrote for the masses and made them laugh. Much of his writing, however, shows his attempt to shake himself free from his reputation as a jester and to project his serious antipathies toward the hypocrisy and sham in society. Some of his works of a satirical nature are pessimistic and bitter; in others, the satire is sugared over by a heavy-hearted comic treatment or by light romance.

Twain's most enduring fame, however, belongs to the period when he wrote pure romance, relatively free from any serious purpose. His recollections of his boyhood surroundings and the rose-colored dreams of his youth produced the Twain masterpieces: *Tom Sawyer, Huckleberry Finn,* and *Life on the Mississippi.* In these great works of American literature Twain loosens his full and unrestrained artistic powers in a sympathetically humorous and tender treatment of days gone by. His technique is realistic, but the rosy glow of memory endows these works with romantic imaginings that elevate them to the rare atmosphere of pure literature. They stand among world literature's best examples of a harmonious blending of reality with the daydream.

A classification of Twain's best works

1. _Pure humor._ Scattered through Twain's voluminous works are his many sketches and burlesque episodes which have little purpose other than to provoke mirth. The best example of his uncanny ability in the field of burlesque and extravagant exaggeration is _The Celebrated Jumping Frog of Calaveras County_ (1867). This droll sketch of a California mining camp wager presents Twain at his best in the telling of tall tales of the western frontier. This early tale and the drawling lectures which Twain had begun to give about the country established his reputation as a foremost American humorist.

2. _Sketches, travel narratives, and lectures._ During his career, Mark Twain produced several volumes of autobiographical incidents, travel sketches, and tall tales. _The Innocents Abroad_ (1869) concerns a tour through Europe and the Holy Land, filled with both humorous and serious impressions of Old World sights and the manners of the peoples. _Roughing It_ (1872) is mainly concerned with the author's life on the frontier and is considered a masterpiece of humorous and both realistic and exaggerated description of the ideals and realities of the raw West. _A Tramp Abroad_ (1880) is the narration of a vagabond journey through Germany, Italy, and Switzerland. _Life on the Mississippi_ (1883), a series of sketches from the viewpoint of a river boat pilot between St. Louis and New Orleans, is the writer's best nonfiction book.

3. _Autobiographical fiction._ Twain's first novel was a satire on the materialistic age in which he lived. _The Gilded Age_ (1873) is a realistic condemnation of the unbridled speculation and greed of ruthless individuals who exploited and destroyed America's natural resources for their personal gain.

During the next 3 years Mark Twain seems to have come to the conclusion that he must compromise both with his age and with his own inclinations in order to maintain his early successes, that he must give his public humor and not serious social criticism. Urged by his wife and friends, Mark Twain retold his boyhood experiences along the great Mississippi river. _The Adventures of Tom Sawyer_ (216) (1876) and _The Adventures of Huckleberry Finn_ (217) (1884) are the results in fiction, and these are the writer's best books. These novels are stories of boys and stand high in the scale of American writings. They are not tales from a boy's point of view but are mature writings woven from the nostalgic memories of Mark Twain. Neither book is entirely free from a looseness of construction but both blend a sympathetic haze of romantic atmosphere with a realistic treatment of nature and character that will cause them to live long among the glories of our literature.

Along with *Life on the Mississippi* (1883), *Tom Sawyer* and *Huckleberry Finn* bring a period of American frontier life into the realms of art, with a tender poetic glow of romance. Here the author gave himself over entirely to golden memories and the youthful optimism which he was still capable of recapturing for a time. There is little to cause one of these books to stand above the other in permanent value in our literature. All 3 show flashes of literary genius; all 3 show their loose ends and careless structural faults. Perhaps *Huckleberry Finn* is a bit stronger in its character delineation and nature description. It is not unreasonable to assume, however, that either *Tom Sawyer* or *Huckleberry Finn* could stand beside *Moby Dick* and *The Scarlet Letter* as the 3 best American novels produced in our literary history to the beginning of the present century.

Clemens made further attempts to indulge again in autobiographical romance some 10 years later: *The Tragedy of Pudd'nhead Wilson* (1894), *Tom Sawyer Abroad* (1894), and *Tom Sawyer Detective* (1896). By this time, however, he had lost the spirit for romantic pioneering and these novels lack the charm and realistic tone of his masterpieces.

4. _Historical romances_. Mark Twain wrote *The Prince and the Pauper* (1882) for his children. Here he presents a light tale of mixed identity between the young English Tudor Prince Edward (later Edward VI) and Tom Canty, a pauper who almost succeeded in being crowned king by mistake. Beneath this light romance Twain attacks the English monarchical system.

A Connecticut Yankee in King Arthur's Court (1889) is another satire veiled as historical romance. Here Twain condemns aristocratic ideals of chivalry as mere cloaks covering hypocrisy and pretense. He brings forward western frontier individualism and classlessness as the ideal for society.

In *Personal Recollections of Joan of Arc* (1896) Twain presents a carefully constructed romanticized historical biography. His satire is directed against the religious system which tried and martyrized the Maid of Orleans.

5. _Twain's final period_. In Mark Twain's final writings, the black despair of his spirit is evident on every page. He had lost

his entire faith in God and man. The buoyant optimism and light mirth of his early writing had completely given way to a despairing pessimism.

The Man That Corrupted Hadleyburg (1900) is the best of Twain's later works. This is a short story in which the author deals directly and relentlessly with the greed and corruption of money madness and how it gradually rotted away the soul of a community.

The enigma of Mark Twain's genius

To many readers and critics Samuel Clemens appears as a literary barbarian, insensitive to and ignorant of the refinements of aesthetic art. To many others, he is the most native American of all our writers and the most sympathetic interpreter of the basic ideals and optimism that characterized the mid-19th century frontier.

Both opinions are correct. Much of Twain's work has little literary value and much of his writing lies in the realm of pure art. There is much looseness of structure, tedious and drawn out verbosity, broad and crude humor, to be found in Twain. But there is also a rich simplicity and brilliance of description and character delineation, a poetic prose at times and a sympathetic humor in abundance. When Twain wrote of individual men or boys and of his early and fundamental pride in the folk life of America, he was inspired. But when he dealt with philosophy, social or political ideas, and was cramped by his personal obsessions, he was childlike in his logic and irregular in his writing. The best of Twain, however, is enough to insure him a permanent place among the immortals of our literature. *Huckleberry Finn* should be read at least twice in the life of every American: once when the reader is young, as a work of juvenile fiction, and again in maturity, as a supreme masterpiece of American literary artistry.

THE RISE OF THE AMERICAN REALISTS

Prior to the Civil War, American life emphasized individualism and the frontier spirit. Our national life was truly romantic and our literature just as truly reflected that spirit. After the war, in the seventies and the eighties, our life was no longer romantic in its national aspects. Romanticism in the gilded age was "gilt and tinsel," artificial and shallow, filled with local color, side-splitting laughter, exaggeration, and a forced pleasantness. During this age, a few voices rose feebly to sound a realistic note, but when they did they were labeled as uninteresting, sordid, and immoral. Mark Twain is a superb example of a spirit who saw the realities around him and longed to write about them. He could bring himself to face contemporary reality squarely only in one novel, *The Gilded Age*. Beyond this work, he dealt in philosophical satire and covered his occasional flashes of resentment with humor and sentimental romance.

Industrialism had conquered Europe and had brought its social problems much earlier than its full effects were felt in America. Here the frontier kept the individual spirit alive longer. In Europe realism had entered literature as a strong force by mid-19th century. It was not until near 1890 in America that industrialism and the disappearance of the frontier brought the general feeling that individual freedom and romance had disappeared from our national life. It was only then that the American reading public was prepared and eager to receive literary exposition of true conditions in the American social scene. It was after 1890, then, that writers could appear and be accepted, who might not only preach a creed of "truthful presentation of material" but who might practice it to the fullest extent and receive approbation as literary artists.

Isolated examples of realistic technique among local colorists

Among the local-color groups of the post-Civil War period, there were 3 writers who, at least in one work, did attempt to present life faithfully as they found it, uncolored by their personal views or by exaggerated and sensational elements.

1. *Edward Eggleston (1837-1902)*, an Indiana clergyman, set out to write of life in the Ohio Valley as he found it, without the colorful tinsel, the exaggerated dialect, and the sensationalism of the dominant local-color groups of writers. He succeeded better than most who declared they had such intentions; his tales are truthful pictures of Indiana home life. His better novels are: *The Circuit Rider* (1874), the story of an itinerant Ohio preacher, and the pair of novels, *The Hoosier Schoolmaster* (1871) and *The Hoosier Schoolboy* (1883), both filled with realistic pictures of life and school conditions in the backwoods regions of Indiana about 1850. All of Eggleston's books are

marred by overpious sentimentalism, melodramatic incidents, and wooden caricature types. Otherwise, they deserve to rank as true and faithful presentations of life.

2. _Joseph Kirkland (1830-1894)_ wrote of the Mississippi Valley. His _Zury; the Meanest Man in Spring County_ (1887) is his one important book, giving a very unromantic and stern picture of western farm life. Like Eggleston, Kirkland was given to moralizing and sentimentality, but aside from these characteristics, his novel is faithful to the language, character, and rustic setting of his geographical area.

3. _Ed Howe (1853-1937),_ the editor of a Kansas newspaper, wrote a grim and powerful treatment of the smugness and cruel aspects of life in two rural villages. _The Story of a Country Town_ (1883) is relentless in its penetrating analysis of the more unwholesome aspects of rural character and society. Despite a tendency toward melodrama, this book has all the realistic, and even naturalistic, technique of the fiction of the early years of the 20th century. It is an important book in the history of our literature; it anticipated a literary movement but was not a part of it. When it was written, Howe's book was ignored by a public and by critics who were unreceptive to unpleasant truth in literature.

Transition from Gilded Age Tinsel to Realism

The transition from the predominant 19th century romanticism in prose to an equally dominant 20th century realistic prose is best represented by 3 writers: _William Dean Howells (1837-1920), Henry James (1843-1916),_ and _Hamlin Garland (1860-1940)_. Before these men, little of our fiction had been produced as the result of a deliberate intention of writers to give entirely truthful presentations of their material. Before these men had ceased to write, the realistic method was the major trend among our greatest writers of fiction. During their careers the method of the romantics in presenting a colored and idealized version of reality had slowly lost ground and new writers had come forward to offer deep and penetrating studies into the reality of a new American society. Howells, James, and Garland did not practice the realistic creed to the extent that they defined it. Their writings were not entirely as Howells phrased the requirements of realism, "nothing more and nothing less than the truthful presentation of material." None of the three men became our first true American realist in literature. Howells shrank from unpleasantness in life and presented only a genteel or pleasant reality. James migrated to England and lost touch with the late century American reality before he wrote his major works. Garland, obsessed with the desire to reform the social and economic conditions of the midwestern farmer, saw only a sullen and ugly side of life in his early writings, and later turned to romantic political dreams of panaceas. But all three writers are American realists by intention, if not entirely so in their production.

Howells: the most influential early realist

William Dean Howells is an important name in our literature as a novelist and as a literary critic. Born in Ohio, Howells became popular and influential throughout the nation and became the most important of the advocates for a realistic method in fiction. Howells and Mark Twain were the first of the western writers to find a friendly reception in New England. Howells, because of his use of themes from the wealthy and aristocratic society of the eastern seaboard and his refined style, became accepted wholeheartedly by the followers of the genteel tradition.*

Howells wrote many plays, a great deal of poetry, sketches, and stories. He produced several books dealing with his travels in Europe. In Europe he had been profoundly impressed by the great Russian realist and humanitarian, Count Leo Tolstoy.

Howells preached the realistic creed in many critical works. The best of these for an understanding of his literary beliefs is *Criticism and Fiction* (1891). This, perhaps, was the most influential argument for realism that operated upon the younger generations of writers toward the turn of the century. In this work, Howells denounced the romanticized fiction of his day and advocated strongly a more democratic approach to American life in writing.

Howells and his literary credo

In his many novels, Howells followed his own theories only a part of the way at times and never all the way. He chose his materials largely from eastern society, wealthy, aristocratic, and refined. He wrote in a simple, clear and graceful style of the foibles and aspirations of both individuals and society in the city and in the country. The truth which Howells sought to convey had its limitations. It must be pleasant truth ordinarily; he usually ignored all other aspects of life. He was seldom as impartial as he proclaimed a good realist should be. His stories are filled with a good deal of sentimentality.

But Howells, by somewhat less than a truly realistic treatment, led American readers and critics to accept realism, and was the greatest single force in securing a national approval of the realistic technique. Howells, himself, was a "romantic" realist in that he endeavored to present life faithfully, but permitted himself to choose only the pleasant realities and to color the results with his own and his characters' concepts of what actuality showed life to be. Howells paved the way as a pioneer for realism and as an enemy of the romantic treatment of life which had prevailed during the entire century. He did more than any other single individual to secure an American tolerance for the commonplace in literary works. He demonstrated time after time that the commonplace could be treated as artistically as the aristocratic and the fanciful.

Two significant novels of Howells

In addition to his voluminous output in other fields, Howells wrote some 25 novels. At least 8 of them deserve to live as landmarks in American literature's climb to realism. Such novels as *A Hazard of New Fortune* (1890), *Indian Summer* (1886), *The Lady of the Aroostook* (1879), *The Landlord at Lion's Head* (1897), and *The Kentons* (1902) are all novels that read well today. In fact, it is often a pleasure to read works that fall somewhat short of the stark, grim, and grimy type of factual reporting of the unpleasant aspects of American life that were to dominate our literature after 1900.

The Rise of Silas Lapham (218) (1885) is perhaps his most finished production. This story of the self-made Colonel Lapham and his family from Vermont and his wholesome reaction to his loss of fortune and prestige in Boston society is well constructed and written in a smooth and simple prose.

A Modern Instance (218) (1881) is a problem novel which provides an interesting contrast to the basic concept advanced in *Silas Lapham*. The former novel deals with the regeneration of character and this work describes its deterioriation in two young lovers who discover their incompatibility in marriage. This novel shows Howells at the height of his powers as a realist, dealing with ordinary people and with the individual and the social aspects of a wrecked marriage.

Henry James: international novelist

Henry James was American only by birth and education. Most of his life was spent abroad and he became a British citizen before his death in 1916. But he is one of the world's foremost modern novelists and exerted a considerable influence upon American realism and should be considered briefly for that reason.

James, the brother of the famous pioneer psychologist, William James, was both wealthy and intellectual. He left America because he felt that American culture was shallow and that American life was based upon false values of materialism and hypocritical sham. In these beliefs he did not stray far from the ideas of many American intellectuals of his generation, including Mark Twain.

Henry James, in his novels, concentrated his efforts upon the psychological portrayal of character through a detailed and leisurely study of his major personages in their contacts with the external environment about them. In this type of novel he is a master, though his studies are cold and emotionless. His style is far from being simple and clear. James was a seeker after truth, but he dresses it in a linguistic style that is elegant, abstruse, and ornate. He had no concern with a democratization of literature; he abhorred the commonplace. His object was psychological analysis on an elegant plane of intellectuality.

James is one of modern literature's most prominent figures. He is American only in that he treated American personages in some of his best novels. In _The Portrait of a Lady_ (1881) the heroine is an American woman who lives in Europe. In _The Ambassadors_ (1903) his intellectual American hero discovers in Paris the satisfactory cultural values which he had missed in the United States. In _The Golden Bowl_ (1904), an American girl, married to an Italian prince, is called upon to face the adultery of her husband with her own stepmother.

Thus James is American only in that many of his characters are typical American intellectuals. His field of study in the novel is psychology and his biases are definitely inclined toward Old World culture and attitudes. This, of course, is no adverse criticism of James as a novelist. It merely establishes the facts that, although James is a major figure in influencing later American psychological novelists and is, in himself, an international figure worthy of study, he did not treat American reality in his works. His realistic tendencies were not aimed in the direction of studies of psychological traits peculiar to Americans.

Hamlin Garland: reformer and propagandist

Garland was born on a Wisconsin farm and was impressed in his boyhood with the drudgery and misery attached to middle border farm life. He taught school, tried his hand at mining, carpentry, and news reporting. While in Boston, teaching and lecturing, he came into contact with Howells and determined to portray the middle border farm life in accordance with the Howells realistic attitude. His first book is his one and only masterpiece of realism: _Main-Travelled Roads_ (1891). It is a collection of stories and sketches of the many miseries and the few joys attendant upon midwestern farm life.

Garland did not have the Howells optimism and genteel attitude; he was pessimistic and despairing. He portrayed the farmer and his family as automatons, caught in a grim set of circumstances that sapped joy and ambition from the human soul and left it dry and spiritless. Garland was the first of the American writers to picture farm life without a romantically idyllic glow.

Garland did not continue with his impartial pictures of the frontier farm. He became concerned with reform of farm conditions and his writing became emotional propagandizing attempts to secure favorable public reaction toward legislative action to relieve the farmer of his burden of backbreaking work and scant return. He had ceased to be an honest teller of tales; he had become a preacher, intent upon delivering his message. He now approached his material with the attitude of a romantic rebel. The objectivity of his early stories was gone.

Garland's most valued book

Garland wrote one of our minor classics in _A Son of the Middle Border_ (1914), an autobiographical narrative of his boyhood. This is an important and well-balanced account of pioneer life on the western farm. Like Mark Twain's _Life on the Mississippi,_ Garland's account is reality, tinged by the romantic glow of mature recollection. Garland's memories of his youth are both bitter and sweet. This book will live alongside that of Twain in our literature as excellent and sympathetic portrayals of frontier life in the 19th century.

Criticism and the socialistic dream in the gilded age

We have noted that many of our writers felt lost and confused in our age of rapid industrial development, land speculation, growth of big business control, and neglect of cultural achievement. Some, like James, fled the country. Others, like Twain, inwardly despaired and became bitter as they continued to play to the taste of the masses. Some, like the local colorists, made themselves at home with their surroundings and catered to popular taste, without personal pessimism or bitterness.

Many writers expressed their distaste of the age in one book, in the form of satire and fictional invective. John Hay's novel, *The Bread-Winners* (1883), Henry Adams, in *Democracy—An American Novel* (1880), and Twain, in *The Gilded Age* (1873), are all isolated attacks on ruthless individuals, economic and social policy, speculation, and big business. It is interesting to note that both Hay's novel and that of Adams were issued anonymously.

There were many other writers in the period who criticized democracy and our weakened public morality and social responsibility. Edward Godkin, who founded *The Nation* (1865), was one of these severe critics of national and individual corruption in our country. Henry George wrote well and extensively of the social injustices that prevailed. We have already noted Hamlin Garland's concern with agricultural problems, which he expressed in such novels as *A Member of the Third House, A Spoil of Office,* and *Jason Edwards: An Average Man* (all issued in 1892). There were many others, whose work is hardly the concern of creative writing except that they sowed the ideas which were to enter a large body of our best fiction after the turn of the century.

Bellamy's "Looking Backward" and "Equality"

There were many in the age who dreamed of socialism and the ideal state. Few in this country had paid much attention to Karl Marx and his system for government and society as expounded in *Capital* (1867-1895). But, following the Civil War, the group of believers in some form of socialized state grew steadily throughout the gilded age. The only writer whose books on socialistic idealism reached the plane of creative writing was Edward Bellamy (1850-1898).

Looking Backward, or 2000-1887 (1888) is a Utopian romance which attempts to outline an American system of socialism, called Nationalism. Julian West, a wealthy young Bostonian, awakens in the year 2000 from an hypnotic sleep that has lasted since 1887, and finds himself in a new world of change that has taken place. The remainder of this book and his sequel, _Equality_ (1897), are concerned with West's discoveries in this ideal world in which class distinctions have vanished and there is no longer poverty or crime. A thin romantic plot runs through the two books, giving them the structure of novels, but the principal aims of the books are, of course, to expose Bellamy's ideas of social, economic, and political reform.

Bellamy's first book enjoyed a sale of 400,000 copies in the first 10 years, and both works are widely read today. Their success grew out of gilded-age conditions and they were highly influential in arousing public demand for social reform. It is difficult to calculate the influence they had on the large body of novelistic writing that turned our fiction, after 1900, into analysis of social problems. As we have noted, there were many attempts among our best writers to redirect American prose toward the presentation of a less romanticized concept of American life and to analyze the conditions in our society which seemed to demand remolding in a direction toward our first principles for an American national state, free from Old World oppression and dedicated to the advancement of all fields of knowledge and cultural achievement, guaranteeing and preserving a wholesome environment for the growth of man's dignity and capacities to create. Thus did the gilded age leave its message to the first of the new generations of writers, who were coming into their creative maturity about the same time that the foremost leaders in all fields of American life today were growing up and learning to read.

Chapter V

MOVEMENTS AND TRENDS IN TWENTIETH CENTURY WRITING

COMPLEXITY OF THE CONTEMPORARY LITERARY SCENE

Most of the books published in the past 60 years or more still crowd the shelves of public and college libraries, though here and there a book that only went through one or two editions has worn out, has been "lost" or deliberately discarded. To find books, published first in the lifetime of living persons, still available in libraries is little of an indication of their permanent worth or value to literature.

A review of this century's writings in the United States must necessarily deal mainly with movements and trends rather than with masterpieces, literary schools, and names of writers for the ages. We are too close to the writers who live with ourselves or our parents to determine even with a reasonable degree of certainty what to expect when time and taste has weeded the long-lived from the short. The older periods have received their "baptism of fire" and their labels, and their writers of lesser importance have been relegated to oblivion by time, the greatest and most cruel of critics, and by the fact that they belonged too much to one period or to one set of social conditions or political circumstances. They contributed little or nothing toward the over-all progress of culture. In one's own times, many authors loom as important this year and are hardly mentioned the next. Permanent values are hard to see except in historical perspective.

Beginnings of the New Creative Period

By 1890, American literature was in the throes of a struggle to determine its future course. It was basically a struggle between romanticism and realism in the method or technique of approach to the raw materials for literary works. There were ample signs that the romantic element was vanishing from our national life and that the new literature would endeavor to reflect the new realities. There was also evidence that great groups of people were loath to accept a writing that faced directly into the actualities of the new social situations and would continue to demand an idealized and colorful substitute.

It was also the period of the beginning of a marked division between a body of writing designed to please the new literate masses of readers in a democracy and one which still traveled in the realms of the aristocratic and intellectual concepts of the few. Should creative writing retire from commonplace reality and simplified treatment or should it abandon its aristocratic stand and cater openly to mass demand and popular taste? Or would literature become divided into two separate bodies of writing, each designed for widely differing audiences (a thing which this writer accepts as the present status of creative writing in the United States)? In short, the problem that is only partially resolved at the present time in all forms of creative endeavor on a world basis, the problem of democratization versus dehumanization of art, was already present in American writing in 1890 and showed signs of producing some extreme forms of writing, in comparison with traditional forms.

By 1890, American literature had become truly national and the old sectional barriers had broken down. Writers had risen, and well west of the eastern seaboard, like Mark Twain, Howells, Garland, and others, who represented the entire nation and whose work was followed with interest throughout the world. By the last decade of the 19th century, the bases for experimentation and new directions in American writing were present. The varied new movements and trends of the present century began during this *fin de siècle** decade—a decade which represented a lull between two creative periods, one just ending and another hardly begun. Twentieth century literature began in the nineties.

Specific Pressures on Literary Directions

To gain even a general understanding of the complex directions which our creative writing has taken, for good or for bad, in this age, we must also understand something of the enormous and violent changes and conflicts which have taken place in

American life and thought since 1890. For, nowhere in the world more than in the United States, have such all-embracing shifts taken place in structure and attitudes of a national society.

Two elements have remained basically constant, and at the present neither shows signs of weakening fundamentally as the strong underlying currents of our literature: a continued democratic development and exploration of native regional themes, both present-day and historical, and a strengthening resistence of individual writers toward becoming subservient to any literary fashion or common ideal. Within these constant tendencies, many seemingly opposing forces operate in a democratic manner: regional cultures versus a national culture, ruralism versus urbanism, individualism versus mass concepts, conservatism versus liberalism or radicalism in ideas and projected reforms, nationalism versus a world view in political philosophy and ethics, a stout young independence in creative art versus a dependence upon older European cultures.

Our literature has reflected the course of American life from its beginning in the colonies and not only has continued to try to interpret our basic democracy and nationalistic feelings, but also to branch into these antithetical currents which harmonize or disagree as they play beneath the surface of our intellectual and political movement forward into time. A literature which attempts all these things is necessarily complex and diffuse in its directions.

A Word about "Popular" Writing

We have noted that our past literary history shows that conformity to standard classifications and the critical opinions of observers of the literary parade do not necessarily provide a test of creative genius or of whether creative writing is the best expression of the best thought, employing imaginative use of experience which is felt or observed by those who reduce it to written form. Writing has survived from the past in spite of nonconformity to those principles to become a part of our cultural heritage. Stowe's *Uncle Tom's Cabin* lives, despite its sentimentalized poverty and lack of literary qualities, What we now consider, perhaps, our greatest novel (Melville's *Moby Dick)* received scant attention in the age in which it was written, even by the most intellectual and supposedly unbiased literary critics of the time. Both works were published as books in the same year, 1852.

And in the age in which we live, an age of masses of readers, a corresponding mass of writing has appeared to satisfy varying tastes. The majority of it, doubtless, is subliterary and has little permanent place in our culture. Unfortunately, in a materialistic democracy, creative achievement is often judged by the same values which determine the worth of technological products. The "best" automobile in our age is one which tends to be the most attractive in external appearance and to give the least troublesome performance during its functional life. Homer's *Iliad* was written many years before Christ, in an age of crude horse-drawn chariots, but this work continues to be recognized by the most cultured minds in every generation as having the qualities which maintain its high worth universally as a work of literature.

A personal reaction to contemporary writing

The writer of this "review" of American literature has no quarrel with contemporary "popular" writing. Creative writing, in an age of mass consumption, no longer seeks to serve all readers any more than a particular model of automobile is designed to be purchased by people of all tastes and of all levels of income in our society. In this century, far more so than in the past, writing caters to various levels of intellectual taste and training and it will continue to do so as long as those levels vary one from the other. Our modern civilization, with its widespread literacy and educational opportunity, has created a demand for "literature" on all levels, a "creative" writing, in prose or poetry, which makes imaginative use of experience, whether felt or observed by its creators. In any future age of democracy and of a literate citizenry, creative writing on two (or more) levels will continue to surround any reader, with its appeal to be purchased and read, whether that appeal be through advertising or through its evident qualities which are recognized from the experience of the potential reader. That the reader is of a "majority" or of a "minority" for which a particular work is written is largely a matter of his training and developed taste for imaginative reading.

The question of "democratizing" or of "dehumanizing" literature is an idle academic one. Both relatively crude "democratic" and an artistic and intellectual "aristocratic" (and all levels between the extreme meanings of these terms) bodies of writings exist in abundance in our age of enlightened democracy and will continue to be produced in future ages.

This writer confesses with little shame that early in adolescence he possessed a taste for comics and for writing which took the forms of "confessions," solutions of crimes by master detectives, and of emotionally sentimental portrayals of melodramatic incidents. He further confesses, with more pride, that he reached a stage of development before physical adolescence had ended when he read both plays of Shakespeare and adventures of *Sherlock Holmes* in the same evening with equal pleasure and with some appreciation of the differing degrees of permanent value each contributed to his sum of intellectual maturity.

Since that period, a quarter of a century ago, this reader's habits have changed only in degree. He now spends most of his time for reading with masterpieces of the world's literary past or with contemporary writing which seems most likely to have permanent place in literature. The remainder of his reading continues to be devoted to the amusement and entertainment he continues to derive from writings of exotic adventure and sentimentality. (He graduated only from "confessions.") He hopes that, to the end of his life, his reading tastes will continue to operate in the same democratic manner.

This writer can find only 2 tendencies with which to quarrel in our contemporary reading habits in this historical review of American literature, which can be little "historical" in this final section. One tendency which disturbs him is the attitude of many readers of the "popular" to deprecate and to build a wall of resistance against the higher levels of creative literary accomplishment because they do not understand its values and are determined to remain deliberately blind to them. Some even take pride in their continued resistance to self-development in the direction of an appreciation and pleasure to be derived from writing which seeks a higher goal than that of mere amusement and entertainment, brought to adolescent levels of expression and emotional appeal—a higher goal of a wider and deeper understanding of life.

The other disturbing factor to this writer is the attitude of haughty superiority which some few of the *cognoscenti* assume in this age. They, in withdrawal from the realities, contribute little toward alleviation of low levels in our reading habits and toward the raising of those habits in the direction of more healthy critical attitudes, combined with wider desire and demand for richer reading experience. We have, and have had, in this country (with exception of some minor tendencies toward the deliberate cultivation of abstruseness) a democratic literature of such uncomplicated nature that this writer cannot believe that any large sector of our population is incapable of understanding and deriving pleasure and benefit from most of what is written in our higher levels of literary expression.

Summary of Trends in 20th Century Creative Writing

In the late years of the 19th century narrative fiction, the novel* and the short story*, had become the most developed forms of literature on a world basis. Both of these fictional forms have received voluminous and varied treatment in contemporary American writing. They continue to be the most exploited forms of creative writing today. Masses of novels and short stories have been produced in our times, appealing to all types of readers, those who seek only the amusing and entertaining aspects of the story itself, vividly and emotionally told, and those who are more exacting and demand beauty of expression, a faithful representation of life, and enlightenment for the mind. On the level of creative literature, fiction had become predominantly realistic toward the close of the 19th century, and this has continued to be its major trend in this century.

No great poets rose immediately to replace the great figures of the romantic school and such isolated individuals as Walt Whitman and Emily Dickinson. In this century, American poetry has had no sustained great movements. Poets have attempted to gain bodies of readers by varied experimental treatment of material, some leaning toward the realistic directions of the novel and others becoming abstruse and artificial in their attempts to carry poetry out of the realms of emotion and sentiment and toward intellectual gymnastics of language and idea. A few great names have risen from this varied experimentation in poetry: Lindsay, Lowell, Frost, Sandburg, Masters, Millay, Benét, Robinson, and a few others. In late years the trend of the younger poets is again toward a simplicity, a directness, and an emotional appeal that American poetry had seen little of in this century.

There had been no great drama movements in the United States prior to this century and none have appeared to date. The single name of Eugene O'Neill has risen to international importance. For the most part, the American theater has continued to be dominated by the purely commercial theater of New York. In recent years, however, art and experimental theaters have blossomed throughout the country, giving some promise that a serious native drama may be in the offing. The major produc-

tion of serious drama in this century has been that of contemporary European playwrights or that of past ages of greatness
in world literatures.

The informal or personal essay has showed the same decline
of popularity in America as is evident in world literatures in
general. American biography and autobiography in this century
has continued to approach pure literature occasionally, an ideal
so difficult to achieve in this genre which would fuse sound
science with effective art. American criticism in this century has
taken enormous strides toward overcoming the inconsistencies
and prejudices of the past century and toward a definitive re-
interpretation of America's literary past.

Plan of discussion in the final section

The final major sections of this "review" will make a
hazardous attempt to elaborate upon the general statements
made above and to simplify the complexities of the contemporary
literary scene somewhat, by treating it as follows: (1) dealing
with each of the major literary types to recent years in a strictly
historical sense with little attempt to evaluate their importance;
(2) defining and analyzing the background and sources for the
shifting trends within each literary type; (3) giving major
emphasis to only a very select group of writers and works which
best seem to represent the trends. Many sources are available
giving detailed biographies and lists of works. Many very brief
digests of works from the contemporary period will be included
in Appendix A; only one representative of each differing trend
will be given detailed treatment there.

I. TRENDS IN PROSE FICTION

Causes of the Forceful Advance of American Realism

Before the Civil War our fiction had been dominated by
romanticism and a tone of imagination and fancy. Early
American life had been a romantic one and the individual spirit
of adventure and of the free development of personal initiative
to dominate the vast frontiers of the nation were faithfully reflected in our writing.

But various forces brought about a gradual shift to a realistic,
and even an exaggerated searching and grimly pessimistic, outlook toward American life. This was a trend that grew in spite
of the continued demand of a large body of readers for writing

that would feed their imaginations with a surface "gilt and tinsel" which they felt they could no longer experience in reality. A false, or "pseudo," romanticism has continued in our writing to the present day, but the major portion of our best creative production became increasingly realistic in its presentation of both pleasant and unpleasant aspects of our society. And, for a time, it seemed that an exaggerated trend toward the presentation of the unpleasant aspects of American life would continue indefinitely into this century.

The forces which brought about this radical change in the literary taste of writers in their choice of subject matter and method of presenting it and of a large body of our reading public were:

1. The rise of industrial centers and business empires as controlling factors in our life and economy.

2. The disappearance of the frontier and of the free land.

3. The concentration of population in cities and the concentration of political and economic power in the hands of big business and the attendant corruption, scandal, and social misery.

4. The rise of organized labor, agricultural, social, and political groups to combat the corruption in land speculation, big commercial interests and political rings, and their interest in the analysis of the evils and miseries in our society.

5. The advances of science, particularly in the field of biology with the theories of Darwin and others, with its methods of microscopic analysis and its early promulgation of deterministic ideas from which man would appear to be a victim of circumstances and not capable of the control of his own destiny.

6. Stemming from the factors mentioned above, the growing spirit of pessimism and fatalistic despair of the intellectual individual and the feeling that he was being smothered under the weight of mass concepts and institutions and that a materialistic democracy would bring about a total eclipse of achievement in the creative arts.

7. The strong influence of European literatures, already dedicated to realism, upon American intellectuals.

8. The advances in transportation, rapid and wide dissemination of facts and ideas in newspapers and magazines, national unity, and the breaking down of the influence of eastern aristocratic groups and their traditions.

9. The rise of national pride and international arrogance and the display of imperialistic policies in the Spanish American War of 1898, the Panama Canal acquisition, the "big stick" policies

of Theodore Roosevelt, and the failure of the ideas for which World War I was fought, brought further degrees of desire for realistic self-appraisal of our democratic society and of its workings.

10. Stemming from factors mentioned above, the notable decline in religious faith and in long-range cherished values, a growing cynicism with individual and collective ideals, leading individual writers to an exaggerated contemplation of the sordid elements of society.

These, and other factors of a like nature, not only contributed to the rise of the realistic method of treating literary material but advanced prose fiction as the literary form that could best express objective reality, free from the subjective emotions and sentimentality of poetry.

Techniques in Our Realistic Fiction

In the discussion of the complex aspects of realistic fiction, certain terms are used by critics to designate varying trends, movements, or shadings of the major idea of a total realistic technique, as opposed to one completely dominated by fancy, untruth, absolute idealism, and lofty flights of emotion and imagination. Since we shall use these critical terms in the discussions below, it is well to glance briefly at ideas as to what distinguishes them one from the other within the range of realistic fiction.

Realism, if applied in the totality of its concepts by writers of fiction, would mean the presentation of life as it is, of things as they are in the time and place selected for treatment, without idealization, sentimentality, or coloration of any sort. The realist does not avoid the commonplace and the ordinary in life; nor does he avoid the unpleasant features of life. The realist seeks his material in both its sordid and its noble aspects. His simple purpose is an entirely truthful presentation of material, in both its surface and its inner aspects. True realism, thus, is not simply photographic, since the camera only shows a surface reality.

A _romantic realist_ would be a writer who presents life as he finds it, but tends to seek only the pleasant in life for his material (such as Howells), or who tempers the unpleasant by his own emotional feelings (such as Garland) or his nostalgic recollections (such as Twain, and Garland in _A Son of the Middle Border_). The historical novelist may be a romantic realist in that his facts may be documented as to events and places, but his treatment of character and manners could scarcely be entirely *real* to others than those who lived at the time being fictionalized. A writer, such as Howells, is sometimes called a _genteel realist_ in that he catered to the traditions and taste of a particular aristocratic New England society in his presentation of reality.

Sometimes the terms *subjective* and *objective* are used in connection with realism. An author may give a truthful presentation certainly if he is "objective," that is, if he gives actual facts, not colored by his own opinions. He may likewise be truthful if his facts are presented in a "subjective" manner, that is, from his own experience or individuality.

The terms _impressionism_ and _expressionism_ are often used to distinguish shadings of the realistic technique. Rather than dwell upon reality of objects, the author may choose to exhibit "impressionistic" moods and sensations which objects make upon him. These moods and impressions may be "truthful presentation" although certainly not photographic observation of the external aspects of life. Likewise, the artist may, by the exhibition of his inner experience or intellectual concepts, give an "expressionistic" vision, not of physical objects, but of ultimate truth. These two rather roundabout techniques border closely upon romanticism and are *realistic* only when the author's purpose is nothing except to exhibit truthful presentation of things as they are or life as it is through these subtle literary devices.

Naturalism. The major extension of realism which received such extensive early development during the 19th century in France, and gradually spread through other European literatures, reaching America toward the end of the century, derived its method from science. The method of naturalism is basically the same as that of realism and aims at a detached, scientific objectivity. However, the naturalist-realist imposes a very definite pessimistic bias upon his interpretation of his materials. He is guided by a deterministic viewpoint that man is not a creature of free will, but is an automaton, moved by forces beyond his control. Literary naturalism developed in most Western literatures from the French Zola, Maupassant, and Flaubert, starting flourishing movements in the novel (and the drama) in England, Russia, Germany, and the Scandinavian countries.

Before 1890 and the disillusionment that had set in as a result of the corruption and social evils coming out of the gilded age, the weak and occasional spirit of naturalism shown by such writers as Melville, Mark Twain, Garland, and others, was little noticed and gained few followers. Americans simply dismissed any such manifestations as sordid, unhealthy, uninteresting, and immoral. But during the nineties, naturalism became a strong aspect of our major literary tendency toward realism and began to subside in our literature only after 1930. At the present, naturalism leaves only a weak trace in the stream of fiction which continues in its broader, saner, and less biased course of "faithful presentation" of American life.

Techniques and Trends Leading Away from Realism

Realism, after all, is simply the literary method which has been chosen by the majority of the best prose writers in this age to present their materials in an artistic written form. Many of our best writers, and the majority of our writers of lesser ability, have departed more or less from the realistic method. And again, some writers have produced a part of their work under the banner of realism and have departed measurably from it in other works of perhaps equally permanent value to literature. The trends away from realism lead, naturally, toward the opposing technique of romanticism. Let us note a few of the intermediate techniques which account for much of our best prose fiction (and most of our worst) in this contemporary period, in which the writer's aim is, to a greater or less degree, a departure from the presentation of things as they are or life as it is.

Sentimental fiction. The sentimental element in writing always gives us a departure from truth. On the one hand, it would be an overindulgence on the part of the writer in emotional reactions and personal feelings which would tend to give the material being presented a false coloration. Another aspect would be the tendency on the part of the writer toward an optimistic overemphasis on the goodness of humanity, a tendency toward allowing wishful thinking or personal religious, moral, or patriotic bias to color the truthful presentation of reality. *Sentimental realism,* of course, is a marked tendency among our writers, particularly when fictionalizing elements in the nation's past history. Sentimental realism, except in a rare few writers, breaks down into shallow romance and seldom produces masterpieces of good creative writing.

Social fiction. The social novel (which received emphasis amounting to a literary movement between 1890-1914) gives the novel a purpose or thesis, calculated to propagandize against some evil present in society (at least in the opinion of the writer). The author, here, would not permit his "truthful presentation" of life to speak for itself, but would introduce personal commentary and thus be suspect of distorting reality to agree in a marked degree with the purpose or thesis he wished the reader to adopt as his own conclusion. Such novels, beyond the immediate period in which they are written, are of more value as documents of historical and sociological attitudes than they are as artistic masterpieces. Literary works, even though they abound in admirable expression and perfection of form, seldom live if they only convey a message to an immediate audience of readers.

Regionalism, exoticism, and the *historical approach.* These three terms are not entirely matters of degree of realism or romanticism. Their significance lies partly in the choice of the raw materials for artistic treatment.

Regionalism would be present in a work in which an author selected deliberately his materials for treatment from the life found in a particular geographical area. He might be of that region and have thorough knowledge of its realities; he might have insufficient contact with the region to be able to portray it and its people faithfully. Or he might have the tendency to treat the regional aspects with a sentimentalized and colorful tone (as the local colorists did in the gilded age), a satirical and prejudiced attitude, or (in the case of the writer who depends upon recollected life in the region) a nostalgic idealism.

Exoticism is characteristic of a large body of our writing which provides escape from reality. Actually, most literature is a means by which a reader may escape from the life he lives into a wider and different life. Exoticism is, in a sense, a league between the author and the reader to escape together to a realm where reality is minimized (a regional novel would be exotic— or alien—to one who does not inhabit the region treated); it may be imaginative (another planet, a Utopia, the subconscious in man's psychological make-up, a South Seas island). Exoticism may be found only in the uncommon or flowered language and style in which the literary artist couches his materials.

All historical novels are *exotic* to a more or less degree, as are the "popular" forms of the sentimental novel. It is easily seen that the presence of exoticism in the writer's choice of materials, outside his and his readers' normal experience, or in his style of writing, leads rapidly away from realism, depending upon the degree to which the *exotic* elements are present in the work. A great deal of our subliterary writing is saturated with exoticism.

The historical approach. One of our most popular forms of fiction deals with historical events and personages. Most of it is almost pure romance. Often the history is distorted and false, and both writer and reader are susceptible to the romantic glamour and emotional bias that are usually present in our view of past happenings or great historical personages. Historical fiction has received a rich treatment in this century by serious writers and by those whose capacity to create is very small indeed.

MAJOR DEVELOPMENTS IN CONTEMPORARY FICTION

A. Naturalism in Prose Fiction

The concentration of population in industrial centers, the dying spirit of individual independence in the face of a vanishing frontier, and the subjection of the individual to the machine brought the proper spirit of helplessness to America which made it receptive to an European type of naturalism by 1890. Man was now to be mercilessly considered by writers as an automaton. The concentration now was to be upon an infinitely detailed exposure of his grosser instincts and upon the animal elements in his behavior. As George Meredith, the English realist, put it: "The naturalist sees the hog in nature, and takes nature for the hog."

This fictional technique of disillusionment and pessimism dominated our best writers of prose (and to an extent our poets also) from 1890 until 1930. After 1930, the influence of naturalism lessened only in degree, for even in the period after World War II some of the greatest writers still produce writings which reflect the same detailed and sordid pessimistic penetration into the muck and slime that can be found in American life.

Naturalism not a true reflection of realism

Naturalism does not present a pleasant picture of American life but apparently, at the height of the movement, it reflected life as our writers saw it. As we recognize, even in the early years of the century, it was not a true reflection of the whole of life. It is biased toward the pessimistic attitude. One of our eminent literary critics (J. Donald Adams) has pictured our most naturalistic writers in a posture from which, while writing, they continually contemplate their navels.

Whether the works of these writers will live long in our literature is not the problem of this review. Undoubtedly some of these writings will live to indicate the low state of morality and social responsibility that have characterized a period of our national development.

Stephen Crane: pioneer in American naturalism

Maggie: a Girl of the Streets (1893) was written when Crane (1871-1900) was only 22. Crane was a frail and neurotic youth with a fiery energy. His interest in the sordid and brutal aspects of New York's Bowery district, which he observed on his beat as a news reporter, led him to pen his episodic analysis of slum conditions in the form of a novelette. Maggie, in order to escape the squalor of her grim surroundings, runs away with Pete, who eventually abandons her. She becomes a prostitute and finally sinks to a level where she welcomes an escape through suicide.

Crane failed to find a publisher who was willing to chance an edition of his unconventional writing. He finally published his grimly impressionistic study himself. It attracted little notice and it was not until 1896 that it was reprinted and immediately hailed as a welcome, though startling, innovation in American writing. Crane had broken with all tradition in the novel in our literature. He was not bitter and had no propagandistic axe to grind, as Garland. He was not genteel, seeking the pleasant in reality, as Howells. He was grimly factual and presented his brutal pictures in the impersonal manner of a news reporter.

Crane's impressionistic masterpiece of war

Crane's other novel is _The Red Badge of Courage_ (219) (1895), American literature's first attempt at a direct and impersonal view of Civil War conditions. Crane's account follows a young New York lad who has volunteered with the Union forces and gradually goes to pieces under gunfire. Crane explained: "It occurred to him that he had never wished to come to war. He had not enlisted of his own free will. He had been dragged by a merciless government."

Crane's naturalistic bias is evident from the first pages. To Crane, young Henry Fleming, like Maggie, was a victim of circumstances which led to his moral disintegration. Crane's objective and effective impressionistic style, where he allows his scenes and characters to register themselves as molded by his own individual temperament, make _The Red Badge of Courage_ one of the masterpieces of the entire naturalistic movement in our literature.

In the last 3 years of his life, Crane concentrated upon the short story, his *The Open Boat* being his most effective contribution in this short fictional medium. This story is a tense and graphic account of 4 men in an open boat, the only survivors of a shipwreck off the Florida coast.

Norris: naturalist with romantic tendencies

Frank Norris (1870-1902), like Crane, turned early to journalism as a career. Like Crane, he was intelligent, vigorous, and daring. Like Crane, a pioneer who contributed much to setting the tone for the early 20th century novel, he died too soon to realize his own potential as a truly great writer. Crane died of tuberculosis and Norris as a consequence of an appendix operation.

Frank Norris was a romantic at heart, and his first writing is romantic, in prose and in verse, written under the influence of Stevenson and Kipling. Also under the influence of Zola in his early period, Norris came to the conclusion that a graceful style and gentle themes belonged to an effeminate past in America and that the new age demanded a straightforward and vigorous masculine expression in which no subject, clean or unclean, would be barred from treatment.

The "brutal" novels

McTeague (220) (1898) is the first Norris contribution toward his rejection of the gentle in literature. This is a brutal story of middle and lower-class life in California. McTeague, pursued by the effects of an unsavory heredity, seeks more and more depraved levels of behavior until he finally involves his wife and her former suitor in a series of violent and degrading incidents which finally lead to the deaths of all three. *McTeague,* written in the same depressing reportorial style as the novels of Crane, leaves the reader with a feeling that he has just closed the doors to a morgue when he finishes the final page.

Vandover and the Brute (published 1914), is another story of human degeneracy where the leading personage fights his own dual nature until the evil destroys the good in his soul and sends him to an ignominious death. This novel was too frank-spoken for publishers in 1899 and had to wait until a public had reached a more receptive level 15 years later.

Norris and the social novel

About the turn of the century, Norris became enthused to

write an epic-like novelistic treatment of the conflicting social forces at work in our country. He chose the subject of wheat and proposed to deal with the production, distribution, and consumption of that important product of the western farms. He lived to write only 2 of his allegorical treatments of his vast subject.

In _The Octopus_ (220) (1901), the western farmer, the producer of the wheat that formed such a vital source of American power and prosperity, is shown to be a tool in the grip of the large railroad companies who control and strangle the free passage of the product toward its markets. In _The Pit_ (221) (1903), the flood of vital wheat is now in the grip of the forces of greed and speculation in the Chicago exchange, the "pit." Norris, in his projected novel, _The Wolf,_ would have carried the important grain to relieve famine in Europe.

Norris's 2 novels of his social trilogy show force and an imaginative use of symbolism. _The Octopus_ is far more naturalistic than _The Pit,_ which shows clearly the curious mingling of realism and romanticism in the author's nature. Both novels show the author's enthusiasm and excitement with his wideranging subject. Norris stands not only as an important pioneer figure in the foreground of the naturalistic movement but also as the pioneer of a long line of sociological novels of this century, although his 2 novels in this direction are not the finished productions that were to come within a few years.

Dreiser: Most Influential of the Naturalists

Theodore Dreiser (1871-1945) wrote his works at the height of receptivity to the naturalistic technique in the United States, and he became its most successful exponent in our literature. Dreiser was born in Indiana, of German parents. He became a reporter and later edited a women's magazine. He served in various other journalistic capacities in the East and Midwest until 1910, when he decided to devote his time entirely to creative writing. Dreiser wrote 6 novels and many essays, stories, drama, and sketches. Dreiser, more than any other single writer, set the tone for American fiction for a quarter of a century. His influence is still felt today in a weak, but continuing, thread of naturalist novels that are published every year.

Early novels and the Dreiser technique

Sister Carrie (1900) is Dreiser's first experiment in the European style of naturalism. This first novel is a rather mild form of naturalism, and results as a rather slow-moving story of a working girl who leaves one lover to join another who seems more likely to succeed. Finally Carrie became successful as an actress as her lover, drifting from failure to failure, suicided, leaving the successful woman unfulfilled and lonely. Dreiser attempts to be convincing in his portrayal of his heroine as a victim of circumstances.

His second novel is _Jennie Gerhardt_ (1911), another story of a woman who is driven through life by chance and fate. Here Dreiser showed marked improvement in his characteristic technique of amassing a body of detail and presenting it with force. Dreiser became more and more the analytical reporter, showing skepticism at all points. He was a careful observer of life around him, but everything, to him, was mechanical and subject to no over-all purpose. He dissected American life with a cold chisel, assigning happiness or sorrow to his characters in an impersonal manner, according to the circumstances which happened to fall to the lot of each because of the hereditary impulses which happened to drive them.

His style is clumsy and confused. He succeeds in drawing his forceful pictures through a sheer mass of observed detail, presented always with the Dreiser view of a tragic and fatalistic existence.

Cowperwood: Dreiser's most thorough portrait

Dreiser wrote 3 novels about the rise and decline of an unscrupulous big business magnate: _The Financier_ (1912), _The Titan_ (1914), and _The Stoic_ (1947). These novels trace the character of Frank Cowperwood from his youthful status as a bank clerk through his long and meteoric career. At the end of the third novel, the hero is dead and his amassed fortune is lost. He had finally returned to a former mistress after divorcing his first wife and being abandoned by his second. After his death, his faithful mistress devotes her life to the reform of American materialism.

"An American Tragedy"

Dreiser wrote his most famous book in 1925. _An American Tragedy_ (221) is a long and sprawling, chaotic, narrative, built around a very flimsy plot. A youth, driven by his destiny, kills his sweetheart and is finally executed. But Dreiser's detailed study of the youth's life and driving forces and the vast amount of detail which he observes in the American social scene is thorough and painstaking. This novel was written at the height of the naturalistic movement in America, and Dreiser was its prophet. The book had an immediate and phenomenal success; it was even hailed as "the great American novel" at the time. Today, its many faults and its thoroughly one-sided pessimistic viewpoint cause it to be regarded simply as the high point in our enthusiastic espousal of naturalism in the novel.

Dreiser and American life

Dreiser's concepts are common to many others of the naturalist group in our century. His people are playthings of destiny, driven by blind forces beyond their control. His concept of life is near an animal existence. Life is chaotic, and spiritual satisfactions have little place in it. To Dreiser, some win through to success in our society because chance places before them better opportunities to grab off material gains or satisfactions of the flesh, and others, through their environmental surroundings, usually induced by a background of hereditary weakness, lose and have no chance of redemption. Dreiser represents a low point in a concept of human life, one that is pessimistic, deterministic, and with little or no hope of dependence upon the effectiveness of the nobler impulses of man.

Other naturalist fiction in our age

The spirit of naturalism, which reached its peak of development with Dreiser, has had many other followers among our writers, some of whom have imitated only certain aspects of the European type of highly detailed and circumstantial treatment which Dreiser employed to such exaggerated degree. Much of the naturalist influence has poured into the social, or problem, novel, with its added propagandistic or reform elements. Much of the objectivity of the older naturalistic approach passed with Dreiser's generation. The naturalist writers after Dreiser have tended toward a very subjective treatment of their material. But the general tone of pessimism and disillusion, the analysis of morbid and depressing aspects of the American scene, continued to be characteristic of a large body of our fiction until very recent years. (See Appendix A, page 222, for brief digests of 20th century realistic novels which involve a strong bias toward naturalism. These digests include summaries of the basic ideas developed by the following notable fiction writers of the contemporary period: Jack London, James T. Farrell, Ernest Hemingway, F. Scott Fitzgerald, Thomas Wolfe, William Faulkner, John Dos Passos, Erskine Caldwell, John O'Hara, Richard Wright, and James Jones.)

B. The Social Fiction

The spirit of disillusion and indignation which swept through our society around the turn of the century did not find its expression entirely in the naturalist principles. Many of our writers were little concerned with the deterministic bias of the naturalists. They saw more direct and curable causes of our social ills: corruption in politics and in other of our institutions, individual greed of speculators and industrialists, and a misdirection of our basic democratic concepts. They saw an aristocratic control over our economy by small groups of big businessmen and politicians, in an alliance for the advancement of their own individual and vested interests. These writers concentrated upon critical attacks in an effort to build up a sensitive social conscience which would lead to mass indignation and demand for reforms.

The early "problem" novels

We have noted in the last chapter on the gilded age that, deep within this period following the Civil War, writers such as Twain, Hay, Adams, and Howe, had written novels which had a sociological purpose, to analyze evil within our economic and social structure. We noted that little public attention was paid them, with exception of the novels of Bellamy which treated the broader ideals of Marxian socialism as well as the immediate American scene.

But from 1903 until after World War I, the American people accepted and demanded more of this type of fiction of self-criticism and social problems. In this early period of popularity, the social novel was definitely a thesis, or problem, novel, in that it studied specific questions of social interest. This form of the realistic novel did not attempt to suggest remedies for the conditions described; it concentrated attention upon an unbiased presentation of facts. The approach was simple and direct and often was little more than mere journalistic reporting, with much of the righteous tone of a moral tract. Most of the best of the early-century social novels are short on the side of artistic structure and expression.

The "muckraker" school

During this early period, the convictions of many that much of our social ill was caused by an alliance of special privilege between unscrupulous big business interests and corrupt politicians, led to a great deal of literary probing into our economic and social institutions in an attempt to expose the malodorous facts. Theodore Roosevelt, angered at the persistent efforts of these literary "detectives," referred (1906) to them as "muckrakers." He was referring to a character in *The Pilgrim's Progress* of John Bunyan who was so busy raking the muck beneath his feet that he did not see a heavenly crown that was above his head. This term stuck in our literary vocabulary and writers who led the crusade to expose the corruption and special privilege in our political and economic structure are known as the "muckraking school*."

More recent sociological fiction

In the twenties the "muckraking" crusade and much of the fiction devoted to the factual-like literary analysis of social problems had subsided and had given way to a more artistic type of realistic delving into our social structure to expose its weaknesses. This later realistic novel, devoted to a social purpose, tended to be humoristically or bitterly satirical in its treatment.

In the thirties the economic depression, which began with the stock market collapse of 1929, provided the major social problems which kept the sociological novel in the forefront of our realistic writing. Many of our finest living writers have devoted at least a part of their production to novels treating the social miseries induced by the depression.

In the fiction of today the sociological novel continues on a minor note, devoted largely to racial problems, particularly to that of the Negro and his position in our social structure. Slum conditions in our cities, vice and crime (particularly juvenile delinquency), and corruption in local politics are social topics which occasionally produce fine novels today. The social aspect of the realist novel is far from dead in our fiction, and bids fair to continue as a potent minor influence in our literature.

The greatest of the muckrakers

The earliest of the muckraking movement were journalists, and their studies appeared in such magazines as *Cosmopolitan, McClure's, Collier's, Everybody's,* and others. Among the foremost of these studies were such exposés as Ida Tarbell's *The History of the Standard Oil Company* (1904) and Lincoln Steffens' *The Shame of the Cities* (1904). These early writings were presented as factual reports of corruption in big business and politics. The studies by Steffens, which he continued until his death in 1936, are considered the most balanced and scientifically produced of the many studies of weaknesses in our local and national political systems. Most of the writings of the muckraking school are reports and do not approach the field of literature.

David Graham Phillips (1867-1911), a newspaper man and romantic novelist, began to turn his zeal against fraud and corruption toward building novels around his studies. He produced *The Cost* (1904) and *The Deluge* (1905), which dealt with the manipulations on the Wall Street stock market. His *The Plum Tree* (1905) dealt with the activities of a political boss. Phillips continued to turn out one novel after the other, dealing with local and national scandal, until he was murdered by a lunatic in 1911.

His greatest novel, *Susan Lenox: Her Fall and Rise* (written in 1908) mingled his exposés of corruption in politics with his naturalistic relation of the career of a country girl who rose to material success as a prostitute. With exception of this novel, the work of Phillips, highly popular in the first quarter of the century, is scarcely read at all today. Time has not dealt kindly with this fiction which depended too much on the factual presentation of dated subject matter and too little on artistic literary treatment.

Sinclair: master of propaganda in fiction

Upton Sinclair (1878-____) is the greatest and most representative of the muckraker aspect of the social novel. Sinclair was well educated and from a prominent Baltimore family. He is one of our best potential creative artists of the century. His early novels and much of his later work show his power to manipulate the language into a forceful prose style. The subject matter of his many novels is largely dated and is no longer of interest.

In 1906, Sinclair assisted in a governmental investigation of the Chicago stockyards, and from this point, Sinclair turned from the genteel realism of his early novels and developed a passionate zeal for social justice. He began to expose the evils of capitalism in a fierce and moving prose. Sinclair has written many novels of this type. *The Jungle* (1906) (228) is an exposé of the filth and corrupt practices he found in the meat-packing plants. This novel is a vivid and powerful appeal for social reform. *The Jungle* remains the best written and most representative of the qualities to be found in the muckraking fiction generally.

For the following 30 years Sinclair produced book after book in which his evangelistic spirit of righteous indignation never flagged. He has been our most effective crusader in the novel and the most severe critic of many of our institutions. He has continued to be an artist in prose writing, whose products are weakened by their obvious bias and emotionalized propagandistic approach. In *King Coal* (1917) and *The Profits of Religion* (1918), he attacked organized religion as a tool in capitalistic hands to keep the poor in contented subjugation. In *The Goose Step* (1923) and *The Goslings* (1924), he attacked the regimentation and one-sided educational diet which he saw imposed upon the school systems by capitalist manipulators. In *The Flivver King* (1937), he turned his searching technique upon the automobile industry.

The later Sinclair and "Lanny Budd"

In 1940, with *World's End,* Sinclair began to trace the career of his hero, the illegitimate son of a munitions manufacturer and an international beauty. In the Lanny Budd series, Sinclair carries his hero through every major world event from World War I to the present. He has written 11 novels in the series through 1953, the entire series bringing the chronicle of events to that date. In this series Sinclair has given up much of his propagandistic zeal and has dealt with the travels and many experiences of his hero in a romantic-realistic fashion. The Lanny Budd novels are, in a sense, historical romances and are unusual in that few of our many writers of the historical novel seem inclined to deal with recent happenings.

Other early sociological fiction

Though few others among the early-century realists showed the crusading zeal and fire of Phillips, Sinclair, and the non-fictional attackers of special privilege and corruption, many writers devoted at least a part of their work to a searching criticism of our economic, political and social institutions. (See Appendix A, page 229, for brief digests of novels by Winston Churchill, Robert Herrick, Jack London, and Ernest Poole.)

The changing tone of social fiction

After World War I, the virulent economic and political criticism of the early-century writers was stilled, with exception of Upton Sinclair, who continued his violent attacks on the minions of capitalism. The social novel continued as a strong tendency in our realistic writing but its temper took new directions, mainly that of a dissection of attitudes and institutions of *bourgeois* society. The focus of attention was principally the small town and the village. The attacks were upon either the spirit of narrowness and smug Puritanism that characterized small-town life or upon the pettiness and greed of small-town leaders.

Though our better realists of the age were to be counted among the attackers, there were a few of our writers of sentimental fiction about the turn of the century who undertook a nostalgic emotionalized view of village life. William Allen White's *A Certain Rich Man (1909)* (230) and Booth Tarkington's *The Gentleman from Indiana (1899)* (231) are among the better novels in which these writers laud the small town as idyllic paradises wherein reside the good and wholesome virtues of American life.

But the picture that the best of the realist novelists of the twenties presented of the American small town was quite a different one. These novelists pictured village life as indescribably dull and resistant to change. The people are pictured as uncultured, intolerant, spiritually narrow, and hypocritical. Businessmen and politicians are portrayed as avaricious, sharp, and backbiting.

Sinclair Lewis (1885-1951)

Lewis was born in a small Minnesota village. He early showed a deep interest in social reform. While at Yale, he dedicated himself to writing as a career. After graduating, he worked for a time as a journalist. His first 6 novels are undistinguished.

In 1920, *Main Street* (231) brought Lewis international fame as a realist and a satirist. This novel is primarily a sociological study of a rural midwestern town. Lewis produced his other 2 most famous social novels within the next 5 years: *Babbitt* (1922) (232), a penetrating study of smug middle-class respectability, and *Arrowsmith* (1925) (232), a conflict between personal high idealism in an individual doctor versus the narrow bigotry in medical practice which would reduce the high-minded scientist to a sordid conformist level of sham and avarice.

The Lewis technique

Lewis continued to produce a novel every 2 years until his death, but none come up to the standard of excellence he set in the 3 novels he wrote in the early twenties. Lewis is perhaps the most influential of our realist novelists. He possessed a phenomenal facility for amassing details and in presenting a unified and plausible picture of American life, with overtones of humorous and slightly malicious satire. Lewis employed an almost photographic realism and was a master at his reproduction of *bourgeois* speech and actions. His satirical humor was mild, but deadly, in creating an atmosphere of dull respectability and unbelievable stupidity in small-town life.

Actually Lewis was at home in his portrayals of *bourgeois* American life. He was himself of it, and he recognized its failings from his own experience. He saw the comic side of his own existence and was a master at the faithful reproduction of his own memories.

Lewis refused the Pulitzer Prize in 1926, but accepted the Nobel Prize in 1930. His *Main Street* and *Babbitt* sold over a half million copies each and have been read in translation the world over. There have been no more successful novels in the century on the higher artistic literary levels.

Sherwood Anderson (1876-1941)

Anderson was born in a small town in Ohio. He, unlike Lewis, became concerned with the inner conflicts of his characters. He saw the American small town as a seething cauldron of indvidual frustration and passion. His approach to small-town life was through individuals who were made unhappy and bitter, according to his views, by the Puritanism and surface virtue and respectability of middle-class life. Anderson leaned very heavily toward the naturalist bias of determinism. His characters are victims of the circumstances in which they were born and raised and from which their spirits could not escape— the atmosphere of narrow smugness and intolerance of middle-class life. Anderson tends, of course, only to study the social misfits of his small-town setting and attempts to trace their ills, in mystically symbolic identification, to the forces of town life which suppress their normal development as balanced and happy individuals.

Anderson's medium for his best work is the short story. _Winesburg, Ohio_ (1919) (232) is the collection which gave him literary fame. These studies of human behavior, of confused and frustrated personalities, continue to be the most representative picture of Anderson's bitter social condemnation, that the misfits of the social scene are mostly created by the very social group which shows the most bitter cruelty toward their confused and twisted souls.

The novel of the depression years

During the years of economic depression in the early thirties, the attention of many of our writers of realist fiction was drawn to the problems in our social life that were induced by the economic collapse itself. Our most enduring social fiction, however, came from writers whose attention was drawn to the wide gulf that existed between the average middle-class American and certain groups of underprivileged individuals. Much of our best fiction in the period between the wars was devoted to studies of migrant agricultural workers, the sharecropper and tenant farmer groups of the South, workers in eastern textile mills, minority racial groups, and city slum populations. The tragic contrast between the privileged and the underprivileged in the American scene produced the best social novels of the thirties and early forties.

John Steinbeck (1902-   )

Steinbeck's liberal and humanitarian views mainly have found expression in his best novels as an ardent desire for agrarian reform in the direction of more widespread individual land ownership. His sharpest barbs have been directed against the almost feudal corporation land ownership in California. Steinbeck was born in Salinas, California, and most of his novels have a California setting.

At his best, Steinbeck is one of the finest prose artists in the century. He is a master of a simple, but lyric, prose style. His lyric prose, combined with his strong leaning to sentiment and symbolism, make his realistic pictures quite often seem out of keeping with his sociological message and the clarity and factual treatment that these themes seem to require. Steinbeck's novels to date are highly varied—some are realistic and some are almost pure romance.

Whimsey, sentiment, and sociology in Steinbeck

Tortilla Flat (1935), the somewhat whimsical and episodic treatment of the joys and tribulations of the *paisanos* of the Monterey Peninsula in California, is sentimental and humorously sympathetic. The little book is beautifully written and highly entertaining, but tends to rouse little of the serious sociological feelings in the mind of the reader that, perhaps, the author intended to convey. Of Mice and Men (1937) is a sentimentalized folk tragedy concerning 2 itinerant farm workers, one of whom is a simple-minded hulk of animal man. The reader is fascinated by the brute animal simplicity of Lennie, but remains impervious to the social import that is attached to the tale. For the most part, Steinbeck has produced highly entertaining tales, with fine psychological penetration and couched in beautiful language, but his serious message is lost beneath the Steinbeck brilliance as a prose stylist and his gentle sympathy.

Steinbeck's artistic masterpiece

The Grapes of Wrath (1939, Pulitzer Prize 1940) (233) is the novel that raised Steinbeck to the level of great prose fiction. This story of the migration of a farm family from the Oklahoma dust bowl to a fertile California valley is a work of masterful descriptive power and artistic realism in character delineation. Steinbeck's chief faults are present: a tendency toward sentiment and an episodic treatment of the narrative. But the language is prose that carries color and meaning beyond the surface of photographic reality. Steinbeck creates an artistic atmosphere in his reporting of observed facts that gives his descriptive passages a depth of conviction and permeating mood. *The Grapes of Wrath* is one of the most convincing social novels of the century as well as being one of our literature's finest examples of beautiful writing.

Problems in the social fiction of today

The social novel continues in popularity in the years since World War II with new concentrations of interest. The war brought international social problems into the fore in American fiction in the years immediately following the conflict. A number of our novels have been produced which deal with dispossessed individuals and minority groups in Europe. None of these is likely to interest readers of the future.

The Negro in fiction

On the American scene the war focused sharp attention upon the American rift between ideals and practice in treatment of the major U.S. minority racial group: the Negro. Since 1940 many novels have appeared in which this social problem has been discussed. Lillian Smith, a Georgia social worker, wrote *Strange Fruit* in 1944, in which the author charged both Negro and white with responsibility in the solution of their mutual difficulties in living together and sharing equally in the fruits of democracy. The novel created a sensation, receiving both blasts of condemnation and high praise as it grew in popularity.

The most forceful realist who is producing books on the subject at present is Richard Wright, a young Negro, born and raised in Mississippi. Wright is a skilled writer, but with a definite naturalist bias. Wright's vivid and forceful narrative tends to concentrate upon the viewpoint of the Negro, and his characters, around whom he builds his social thesis, tend to represent the dregs of his race. His *Native Son (1940)* (227) established Wright as the leading Negro author in our contemporary literature. Since this novel, Wright has concentrated largely upon recollections of his own boyhood and upon building a store of folklore and historical data of his race. His latest book, *Black Power (1954)*, is a study of the contemporary Negro in Africa.

The atom bomb and juvenile delinquency

The war also brought 2 other social problems into sharp focus in our current writing: the possible social effects of atomic warfare and crime in the younger age groups. Although several fictional treatments of atomic warfare have appeared, none are of literary merit and all tend to hypothetical romance. The problem of the child delinquent has also received bulky treatment, but scarcely any that merits serious literary consideration. The most sensational fictional treatment so far was *The Bad Seed* (1954), a highly naturalistic treatment of an 8-year-old murderess. It enjoyed a long run in the dramatic adaptation by Maxwell Anderson and has recently been released in a movie version. Both the atomic bomb and juvenile delinquency have been dealt with much more effectively and convincingly in non-fictional studies than in the novel.

C. Genteel Realism

Standing at almost the opposite pole from naturalism, within the meaning of the term realism as a straightforward presentation of life as it is, there has been in this century a group of writers who followed in the footsteps of Howells and James—the continuators of the genteel tradition. These writers have attempted to present a realistic view of life, but they have carefully chosen their materials from select areas of American society. They are aristocratic writers who deliberately cultivate themes connected with the conventional and established codes of upper-class morality. They deliberately avoid shoddiness, vulgarity, and themes with significant social problems.

These writers have aimed primarily at finished technique, both in expression and in skillful integration of character and plot. They concern themselves with perfection of design and composition, clear and dignified expression. They strive for finished novels that will reflect only good manners and elegance. These writers, as James, are concerned with psychology and the logical and authentic development of character.

The leading figures of our literature of this century in the tradition of genteel writing have been women: _Edith Wharton (1863-1937)_ and _Willa Cather (1874-1947)_. Each has operated in widely differing environments but both have aimed at an identical refinement of novelistic art that they considered could be achieved only with _significant_ material. The refined expression of both women shows only one basic distinction. Mrs. Wharton is mildly satirical and Willa Cather is entirely serious and there is little to detract from her cool and direct approach to character and plot development. Both women have produced some of the most smoothly flowing and sympathetically imaginative realistic fiction of our time.

Edith Wharton's approach to realism

Edith Wharton was of a distinguished New York family. She was privately educated at home and abroad, and in every sense was of the aristocratic society about which she wrote most of her novels. She was concerned with beauty of expression and refinement of theme. She also sought to express faithfully the life and problems of her society. Her realism is tinged with a gentle satire. Edith Wharton's novels approach the upper classes with much the same technique that Sinclair Lewis employed in his middle-class settings. Mrs. Wharton's approach, however, had little of a social purpose; she was concerned almost entirely with an artistic pattern within which to analyze social manners within a refined tradition. _The House of Mirth (1905)_ (233), the story of a girl who is ostracized from her group for unconventional behavior, is representative of the best of Mrs. Wharton's many novels.

In 1911, Mrs. Wharton wrote *Ethan Frome* (234), a novelette dealing with simple New England people, one of the rare instances where she departed from her ironic depiction of aristocratic manners. _Ethan Frome_ is considered a masterpiece of objective realism and fine character portrayal. This little work is likely to endure in our literature much longer than the many longer novels that best characterize Mrs. Wharton's approach to realism.

Willa Cather's approach to realism

Willa Cather grew up in Nebraska, spending the greater part of her formative years among European immigrant groups. When she began her writing career, her first desire was to reproduce in artistic fiction the memories of those Scandanavian and Bohemian peoples with whom she had been intimate for many years. Her best novel of this early period is _My Antonia_ (1918) (235), the tender and sympathetic tale of a Bohemian immigrant girl and her hardships on the Nebraskan frontier.

In Willa Cather's second group of novels, she deplores the encroaching spirit of material selfishness that is invading the gentle and kindly midwestern neighborliness that she recalled from her youth.

When Miss Cather realized she had exhausted her fund of recollected material of the Midwest, she turned her attention to the pioneering efforts of the Catholic Church in the Southwest and in Canada. Her best-known work from this period is _Death Comes for the Archbishop (1927)_ (235).

Willa Cather, like Edith Wharton, was little concerned with social, economic, or political problems. Like her fellow leader in our 20th century genteel realism, she was concerned with a polished artistic production and with the beauties which could be found in reality.

D. Sentimental Realism

In this century of a dominant realism in fiction, many writers have followed the basic technique but have had little of the realist attitude or spirit. Much of our most popular fiction, in terms of book sales, has had a generous heaping of sentimentality imposed upon a thinly pursued realist method. These novelists have usually purported to present American life as it is, but in reality, have colored their efforts highly with personal pride, patriotism, and optimism. They are the seekers of a pleasant surface reality, gentle conflict, emotionalized situations, and happy endings.

Booth Tarkington (1869-1946) produced many novels which are skilled representations of surface reality. They are all biased toward an abiding American faith in the proposition that virtue and integrity always emerge triumphant. _The Magnificent Ambersons_ (1918) (235) is a fine example of the sort of fiction that has made Tarkington one of our most read authors in the century.

Edna Ferber _(So Big, Show Boat, Cimarron, Giant)_, Kathleen Norris _(Foolish Virgin, Heartbroken Melody)_, and Fanny Hurst _(Humoresque, Mannequin, Hallelujah, Anywoman)_ are other names, only slightly below Tarkington in ability, who have provided reading in the realm of sentimental realism in this century on a popular subliterary level.

E. Realism and the Regional Novel

With the strong national spirit that swept through America after the Civil War, came increasing interest in fiction which concentrated its attention upon a more or less accurate representation of the peoples, manners, and ideas of particular areas of the country. The _local colorists_ met the popular demand with varied treatments of the South, Midwest, Far West, and New England in highly romanticized fiction. With the rise of realism, this search for the rich regional materials continued unabated, the glitter and tinsel of the local-color technique giving way to a sympathetic or satiric realism in many authors.

In this century, the regional aspect of our fiction has been a continually invigorating one. Except in historical novels generally, the treatment in the last few years in our better creative writing has been a realistic one, with the author's approach being objective or subjective. The subjective approach is, of course, very strong in the regional novel, many writers depending upon memory to supply much of the detail of the region in which they once lived, or of the prior period being treated.

Regional peoples have been treated both lovingly and satirically. Naturalism, objective or subjective realism, and the more genteel and sentimental approaches are found in our regional fiction. Often the treatment is purely romantic and imaginatively fanciful.

Manifestation of a people's literature

Much of our literature devoted too intensely to regional matter is of little interest in other parts of the world, and much of it will serve only a temporary reading public. But some great fiction has risen and will rise from this very American interest in our own colorful landscape and the peoples who inhabit it, in city and in the country. The intense interest in regional themes in our creative fiction is a healthy indication that our national culture increasingly will reflect the spirit and aspirations of a democratic people, cognizant of the nature of the parts that make up the whole State.

See Appendix A, page 236, for reference to digests of recent novels dealing with the landscape, the peoples, and their manners and traditions in various areas of the United States.

F.   The Historical Novel

Since 1900, the historical novel has gained steadily in popularity until today few of our major fiction writers have failed to attempt at least one work dealing with some phase of American history. Many writers of popular fiction, who cater to mass demand for high adventure, colorful pageantry, and generous helpings of sentimentality, have produced a plethora of subliterary historical novels within recent years. Most of the mass of historical novels represent, of course, poor writing and erroneous history. The most popular of these subliterary "historical romances" of recent years was the single work of Margaret Mitchell, _Gone With the Wind_ (1937), a long narrative dealing with the Civil War and the Reconstruction period. This novel sold over 1,500,000 copies in the first year, making it the fastest-selling novel in U.S. publishing history. To date it has sold well above the 5 million mark in English. It also sold well in its more than 20 translations into foreign languages, the German edition alone having sold nearly 750,000 copies.

Values and the historical novel

It is extremely difficult to predict which of the historical novels are most likely to prove permanent contributions to our body of best creative writings. Many of the historical novels are well written and have a sound basis in history. All such novels are highly subject to the weaknesses inherent in sentimentality and romance. In a sense, all history is romance, and particularly so are the events of the recorded past of one's own nation.

The historical novel is closely allied to the regional novel (many of which are historical novels) in technique and the continued popularity of this type of a blending of realism and romanticism in our writing is but another indication of the healthy interest of Americans in the rich resources of our soil and peoples, past and present.

Whether the spirit of the historical novel tends to the realistic or to the romantic, to sentimental or satiric treatments, to a historical panorama of events and places, or to imaginative concentration upon character development, great numbers of these accounts will continue to be created and read in the writing of a literate people, interested in their own national heritage.

Major writers of historical novels

On the more popular, and hence more sentimental and romantic level these writers have appealed to masses of readers in this century: Zane Grey, Stewart Edward White, Emerson Hough, Edna Ferber, John Fox, Owen Wister, Van Wyck Mason, and many others.

On the side of more serious attempts to recapture historical reality and to create an aesthetic work, these authors rank high for at least one work: Winston Churchill, Walter D. Edmonds, Kenneth Roberts, Mary Johnston, Gertrude Atherton, James Boyd, Elizabeth Madox Roberts, Ellen Glasgow, and many others. (See Appendix A, page 236, for brief digests of representative historical novels of recent years, which also contain a regional interest.

G. Exoticism and Romance in Fiction

With the rise of realism and its naturalistic aspect in the late years of the 19th century, there came a corresponding surge of exotic and imaginatively fanciful fiction to satisfy the demands of large sectors of our literate masses of readers. To many the new realistic methods produced only sordid, cheerless, and bitter pictures of life. These many readers demanded optimism, sweetness, and the thrill of high adventure. Many readers had tired of the local colorists' versions of the American scene and yearned to be stimulated by the call of far-off places. They longed for vicarious escape into some realm of the unfamiliar. The historical romance (see above) satisfied only a part of this craving for writing which would deal with themes alien to the workaday American scene.

Stimulus from England

In the last years of the old century, American readers were excited by the wave of exotic fiction and poetry which poured into our bookstores from England. They were carried to the South Seas by Stevenson, to India by Kipling, to Japan by Hearn. H. Rider Haggard, Sir Anthony Hope, and others roamed the far reaches of space and time to carry their readers into realms of strangeness and romantic fancy. H. G. Wells had begun to produce a type of scientific fantasy which reached into other worlds. Conan Doyle had created his superdetective, Sherlock Holmes, who was gifted with uncanny powers for ferreting out the weird and exotic crimes of master criminals.

American popular exoticism

American writers rose in numbers to answer the call for something more exciting than the familiar events and peoples of the everyday home front activities. Lew Wallace had carried readers back into the splendors of Aztec Mexico (The Fair God) in 1873 and to the glories of ancient Rome (Ben Hur) as early as 1880. About 1900, the wave of enthusiasm for fiction in which both the writer and his audience could flee together to realms of fanciful fact, where reality made few demands, produced scores of works. Books such as Charles Major's *When Knighthood Was in Flower* (1898), Booth Tarkington's *Monsieur Beaucaire* (1900), and George Barr McCutcheon's *Graustark* (1901) precipitated a revival of romance on the popular reading level, a false or "pseudo" romanticism of escape to alien and fanciful realms of the imagination.

On the popular level of writing, with little artistic concept, this tide of exotic fiction has continued unabated to the present. Many themes have been exploited by such writers as James

Oliver Curwood (the north woods of Canada and Alaska), Nordoff and Hall (the South Seas), Edgar Rice Burroughs (creator of Tarzan, a neoprimitive superhuman), and many others. Today it is apparent that the detective story and the historical romance (particularly of the western frontier) are the most exploited themes which provide escape from reality for millions of American readers. In the last 20 years there has been a wave of interest in the popular novel which attempts to create for the modern reader a revived sense of Christian spirituality by the exploitation of New Testament themes. *The Robe* (1942) of Lloyd Douglas has been the most phenomenally successful of these books which treat biblical themes in an exotic manner.

Exoticism among the better contemporary novelists

By 1920 many of our best fiction writers were devoting all or a part of their production to the novel of exotic theme. These writers have carried exotic romanticism into a level approaching pure literature through their command of language, their sense of integration of plot structure, and their devotion to a serious purpose other than that of providing a pure escape valve for the imaginations of reality-bound readers.

Perhaps the 2 most successful of the better writers of exotic fiction in the century (aside from writers of historical romances which involve varying degrees of exoticism) have approached their escapist matter from widely differing directions. Pearl Buck (1892-   ), winner of both the Pulitzer and Nobel prizes, has devoted most of her production to Chinese peasant life. *The Good Earth* (1931) (239) is representative of her best efforts to make this ancient culture comprehensible to Western readers. James Branch Cabell (1879-1958) has created a mythical middle-age country of Poictesme to which he returns to develop his dreamlike tales of fantasy. Cabell is a romantic with a difference. He uses his exotic creations to direct barbs of humorous and ironical satire at the ideals of modern society: religion, patriotism, romantic love. *Jurgen* (1919) (240) is representative of Cabell's voluminous productions.

The Short Story

Hawthorne and Poe were the pioneers in the development of the modern short fictional form (average 5,000 words) in America which has received the name of *short story** in literatures. The intense popularity of this form in the past 70 years is probably due largely to the phenomenal demand of magazines for brief, but complete, treatment of imaginative themes for hurried American readers. The short story appears in all levels of excellence. Few writers, whether their major production be drama, the novel, or poetry, fail to turn out at least a few short stories in the course of their careers. Clever fabricators of imaginative tales realize early that financial returns are immediate in the magazine market. The result is that the American short story has become fairly well standardized and is, in a sense, an industry. American colleges offer courses on how to write and market short stories. Hence this brief fictional form has come under a good deal of suspicion in considerations of creative literature.

The short story, whatever its shortcomings in lack of space for proper development of character and setting, is the most popular form of writing and it is not likely that its vogue is a temporary one. It will continue to attract writing talents, distinguished and otherwise.

Development of the contemporary short story

The American reader of the post-Civil War period was fed with the local colorist tales of Bret Harte, Mark Twain, Joel Chandler Harris, and others. Soon other writers, mainly journalists, entered the field and began to deviate from the purely local-color aspect of the popular writing of the age. Such writers as Frank R. Stockton (*The Lady, or the Tiger?*) and Richard Harding Davis (*Gallegher*) began to exploit sentimentality and a normal human curiosity in their themes. The popular American short story was relatively well established, in form and the sentimental appeal of its themes, by 1900.

During the first decade of the 20th century a phenomenally successful short story writer was William Sydney Porter (1862-1910), who wrote under the name of O. Henry. Porter was an adventurer, bank clerk, and news reporter who possessed the remarkable ability to turn out hundreds of catchy and colorful tales of human types to be found in the masses of humanity from the lower economic levels of society and from the underworld. O. Henry's stories are full of evidence of hasty writing and sentimentality, but his formula of the surprise ending and his journalistic technique of racy and rapid-moving prose won him millions of readers in his lifetime and after. The influence of O.

Henry has been the greatest single standardizing factor in the American short story of this century.

O. Henry's most representative collection is *The Four Million* (1906), romantic portrayals of pathos and sentiment surrounding the lives of shop girls, vagabonds, burglars, and other types of humanity to be found in East Side New York.

Recent efforts to break away from the "formula" story

Since O. Henry's day, the majority of the higher type, or slick-paper, magazines have followed the formula set down by this early-century popularizer of the short story. However, many experimental forms of the more artistic short story have been exploited, and the short story has followed all the methods and techniques developed in the novel and has attracted the attention of our best writers. Some have approached the short fictional medium in a highly subjective manner (William Faulkner, William Saroyan, Conrad Aiken, Sherwood Anderson), while others have attempted a complete objectivity (Ernest Hemingway, Erskine Caldwell). Though the majority of our most brilliant writers of novels, drama, and poetry have developed one or another of the experimental types of short stories, few writers have depended upon this genre for their major reputation. A few writers, however, are best known for their production in this short fictional form: Katherine Anne Porter, Kay Boyle, Mark Schorer, James Thurber, and others.

But whether the short story is treated popularly and romantically, depending upon incidents, sketchily drawn characters, and the surprise ending for its effects, in the manner of O. Henry, or more in the artistic and experimental manner of the selections which young writers began to produce for such magazines as *The New Yorker, Esquire,* and *Story,* its popularity has continued to be undiminished since the early years of the century. Its production has attracted an equally wide range of distinguished and undistinguished writing talent during recent years. For the huge magazine market, whether slick or pulp, the short story is in greater demand than all other forms of writing. A number of anthologies of recent short stories appear every year. Rarely, however, does a book collection by a single author achieve the sales accorded the anthologies.

II.   TRENDS IN POETRY

Since the deaths of the last of the great romantics and such isolated giants of verse as Walt Whitman and Emily Dickinson, American poetry has gone through varied periods of experimentation and has gained and lost a reading public several times. No great schools or movements have commanded large followings. Most of the best poetry has been produced by individual writers, unassociated with particular movements. The 2 great 19th century figures of Whitman and Dickinson have continued to influence deeply the most outstanding poets of this country. But for the most part and until recent years, American poetry had shown a continuing dependence upon English models and had suffered the same decline of reader interest as was manifested in England after the death of Tennyson in 1892, the same year Whitman died.

Some causes for decline in poetry

Some have assigned the decline of great poetry, both in England and America during the 1890's, to the rise of the novel and its realistic technique—a technique unsuited to lyric expression. The spirit of doubt, cynicism, and commercialism that brought the pessimistic determinism of the naturalistic technique and the muckraking journalistic approach to the fore in the novel undoubtedly had a great deal to do with causing poetry to desert the emotions and to seek to rationalize life. Poets became experimental, deserting both emotion and the metrical patterns of the past, and each poet attempted to develop an individual language and verse pattern. Poetry became intellectual and cold and more and more came to be read only by small select groups who might understand (or pretend to understand) what the poets were attempting to convey. Too much poetry was merely poor prose with clever language patterns calculated to tax the mental capacity and accumulated knowledge of the reader, rather than to appeal to his feelings and emotional depth. Few poets escaped this craze to experiment on the plane of cerebral gymnastics, but most of the reading public for poetry escaped to swell the mounting mass of readers for the novel and the short story or depended upon the production of the poets of the past or the continuing strain of sentimental or narrative second-rate verse being turned out by such poets as James Whitcomb Riley, Robert Service, or Edgar Guest.

A sign of renascence in American poetry

In the past few years, however, American poetry seems to be returning somewhat toward greater simplicity and directness. The younger poets of today return more and more to a language of beauty and rhythm and a content of feeling and emotion. Doubt, pessimism, uncertainty, and puzzling intellectual patterns are vanishing, being replaced by simple faith and certainty in idea and the old metrical patterns in form. Facts in verse are giving way to uplifting vision in recent American poetry. The rhyme and meter of the great poets of the past are no longer considered childish and immature. American poetry is becoming, once again, lyrical and artistically expressive of normal emotion. And American poetry is capable of acquiring again the large audience it once possessed, a people who, more than any previous generation, are overfed with science and fact, a materialistic spirit, gnawing pessimism, doubt, and fear—a people receptive to the literary medium that can communicate to them beauty of spirit and ennobling vision through direct and uncomplicated appeal to the emotions and the feelings which compose one undying side of man's dual nature, whatever be the external pressures of the age or the society in which he lives.

American Poetry Since Whitman
From 1890 to 1912

For 2 decades after the death of Whitman, American poetry stagnated, and public interest was low in this branch of literary art. James Whitcomb Riley, with his folksy sentimentalism, was the poetic voice who recalled for many readers of the age the pleasures of rural childhood. The better poets had little original to say. For the most part, they continued to produce polished verse in the manner of the English romantics: Shelley, Keats, and the Victorian, Tennyson. The poetry of Thomas Bailey Aldrich (1837-1907), Edward Rowland Sill (1841-1887), and Richard Watson Gilder (1844-1909) was elegant, polished, and sweet, but it was lifeless and dull. One poet, Richard Hovey (1864-1900), strove to introduce a rugged spirit of adventure into his vibrant vagabond songs. William Vaughn Moody (1869-1910), the most promising of the group, who died at the age of 41, possessed a fiery social conscience in his youth and joined the novelists of the day in bringing themes of social injustice and national evils into his verse. But none of these poets succeeded in changing the low ebb of public interest in poetry, and none stirred young writers of genius to follow them.

From 1912 to 1925

American poetry of the transition period from the 19th to the 20th century, unlike the novel, contained little indication that a major revolution in verse and a sudden revival of public interest were just over the horizon. From the founding of Harriet Monroe's little magazine, *Poetry,* in 1912, until the death of Amy Lowell in 1925, a new poetry burst forth upon the American literary scene with the splendid brilliance of fireworks and was eagerly received by a new and numerous mass of readers. Volumes of poetry and poetic criticism flooded the market, and new poets sprang up almost overnight to supply the amazing demand for verse, whether rhythmical or not. This new poetry renascence began as a spontaneous and fresh stream after the most dry and unpoetic period of American literary history and died as suddenly as it began, as the vast new audience which it had won deserted the older poets, who had begun with fresh perspectives and had ended with dry cynicism. The younger poets had no worthy banner to follow and created nothing new of their own. American poetry slipped once again into the doldrums in which it had floundered around the turn of the century.

The new poetry and its characteristics

The upswing of interest in poetry in England and the United States occurred almost simultaneously. English poetry had showed the same lack of direction and scant public interest when its last great 19th century poet, Tennyson, died in 1892, as did American poetry after the death of Whitman in the same year. In 1911, John Masefield published his first collection of poems and English poetry began its sudden revival. The American renascence dates from 1912 with the appearance of *Poetry,* a magazine devoted exclusively to the publication and criticism of verse. During the following few years many other periodicals devoted increasing space to poetry and many poetry magazines flourished for a while. Publishers responded to public demand by issuing many volumes of the new verse. During a brief period volumes of verse were bought and read on a scale comparable to that of the production and sale of novels. Never before or since has there been an equal outpouring of fresh and vigorous verse and an equal public demand for more of the same.

Actually, the new and tremendous enthusiasm for poetry was not initiated by a "school," nor did it become a unified literary movement. The tidal wave of poetry was created by individual poets whose creative inspirations came from varied sources. Many terms have been employed to attempt to describe the basic characteristics of the verse of the period. There were many isolated movements, cults, and theories and such terms as "free verse," "vers libre," "imagism," "pure" poetry, "vorticism," "polyphonic prose," and many others were heard for a while to describe some particular phase of this verse of the period which, today, is rather generally called *new poetry* to distinguish it from older varieties of traditional verse.

In general, the adherents of the new poetry demanded a *freedom* from the metrical controls of traditional poetry. The new poetry is not to bar any form of verse, regardless of whether or not it follows any of the traditional rules. Each poet is to use whatever form he pleases or create new ones to best express what he has to say. The new poets felt also that poetry should depict the present and that no subject should be deemed outside the realm of verse, whether it be ugly or beautiful. The new verse should be extremely modern and should include and express all the brilliant advances of technology, psychology, and development of the human intellect. Therefore an entirely new vocabulary and a new set of *images* were to be created to take the place of outworn symbols for ideas and objects. The atmosphere was one of experimentation and the objective methods of science were to be applied to subject matter. Lyric poetry traditionally had been subjective, the emphasis being upon a projection of the poet's own emotions and feelings in regard to external life. This attempt of the new poets at detachment and impersonal utterance is perhaps the most profound distinction of the new poetry from the old.

Of course, these new attitudes were not peculiar to America. The French poets had experimented with symbolism* and what they termed Parnassism* in the late 19th century and had found imitators in England before the turn of the century. Spanish American poets had flocked to the French banners and had developed their own *Modernista* movement, headed by Rubén Darío, before the dawn of the new century. Darío had rallied the poets of Spain to his standards, and the American Whitman was recognized throughout the European and the southern American world as a "modernist." By the World War I period, the new "free" verse was practised by the leading poets in every world literature. The new poetry in the United States owed its being to the mounting influence of Whitman and the "discovery" of Emily Dickinson, on the one hand, and to the attention the new poets were paying to the foreign movements, particularly the French and the English imitators of the French innovations.

The more prominent of the new poets

The new poets are to be counted in the hundreds. One critic, in 1923, was only half joking when he stated that the parade of poets was so long that there was little public left to view it. Of this long parade of new poets many names are remembered today, but already criticism and time have operated to give us a few outstanding names from this most notable period of American poetry in the present century.

Edwin Arlington Robinson (1869-1935)

Robinson, born in Maine, is the most direct American precursor of the new poetry. Before the turn of the century he cultivated the traditional metrical forms and was turning out verse with a clear and direct style of his own for years before the revival of interest in poetic art brought him to the attention of more than a limited circle of readers. Today Robinson is considered one of the most highly individual poets of his time and as a finished craftsman. Robinson's production is voluminous and distinguished among many poets who failed to achieve originality except for a few poems. Robinson is perhaps to be rated our greatest poet between Whitman and Robert Frost.

Robinson was a new-century romantic and his best verse all reveals his longing for the freer individual spirit of past ages and his dissatisfaction with modern materialistic society. He was interested basically in the spirit of individual man and cared little about the external trappings of social organization in any particular age. He is particularly noted for his character sketches in verse and for his long poems dealing with King Arthur and his Knights of the Round Table and for his dramatic monologue*, *Ben Jonson Entertains a Man from Stratford,* in which a very human portrayal of Shakespeare is revealed through the words of close friends.

Lindsay, Masters, and Sandburg: the prairie poets

Throughout his verse and prose criticism, Whitman had pleaded for a native school of American poets—poets who would give a robust lyric expression to the beauties and the potentialities of America. He said: "We must have new words, new potentialities of speech." In his *As a Strong Bird on Pinions Free* (1872), he had laid down the challenge for young poets to follow him into a "free" verse to depict the American scene.

> The conceits of the poets of other lands I bring thee not,
> Nor the compliments that have served their turn so long,
> Nor rhyme—nor the classics—nor perfume of foreign court,
>   or indoor library!
> But an odor I'd bring to-day as from forests of pine in the
>   north, in Maine—or breath of an Illinois prairie,
> With open airs of Virginia, or Georgia, or Tennessee—or
>   from Texas uplands, or Florida's glades.

And, with the new century, the West gave us three poets who, though tardy in appearing, took up the challenge of the vigorous Whitman and gave us the most robust verse of the new poets.

Poetic evangelist of a gospel of beauty

1. *Vachel Lindsay (1879-1931)*, born in Illinois, attended Hiram College, and studied art in Chicago and New York. He was a born minstrel and had the true spirit of the pioneer, projected into the 20th century. He began to wander, much as a beggar and a vagabond, singing for his supper. He lectured and read his own verse in dramatic fashion to groups and individuals throughout the land.

In his jingling verse, Lindsay preached a gospel of beauty in booming tones. He had a romantic faith in nature and was intensely patriotic, religious, and democratic. He scorned no subject as unfit for his melodic recitations. All his best verse is dramatic and full of the fervor of humanitarianism and piety. He promoted his high moral idealism with a crusading zeal and said: "I would rouse the Abraham Lincoln in you all."

> A bronzed lank man! His suit of ancient black,
> A famous high top-hat and plain worn shawl
> Make him the quaint great figure that men love,
> The prairie-lawyer, master of us all.

He cannot sleep upon his hillside now.
He is among us:—as in times before!
And we who toss and lie awake for long
Breathe deep, and start, to see him pass the door.

His head is bowed. He thinks on men and kings.
Yea, when the sick world cries, how can he sleep?
Too many peasants fight, they know not why,
Too many homesteads in black terror weep . . .
    (from *Abraham Lincoln Walks at Midnight*—1914)

Lindsay's verse is jingle and syncopation. It is material for the vaudeville monologist, the college yell leader, or the fiery evangelist, but it is American in every line. He chanted of the Negro and his brutish superstitions, his revivals and his hopes.

Fat black bucks in a wine-barrel room,
Barrel-house kings, with feet unstable,
Sagged and reeled and pounded on the table,
Pounded on the table,
Beat an empty barrel with the handle of a broom,
Hard as they were able,
Boom, boom, BOOM.
With a silk umbrella and the handle of a broom,
Boomlay, boomlay, boomlay, BOOM.
Then I had religion, Then I had a vision.
I could not turn from their revel in derision . . .
    (from *The Congo*)

He was filled with the thrill of the tones of the calliope steam organ at county fairs.

"I am the Kallyope, Kallyope, Kallyope,
Tooting hope, tooting hope, tooting hope, tooting hope.
Willy, willy, willy wah Hoo!"
    (from *The Kallyope*)

He never failed to bring an evangelical message of spirituality to his audiences.

O, shout Salvation! It was good to see
Kings and Princes by the Lamb set free.
The banjos rattled and the tambourines
Jing-jing-jingled in the hands of Queens . . .
    (from *General William Booth Enters into Heaven*)

Vachel Lindsay's verse is perhaps not great poetry and is undoubtedly filled with fantastic excesses of poetic taste and vocabulary, but it is likely to live long for its native color and its message of optimism in an age of a predominant cynicism and pessimism in American literary expression. Vachel Lindsay is our best representative in poetry of the cheerful reformer who, in his lifetime, went forth personally to evangelize art and whose verse remains to fire the blood of the reader with genuine American emotion.

Master of poetic naturalism

2. _Edgar Lee Masters (1869-1950)_ was born in Kansas but at an early age was removed to the family home in the small town of Petersburg, Illinois. Masters became a lawyer and began his practice in Chicago. He soon gained a reputation as a political and economic liberal.

Masters wrote a good deal of verse in imitation of the English romantics and Victorians which attracted little notice. But his _Spoon River Anthology_, published first in successive issues of the _St. Louis Mirror_ and issued as a book immediately afterward in 1915, was an instant and shocking success in our literature. Everyone read the book and the criticisms were many, favorable and adverse. Masters had both scandalized America and secured the greatest poetic triumph since Whitman's _Leaves of Grass_. Masters continued to pen both conventional and "free" verse until his death, but his fame will continue to be associated with his one notorious volume.

The _Spoon River Anthology_ contains some 250 soliloquies, spoken by the dead of the village graveyard of Spoon River. Each deceased individual gives an honest epitaph for himself in unrhymed realistic verse which is more like a cadenced prose. In his brief poems, Masters gives a grim exposure of the inner souls of his villagers, most of whom were frustrated in life and filled with disillusion not revealed on the headstones which meet the eye above their graves.

A typical example of Masters' depressing view of the true thoughts of American villagers is the soliloquy spoken by the spirit of the well-to-do farmer, Abel Melveny:

> I bought every kind of machine that's known—
> Grinders, shellers, planters, mowers,
> Mills and rakes and ploughs and threshers—
> And all of them stood in the rain and sun,

> Getting rusted, warped and battered,
> For I had no sheds to store them in,
> And no use for most of them.
> And toward the last, when I thought it over,
> There by my window, growing clearer
> About myself, as my pulse slowed down,
> And looked at one of the mills I bought—
> Which I didn't have the slightest use of,
> As things turned out, and I never ran—
> A fine machine, once brightly varnished,
> And eager to do its work,
> Now with its paint washed off—
> I saw myself as a good machine
> That Life had never used.

Masters introduced the same penetrating deterministic naturalism into poetry that Sherwood Anderson was to capitalize upon in his prose collection of stories *(Winesburg, Ohio)*, 4 years later. Both books are masterpieces of psychological penetration into the inner spirits of frustrated beings. Both books became immediately famous and represent landmarks of contemporary American literature and show the extent to which our literary writers have gone in critical penetration into the sordid hopelessness of individual lives. Both books are unforgettable and indispensable reading for one who, whether he end in condemnation or praise, seeks to explore the major productions of our best writing during the century.

Vigorous interpreter of the commonplace

3. _Carl Sandburg (1878-____)_ was born into a Swedish immigrant family in Illinois. He worked as a laborer and went to Puerto Rico as a soldier in the Spanish-American War. After graduating from Lombard College, he became a journalist and organizer for the Social Democratic party in Wisconsin.

His early efforts received little recognition until *Poetry* published some of his very vigorous free verse in 1914. Particularly did his short poem, *Chicago,* rouse critical controversy and gained for Sandburg a large reading public:

> Hog Butcher for the World
> Tool Maker, Stacker of Wheat,
> Player with Railroads and the Nation's Freight
>   Handler;
> Stormy, husky, brawling,
> City of the Big Shoulders: . . .

Sandburg had learned his force and simplicity of expression from Whitman and he had acquired his material from his contacts with American life as a harvest worker, porter, bootblack, hotel dishwasher, milk-wagon driver, and political organizer. He added to these experiences his robust faith in the American workingman and his store of intimate knowledge gained by acute observation.

He was a mystic interpreter of the American scenes he knew best—Chicago and the open prairies of the Midwest—and he sought to harmonize and interpret the spirit common to both environments and to reveal the sordid and the ennobling aspects of life that he found there.

> Can a man sit at a desk in a skyscraper in Chicago
> and be a harnessmaker in a corn town in Iowa
> and feel the tall grass coming up in June
> and the ache of the cottonwood trees
> singing with the prairie wind?
>
> (from *Portrait*)

Sandburg had the humanitarian's sympathy for society and its problems but he was neither evangelist nor propagandist. He was of a robust and rough nature and most of his poetry is a fearless interpretation of a violent age in American life. Sandburg's nature was that of a tender and compassionate individual but he was capable of raising his voice to hurl vituperative colloquial expression in verse when he wrote of hypocrisy, greed, and oppression. It is this expression of Sandburg which is most subject to the charge that it is unpoetic.

> You come along . . . tearing your shirt . . . yelling about Jesus.
>   Where do you get that stuff?
>   What do you know about Jesus?
> Jesus had a way of talking soft and outside of a few bankers
>   and higher-ups among the con men of Jerusalem everybody
>   liked to have this Jesus around because he never made
>   any false passes and everything he said went and he
>   helped the sick and gave the people hope.
>
>   . . . . .
>
> I like to watch a good four-flusher work, but not when he
>   starts people puking and calling for the doctors.
> I like a man that's got nerve and can pull off a great original
>   performance, but you—you're only a bughouse pedlar

of second-hand gospel—you're only shoving out a phoney imitation of the goods this Jesus wanted free as air and sunlight . . .

(from *To a Contemporary Bunkshooter*—1914)

As a poet Sandburg is thoroughly unconventional. His language is colloquial and much of his production is as earthy and harsh as are his themes. His poetry is absolutely "free" and goes to the roots of reality for its effects. But Sandburg is also a poet of quiet beauty and has written many poems in which his figures are tender and soft in their startling revelation.

Fog
The fog comes
on little cat feet.

It sits looking
Over harbor and city
On silent haunches
And then, moves on.

Carl Sandburg, in addition to his many verse collections, has produced many stories for children and a popular compilation of ballads and folk songs called *The American Songbag* (1927). His monumental 6 volume biography of Lincoln is carefully documented history that Sandburg has brought to the level of a popular literary masterpiece by his exquisite prose style and his enthusiastic sympathy for his subject. *Abraham Lincoln: The Prairie Years* and *The War Years* was abridged to 1 volume by the author in 1954, and is enjoying a second wave of popularity in this form.

Whitman, Lindsay, and Sandburg have left a production which, as unorthodox and as unpoetic as much of it may be, has caught a distinctive flavor of the American idiom and way of thinking which no other of our poets has captured. Perhaps it isn't poetry and perhaps it isn't exactly prose; but it is a vibrant and indispensable sector of great native American literary expression.

Ezra Pound and the spread of imagism*

Ezra Pound (1885-   ), though born in Idaho and educated in American schools, has spent little of his writing career in America. A rebellious and restless intellectual, Pound has produced many volumes of poetry and prose in which he has pursued varied techniques and themes—all of them exotic and associated with the most esoteric and "arty" of the European aristocratic artistic groups.

Pound's principal influence upon the poetic renascence in America was through the young poets who had become attracted by his poetic theories and had gathered around the master in London to imitate his experimental verse, largely based on French sources. Pound published a small anthology of verse written by his English and American protégés in 1914, called *Des Imagists*. This little volume and the enthusiasm of his chief American disciple, Amy Lowell, served to foment the most radically experimental revolution in American poetry in the century which, for a period of 10 years, attracted to poetry the most numerous reading public that the genre has possessed in our literary history.

Amy Lowell: leader of American imagism

Amy Lowell (1873-1925) was a brilliant member of a Massachusetts family of aristocratic background. She began publishing her first poems in 1910. Her early verse was conventional and based on classical models. Her association with Ezra Pound and his group of young imagist enthusiasts in England gave her the incentive she needed to bring all her keen intellect to bear upon her poetic art. She issued her collection, *Sword Blades and Poppy Seeds,* in 1914 and became the acknowledged leader of the *imagist* sector of the new poetry. Most of our poets of the period followed the imagist principles laid down by Miss Lowell in at least a part of their work. Of course, upon analysis, it becomes evident that much of imagist theory had already been practiced by such poets as Whitman, Emily Dickinson, Vachel Lindsay, and Carl Sandburg.

Amy Lowell, first of all, felt that poetry should be freed from metrical controls and the accepted, and cliché, imagery of conventional verse of the past. The language of imagist verse must be common speech and there must be absolute freedom in choice of subject matter. The poet must present modern life in clear and concentrated images—concrete, firm, and precise. There must be no giving way to sentimentality. All images must be sharp and clear-cut.

One of Amy Lowell's most famous poems is *Patterns,* a dramatic monologue in which an English lady walks in her garden and thinks of her betrothed, recently killed in action in France. In crystalline impressions, the lady etches for the reader the sharp and cold pattern of her life.

> I walk down the garden paths,
> And all the daffodils
> Are blowing, and the bright blue squills.
> I walk down the patterned garden-paths
> In my stiff, brocaded gown.
> With my powdered hair and jewelled fan,
> I too am a rare
> Pattern . . .
>
> . . . . . .
>
> In a month he would have been my husband.
> In a month, here, underneath this lime,
> We would have broken the pattern;
> He for me, and I for him, . . .
>
> . . . . . .
>
> I shall go
> Up and down,
> In my gown.
> Gorgeously arrayed,
> Boned and stayed.
> And the softness of my body will be guarded
>   from embrace
> By each button, hook, and lace.
> For the man who would loose me is dead,
> Fighting with the Duke in Flanders,
> In a pattern called a war.
> Christ! What are patterns for?

Amy Lowell wrote 8 volumes of poetry, and her followers wrote many more from 1914 to 1925. She had made *imagism* a magic word in our poetry, and her influence continues to the present in much of our verse. Her death in 1925 was somewhat of an event for national mourning. But her "school" collapsed with her passing. She was the magic and compelling force that projected what might have been a very minor fad in our poetry into a poetic revolution. She made an immense contribution to our literature. Amy Lowell brought a reading public back to poetry after a quarter of a century of disinterest and she stimulated a renewed enthusiasm for the writing of verse. She failed to create an enduring movement but she helped to bring to a focus the great contribution of Whitman and Dickinson toward a distinctly native American poetry of this century.

Other aspects of poetic experimentation

Many were the attempts to achieve new linguistic effects and to create new forms in the period of the height of popularity of the imagists. John Gould Fletcher, Alfred Kreymborg, and H. D. (Hilda Doolittle) are representative names among the many poets who basked in the glow cast by Amy Lowell and attempted to carry imagism to its ultimate and more insane extremes.

To list even the names of those who issued poetry during this verse-mad period would fill pages and to quote the extremes of the unconventional verse would fill many volumes.

> 'Twixt the dawn and the dusk of each lyrical day
> There's another school started, and all of them pay.

Impressions of all our normal concepts of life and nature suffered strange contortions as more and more fantastic images poured forth in books and in short-lived poetry magazines.

Eliot and his influence in the interwar period

T. S. Eliot (1888-   ), an international intellectual, was American born but has lived most of his life in England and became a British subject in 1927. Eliot was a leader in a new and metaphysical* type of verse, exemplified best in his _The Waste Land_ (1922). Like Lafcadio Hearn, Ezra Pound, and Gertrude Stein, Eliot was more of an influence upon our writers than he was a part of our literature in his production. Eliot, pessimistic and intellectual, ranged through the aesthetic circles of European "ivory tower" groups. He led many of our poets in the twenties and early thirties into a verse that had no roots in emotion but was simply a fabric of intellectual word patterns. These poets produced little that is read today by the average reader. They are all poets for the small circles of intellectuals who wish to pit their mental capacities and exotic vocabulary against the intricate concepts and cultural references which these poets poured out in a steady stream for a period of almost 15 years.

With the poetic innovations of language and the striving for a cold and polished intellectual form, inspired by Eliot and others of the European groups, came a cynicism and excessive rationalization to our poetry in the twenties and early thirties which almost rendered it emotionally dead. _Elinor Wylie (1885-1928)_ was typical of a disillusioned and pessimistic generation of American poets.

> Now let no charitable hope
> Confuse my mind with images
> Of eagle and of antelope;
> I am in nature none of these.
>
> I was, being human, born alone;
> I am, being woman, hard beset;
> I live by squeezing from a stone
> The little nourishment I get.
>
> In masks outrageous and austere
> The years go by in single file;
> But none has merited my fear,
> And none has quite escaped my smile.
>
> (_Let No Charitable Hope_—1922)

Some poets of this experimental postwar generation carried their cynicism and disillusion into a sort of typographical insanity, a poetry where punctuation and the accepted guides for English usage were completely discarded. Typical of this form of poetic madness is _E. E. Cummings (1894-   )_, who returned saddened from the war and has continued to produce his particular forms of poetic experimentation to the present day. To find meaning in much of the jumbled typography of the verse of Cummings is a challenge to any reader, however much of a hardened intellectual sophisticate he may be. But no reader, who wishes to taste the extremes in literary expression, should fail to browse through the volume _Poems (1923-1954)_ of E. E. Cummings.

Other outstanding poets, whose major work was produced during the early experimental periods of the century and whose verse shows the same highly polished craftsmanship, cynicism, and lack of emotional depth are: _Edna St. Vincent Millay (1892-1950), Hart Crane (1899-1932), Robinson Jeffers (1887-   )_, and _Wallace Stevens (1879-1955)_.

Poets who escaped the experimental debacle in verse

Some of our poets of the early century were only lightly influenced by the violence and the extremes of the experimental tendencies. Carl Sandburg and Vachel Lindsay continued as robust individuals, following in the footsteps of Whitman in their messages of the strength and weakness of democracy. Masters, after his famous experiment in poetic naturalism *(Spoon River Anthology)* continued to pen traditional verse until recent years.

One of the most traditional and sweetly romantic of the popular poets of the century was <u>Sara Teasdale (1884-1933)</u>. A quiet lyric voice that sang simply and emotionally of love and nature in the midst of the strident voices of the poetic revolution was, perhaps, out of tune with the times. But Sara Teasdale continues in popularity with her lyrical simplicity and optimism, reminiscent of the romantic poets of the nineteenth century.

> In the silver light after a storm,
>   Under dripping boughs of bright new green,
> I take the low path to hear the meadowlarks
>   Alone and high-hearted, as if I were a queen.
>
> What have I to fear in life or death
>   Who have known three things: the kiss in the night,
> The white flying joy when a song is born,
>   And meadowlarks whistling in silver light.
>
>   (*Meadowlarks*—1920)

<u>Stephen Vincent Benét (1898-1943)</u> was another of the popular poets of the century who escaped the cynicism and the naturalism of the experimental generation. Benét had romantic tendencies and combined his penchant toward idealism with realistic narrative in verse. Benét is best known for *John Brown's Body* (1928), a long narrative poem of the Civil War. The book-length poem was immediately popular and lives today as a realistic expression of the soul of America. The poem is awkward and verbose in spots; Benét alternates from lack of unity in narrative to some of the most vivid and realistic passages to be found in poetry. Here and there his passages become simple lyrical romance at its best.

Despite Benét's crudities, his is an optimistic and a fresh voice in dealing with our country's past. *John Brown's Body* (Pulitzer Prize, 1929) is a landmark in the century's creative writing. Benét was not the poet that Whitman was, but he made a noble effort to reach the American muse and to record all

the diversity of the broad land—and for many readers of the
past generation, he succeeded.

> American muse, whose strong and diverse heart
> So many men have tried to understand
> But only made it smaller with their art,
> Because you are as various as your land, . . .
>
> . . . . . .
> I only bring a cup of silver air.
> Yet, in your casualness, receive it there.
>
> Receive the dream too haughty for the breast,
> Receive the words that should have walked as bold
> As the storm walks along the mountain-crest
> And are like beggars whining in the cold.
>
> . . . . . .
> Receive them all—and should you choose to touch them
> With one slant ray of quick, American light,
> Even the dust will have no power to smutch them,
> Even the worst will glitter in the night.
>
> If not—the dry bones littered by the way
> May still point giants toward their golden prey.
> (From the *Invocation, John Brown's Body*)

Poet of social and political import

Many others of our poets exposed themselves only lightly
to the experimental techniques and went on to produce a great
deal of individual verse within the general freedom of the new
poetry. Of these one of the most strident poetic voices of the
century has been that of *Archibald MacLeish (1892-   )*.
In his first period of experimentation he was a thorough disciple
of Eliot and Pound. His early poetry is the voice of a hopeless
individual caught in the chaotic pessimism of the postwar
period.

But after 1930, MacLeish became vitally interested in national, political, and cultural aspects of the American scene and
in the threats to our freedom from fascism. He became the
leading social and civil poet of our century. MacLeish has won
the Pulitzer Prize twice *(Conquistador,* 1933 and *Collected
Poems, 1917-1952,* 1952).

MacLeish's poetry iş a reflection of all the various poetic
manners and styles of the century, and he has utilized all the
cross currents of political and social philosophy as themes for

his verse. He remains a diffuse but versatile poet whose popular and timely production has given him a steady following of many readers to the present time. Some of his poetry invariably finds a place in all of the anthologies of the century's poetic achievement.

The century's greatest regional poet

Robert Frost (1874-   ) was born in San Francisco. But at the age of 10 he was taken to New England and his brilliant and long poetic career has been dedicated to a restrained emotional lyric interpretation of the characteristic flavor of New England rural life.

Frost attended Dartmouth and Harvard for brief periods. He has served as bobbin boy in a New England mill, made shoes, edited a country newspaper, taught school, and labored as a farmer. Frost learned the New England rural setting and its humanity at first hand and has chosen the most prosaic of country themes with which to create his unforgettable visions— perhaps the greatest lyric achievement in our literature since Whitman.

Frost took from the new poetry its language of the commonplace, but his is a vernacular free from weird and strange images and from the slang and roughness of Sandburg and Lindsay. His verse portraits of rural simplicity are direct, unaffected, and beautifully sensitive to realistic detail. Frost loved the earth and his neighbors who wrested their meager living from the rocky hillsides, and his expression of their language and their inner thoughts and natural surroundings is work of artistic perfection and craftsmanship.

Frost agreed with the imagists that poetic meaning should be precise and concentrated. With them, he never sentimentalized or drew conclusions. But he brought to his phrasing a sympathy for common humanity and quiet overtones of humor and spiritual significance. His simplicity and direct phrasing of reality is deceiving; his verse contains more meaning than at first meets the eye. Frost drew realistic pictures of a region and its inhabitants, but he also left his deep personal humanitarianism in his verse. His poetry treats the surface of one region but his message is a universal one.

In _Mending Walls (1913)_ the poet meditates as he reluctantly follows his neighbor along the old stone fence between their properties, replacing stones that have fallen as a result of the winter's chill or have been displaced by rabbit hunters.

> Something there is that doesn't love a wall,
>
> . . . . . .
>
> We keep the wall between us as we go.
> To each the boulders that have fallen to each.
>
> . . . . . .
>
> We wear our fingers rough with handling them.
> Oh, just another kind of out-door game,
> One on a side. It comes to little more:
> There where it is we do not need the wall:
> He is all pine and I am apple-orchard.
> My apple trees will never get across
> And eat the cones under his pines, I tell him.
> He only says, "Good fences make good neighbors."

The poet remains unconvinced, as there is no need for a fence between good friends with no animals to keep from one another's crops, but his taciturn farmer friend can only take his reasons and his pride from his ancestors.

> He will not go behind his father's saying,
> And he likes having thought of it so well
> He says again, "Good fences make good neighbors."

Robert Frost, winner 4 times of the Pulitzer Prize, has penned his simple verse of rural life and unsophisticated philosophy for 50 years. His art has steadily deepened and his lyric force and beauty have lost nothing of youthful freshness. They have rather acquired a deeper beauty and a more mellow wisdom throughout the century. Frost has been unequaled in the century for his profound sense of the American spirit. The bulk of his work will likely be read in fresh editions by future generations of Americans who will find only occasional selections in anthologies from most of the other poets of the first half of the 20th century.

One of Frost's most lyrical pieces is the little poem that records the poet's whim to stop his sleigh one evening to watch the snow fall among the trees of a lonely woods.

> Whose woods these are I think I know.
> His house is in the village though;
> He will not see me stopping here
> To watch his woods fill up with snow.
>
> My little horse must think it queer
> To stop without a farmhouse near
> Between the woods and the frozen lake
> The darkest evening of the year.

He gives his harness bells a shake
To ask if there is some mistake.
The only other sound's the sweep
Of easy wind and downy flake.

The woods are lovely, dark and deep
But I have promises to keep,
And miles to go before I sleep,
And miles to go before I sleep.
(*Stopping by Woods on a Snowy Evening*—1923)

American poetry since World War II

The poetic renaissance in America, beginning with the imagists and stretching into the postwar period with varied and new extremes of experimentation, is associated closely with the World War I atmosphere and the era of disillusion following the world conflict. Of course, a new poetry, the basic inspiration for most of this century's outstanding poetic production, predated the war, and its native roots are found deep in the work of Walt Whitman and Emily Dickinson.

When World War II ended in 1945, no such new movements or experimental tendencies were evident. The older poets still held the center of public interest—poets who had been influenced one way or another by the new poetry innovations (Vachel Lindsay, Edgar Lee Masters, Carl Sandburg, Edna St. Vincent Millay, and others). These poets had established their reputations, had a steady following of readers, and were producing volumes almost yearly. They were competing in public interest with reprints and collections from their 19th century masters— Walt Whitman and Emily Dickinson.

The poets who had been affected most strongly by the more daring and the more intellectual innovations of the twenties (such poets as E. E. Cummings, Alfred Kreymborg, William Carlos Williams, and many others) added little to their reputations, but continued to create largely in the same experimental veins which had given them an early audience. Past mid-century, the two groups of older poets continued to hold their audiences and the two poets who provided direct inspiration for the later group, T. S. Eliot and Ezra Pound, were receiving a great deal of critical appreciation and new groups of readers.

In 1950, three of the major awards for poetry in the United States went to Carl Sandburg, Conrad Aiken, and William Carlos Williams, all poets once regarded as "experimental." In the years since 1950, the older groups have received a large share of literary awards. It would seem that today at least some of the new poets, or "free" poets, have won recognition as solid figures in our permanent body of literature.

Characteristics of the young poets

Although no new movements or marked innovations are present in the last years, there are signs that most of the young poets are not following the older groups. Their verse is less burdened with the social and political problems of mankind, the disillusion and hopelessness of the individual, and the tendencies toward metaphysics, philosophy, and the creation of mental gymnastics in verse for select groups of intellectual readers. Style in the younger poets is more simple, direct, and less cerebral. The springs of emotion and feeling, that seemed nearly dry for a quarter of a century, seem to be filling up again. A major theme of American poetry since the last war is the general dismay of modern man in his failure to utilize his potentialities to achieve a satisfying faith and a feeling of security and individual worth. But, unlike the hard tone of interwar poetry, this new verse is a refreshing search for truth, not a cynical disillusionment that consigned individual man and mankind to nothingness. Even some of the older poets, such as Robert Frost, have turned much of their late production to a search for spiritual values. This is, perhaps (as in the novel), the most outstanding innovation in poetic themes in the last decade.

In the past few years, the publication of volumes of poetry has risen steadily—not yet, of course, equaling the phenomenal publication of verse of the early years of the new poetry renascence from 1914-1920. But public demand for poetry at the bookstores in the past few years indicates a renewed interest of Americans in the creative literary agency that is best designed to uplift the spirit of man and provide satisfaction for deep-seated cravings for faith and optimistic vision. Today's generation of readers is one surfeited with facts and scientific (or pseudo-scientific) rationalization. It is a generation, assailed by doubt, that is starved for vision and grasping at what it can feel are certainties. The "ivory tower" verse and the ultrasophisticated egoistic outpourings of small groups of intellectual aesthetes will not reach a wider audience today. The young poets have a large audience, and a much larger potential one, that will demand that the poet speak to them in terms that they can comprehend and in tones of hope and pride in man's basic worth and aspirations.

Need for reappraisal of movements and schools

As one glances back over the past century's accomplishment in American poetry, he is impressed that our poets, most read today and discussed favorably by critics, have been largely independent of movements and schools and only a part of their production can be classified under the conventional literary labels of the past. Late criticism is tending to conclude that a de-emphasis of the importance of schools and movements is a desirable trend. Poetic genius and inspiration, as all creative ability in individuals, is but hampered and stultified by mass labels and concepts. The greatest poets of this century have been the greatest rebels; Walt Whitman, perhaps the greatest poet in our literature, was the supreme rebel of them all.

III. DIRECTIONS IN DRAMA

Summary of American Drama to 1910

A native American drama has been mentioned only once in this review (pages 26-27). Plays continued to be written and produced in our major cities after the period discussed in an early chapter, but little fine native drama was added to our literature. The reasons behind the scarcity of drama in America during 200 years of our literary history are not hard to find.

1. The legal and religious restrictions and taboos during the Colonial period in most of the areas of the eastern seaboard, combined with the hard conditions which afforded little leisure for theater-going.

2. From the Revolutionary period forward, our writers were in almost complete subservience to English inspiration and models. The continued hatred of the Puritans for the theater and their domination over play production in England led to the same dearth of other than patriotic plays, melodramas, and farce comedy in the early days of our national existence.

3. The drama of the romantic revival in England was almost wholly "closet drama," of a highly declamatory type, designed to advance personal romantic ideas and theories through highly artificial plots, or of highly exotic (preferably Oriental) themes.

Again, the American writers, following in the footsteps of the early English romantics, produced very artificial plays, when they produced any at all.

4. Throughout our early national period, interest of the theater-going public centered upon romantic dramatization of our historical past and upon melodramatic presentation of patriotic ideals of democracy. Also, during the period, much Elizabethan drama and adaptations of French classical plays were being produced in America, both by local companies and touring groups from England. During the period a rare, but fine, American comedy of manners (*Fashion,* 1845) was written by Mrs. Anna Cora Mowatt.

5. During the 19th century, there was little to encourage writers to attempt serious drama. English literary prestige and cultural advantages, plus the free piracy of English writing in this country, made the writing of drama highly hazardous and unprofitable. Also, our lack of an adequate copyright law gave the dramatist no protection within the United States. He might finance a production of one of his own plays and find that a rival company was already in production with the same play.

The greatest names in American drama before the Civil War are those of Nathaniel Parker Willis and George Henry Boker, both residents of Philadelphia. Both men wrote excellent blank verse drama dealing with exotic medieval, classical, or Renaissance settings.

In the local-color period from 1860-1890, our new transportation system gave rise to many traveling companies of actors. However, the many plays produced in this period were on the level of melodramatic thrillers and exotic and colorful spectacles.

Toward the end of the 19th century a powerful modern theater was being developed in Europe, with Chekhov, Gorky, Ibsen, Strindberg, Hauptmann, Schnitzler, Maeterlinck, D'Annunzio, and Shaw—a theater of penetrating studies into character and social manners. The most noted of our dramatists of the period was Clyde Fitch (1865-1909) who, among his many melodramas and adaptations of French and German farces, did manage to write two or three plays with depth of characterization and social import. His best play is *The Truth* (1906).

The American theater, to 1910, was largely a commercial one, despite the efforts of a few producers of the calibre of David Belasco to raise its level above that of pure profit; drama and literature seldom met on a common ground. Before 1910, public demand in literature had been conditioned to the novel, poetry, and the short story. People attended the theater for pure entertainment and demanded all the dramatic trickery in the authors' and producers' range of possibility to give them thrills, awesome settings, and sentimental emotional experiences. Our theater has a history before 1910, and there are some scattered plays of literary merit, but there is little of drama as a full-fledged genre in our literature until after that date.

A Period of Drama Revival

Beginning just prior to World War I and continuing until the period of the great economic depression, American drama entered into a period of feverish activity and playwriting and production took a long step toward the establishment of drama as one of the major genres of our literature. Directors and producers sprang up who were interested in studying the techniques of the established European theaters, in raising the artistic level of American play production, and in educating audiences to appreciate a more elevated dramatic fare than they had hitherto brought before them. Playwrights rose to cater to the more refined demands of the commercial directors and producers. For a period of 20 years, not only were the best modern European and classical plays given adequate production in America, but the artistic level of our own drama rose rapidly. The most notable figure of the period and our first dramatist to command world attention and praise was Eugene O'Neill, our literature's greatest dramatist to date.

A second phase of the period of drama revival was the creation of little theater, art theater, or drama workshop movements throughout the country—a series of experimental theaters established by private groups in most of our major cities and by universities and colleges. Although the art theater movement suffered during the depression years (1930-1940), it has mushroomed during the last 15 years to cover the country with a network of experimental theaters. Some of these art theaters are seasonal and draw much of the best acting talent in the country during the summer months to barns and temporary playhouses of all sorts throughout the land. Others of these experimental theaters, such as the Pasadena Playhouse in California, are permanent establishments and function throughout the year with classes in playwriting, acting, directing, scenery design, etc. Some are self-sustaining and others are supported partially by various grants and wealthy patrons of theatrical arts. By 1918 there were more than 50·little theaters in the country, and today they number in the hundreds.

Commercial and Experimental Drama Since 1940

The depression years killed much of the commercial interest in drama experimentatión. Today, the commercial theater is conservative and its interest is largely centered in New York. Although some plays tour the country with professional casts they are usually popular New York productions that have had long runs there. The early-century renaissance and the phenomenal success of the art theaters and drama workshops have succeeded in raising the level of audience interest in fine drama during the century, but the stimulus for young playwrights to produce serious artistic drama is still sadly lacking, because of high costs of production and the conservatism of the New York producers.

The effects of television on drama are hard to predict today. Large profits are forthcoming from television producers, but the demand has been mostly for plays that will command a large popular viewing audience. Much of the drama produced on television in its early days was simple adaptations of fiction. Today, however, some commercial interests are sponsoring drama periods in which original and serious drama experiments are being carried out. In the years after 1953, drama production on television is noticeably rising in artistic quality. The effects are also noticeable in the motion picture industry. In the past two or three years Hollywood has concentrated upon an increasing number of carefully produced classic literary masterpieces (notably *Moby Dick, War and Peace*).

Eugene O'Neill: greatest American dramatist

Eugene O'Neill (1888-1953), the one figure of national and international importance in American dramatic literature, was born in New York City. His father was a popular actor. O'Neill, after an unsuccessful year at Princeton, spent some 8 years of vagabond life in various parts of the world. His first play, a one-act melodrama called *Bound East for Cardiff*, was produced in 1915 by a vacationing Greenwich Village, New York, theater group who were producing plays in a deserted fish house in Provincetown, Massachusetts.

By 1920, O'Neill had abandoned his early penchant for writing plays that were poetic and wholly romantic and exotic in tone and turned his attention to realism and to psychological interpretation of character. His first successful production was _Beyond the Horizon_ (produced in New York in 1920), a naturalistic study of 3 people who make wrong decisions in life and end in grim and tragic frustration. _Anna Christie_ (1922), another study of frustrated lives, is one of O'Neill's best creations in its dramatic intensity and atmosphere of absolute realism.

O'Neill's best plays were written in a period of 11 years (1920-1931). He produced no plays for 12 years after 1934. When he came back to the theater in 1946 with _The Iceman Cometh,_ he had no new techniques or ideas to offer.

In _Desire under the Elms_ (1924), he converts a brutal plot into refined and poetic tragedy. _The Emperor Jones_ (1920) and _The Hairy Ape_ (1922) are melodramatic studies of distortion of the human mind. In both plays his principal character reverts to primitive superstition or to animal brutality. In _The Great God Brown_ (1926), _Strange Interlude_ (1928), and _Mourning Becomes Electra_ (1931), O'Neill successfully attempts elaborate experiments in psychological tragedy.

O'Neill's nature was restless, and his plays reflect his interest in analyzing the elements of unrest in man's nature. His plays roam through a variety of styles and experimental techniques. He was strongly influenced by the theories of Sigmund Freud and the expressionism* of the European dramatists of his day, particularly Hauptmann and Strindberg. His production ranges from the brutally realistic to exotic and violently melodramatic romance.

O'Neill's greatest strength lies in his remarkable experiments in seeking literary expression for the deeper meanings of life. He did not hesitate to be unconventional or unorthodox in his tireless analysis. He roamed through the inner realms of the human spirit and he took every stylistic and mental attitude toward his subjects that he felt would serve to bring his ideas best to focus. His style is rich and earthy. His best plays are abnormally long and difficult to stage and are usually avoided by the commercial theater. His weaknesses are all bound up in the word extravagance: extravagance of realism and of romanticism, extravagance in stretching the limitations of drama and the capacity of the theater to produce his plays properly. But Eugene O'Neill is the single great dramatist in our literature. His work has won the Pulitzer Prize 4 times (1920, 1922, 1928, 1957) and the Nobel Prize in 1936. (See Appendix A, page 241, for digests of typical plays of O'Neill.)

Other playwrights of the contemporary period

Definitely below O'Neill in creative stature are many writers of American plays in the past 40 years. Almost all these writers have directed their efforts toward the New York commercial theater. All of their product has the faults inherent in that aim when considered as drama for the ages. None has possessed the daring of Eugene O'Neill in experimental drama and none has commanded the serious attention of the older and more mature European theater; none has international reputation but O'Neill. All have been practical playwrights and have been interested in producing dramatic vehicles that would have immediate and calculated effectiveness with producers and audiences. All have entered the competitive race for popularity with present-day audiences, and hence most of their work is topical·and dated and lacks the prolonged appeal that makes for universality and life as literature. Little of the drama of the commercial theater of today would speak to generations to come. Most of our playwrights are men of the theater, rather than real dramatists.

Among the leading writers of plays in the past years are: Maxwell Anderson *(Winterset, The Masque of Kings, High Tor)*, Sidney Howard *(They Knew What They Wanted)*, Philip Barry *(The Philadelphia Story)*, George Kelly *(Craig's Wife)*, Robert Anderson *(Abe Lincoln in Illinois)*, Tennessee Williams *(The Glass Menagerie, A Streetcar Named Desire)*, and many others.

IV. MISCELLANEOUS CREATIVE WRITING OF THE CENTURY

A large sector of the sum total of any literature does not fit the classifications of fiction, poetry, or drama, the literary genres ordinarily grouped into the broad classification of *belles-lettres*. To speak of American "letters," of course, would comprehend these additional classifications. Literature interpreted broadly as "best writings" would also seem to include them.

Didactic literature*, or that which tends to be scientific or technical, enters into the realm of aesthetic or creative writing at the point where the author has injected into his basic purpose of presenting facts or teaching, an imaginative use of experience and the impressions he has received from his subject matter through the senses. To enter the realm of *belles-lettres,* of course, such writing would necessarily be couched in beautiful expression of literary language and involve the elements of fine style and expert craftsmanship. A final test of whether such a didactic work meets the requirements of polite literature would be, of course, that it is read for culture and entertainment, aside from the factual or moral instruction it might contain.

There has been a great deal of fine writing in the United States during the present century, outside of the realm of *belles-lettres,* which will, perhaps, compete with Emerson's *Essays,* Lincoln's *Gettysburg Address,* or Franklin's *Autobiography* for places in our permanent body of literature, after the cruel hand of time has weeded out that which will have no appeal to future generations of readers. This review, concerned principally with *belles-lettres,* can mention only a few writers whose work shows promise of becoming of some interest to readers other than of the present-day generation.

The Essay

Since 1900, the informal or personal essay*, so strongly developed in the 19th century, has not been popular with readers or writers in the United States or in England. Essays in this century, in both countries, have become more formal and expository, devoted to social, economic, political, and moral issues of the age. The essay has largely become the "article" in this century.

There have been, however, some who have carried the tone of intimate informality of the essay of the past century into the present age. John Burroughs (1837-1921) produced volumes of sensitive nature studies. Also dealing with the flora and fauna of nature, the following writers have brought a rich prose style and a personal enthusiasm to lighten the scientific accuracy of their observations: Henry Van Dyke (1852-1933), Dallas Sharp (1870-1929), William Beebe (1877-   ), and Donald Culross Peattie (1898-   ).

Individual and conversational expression of personal points of view on human foibles (a type of essay in which Oliver Wendell Holmes was master in the last century) has received only a sporadic development in this century. Samuel McChord Crothers (1857-1928), Logan Pearsall Smith (1865-1946), Agnes Repplier (1858-1950), and Katherine Fullerton Gerould (1879-1944) are present-century defenders of the genteel and traditional in manners and morals.

The treatment of economic and political themes in the formal expository essay has had some outstanding masters of language and technique, among whom are James Truslow Adams (1878-   ), Walter Lippmann (1889-   ), and Stuart Chase (1888-   ).

The short essay, printed in the columns of daily newspapers, became more and more popular as the century advanced. Columnists have numbered in the hundreds in the century and some have achieved reputations as fine creative writers on a multitude of miscellaneous subjects of interest to the average American. The founding of the *New Yorker* magazine in 1925 began an era of a higher type of artistic column than had hitherto been seen in the dailies. Soon other magazines followed, and the slick magazine essay is an outstanding feature of writing today. Some writers who have approached literature with many of their essays, or articles, during the century are: Ed Howe, O. O. McIntyre, Clifton Fadiman, Heywood Broun, Westbrook Pegler, George Ade, Walter Winchell, Ben Hecht, Franklin P. Adams, Christopher Morley, Dorothy Thompson, Mrs. Franklin D. Roosevelt, Don Marquis, Robert Benchley, Alexander Woollcott, Clarence Day, Will Rogers, James Thurber, and many others. The last 6 names are noted for their varied humorous or sentimentalized approaches to life and manners. Ogden Nash, Franklin P. Adams, Dorothy Parker, Margaret Fishback, and others, have achieved reputations for their *vers de société* (epigrammatic and humorous verse with jingling rhyme, the purpose of which is satire and commentary upon social manners and timely topics).

Woodrow Wilson, Herbert Clark Hoover, Franklin Delano Roosevelt, and other able political figures of the times have contributed fine examples of the oratorical essay, many of which will deserve place in future anthologies of the total body of American letters.

Biography, Autobiography, and History

Biography involves an indispensable mixture of science and art, and its success as literature is dependent largely upon the author's manipulation of language and the sympathetic treatment that he brings to his subject. Biographies that combine the characteristics of sound science and good art are necessarily rare. Fictionalized biography often becomes nothing more than a historical novel, and factual research and documentation tend to lead rapidly away from aesthetic writing.

In numbers, autobiographies have fallen far short of biographies in our writing. However, the literary qualities of the top-ranking autobiographies have tended to be judged superior to those of the better biographies. Perhaps the fast pace of American life, our interest in externals rather than in introspection, the absence of a rich social and religious life are antidotes to the deep introversion and self-analytical attitude that seem to be requisites for a richly developed genre of autobiography.

History may reach the level of fine writing by the same route as biography and its hazards are the same, essentially. History, in the realm of literature, must be a combination of sound science and good art.

Literary Criticism*

American criticism is coming of age in the contemporary period. The 18th and 19th centuries produced very few significant theories, and most of the critical judgment of the past had been highly biased and inconsistent. There was much individual gossip about books, based upon few standards other than whim; books were condemned simply because the author seemed a little queer and was thought to be atheistic because of his mystical ideas by staid New England critics (Melville). Most of our 19th century criticism was of the genteel tradition and aimed to preserve and perpetuate an opinion considered suitable for belief of a limited circle of aristocratic tradition. The critical axes fell wherever anything appeared that tended to disturb the unruffled surface of the "proper" (Whitman was condemned roundly by this critical monopoly until after the beginning of this century.)

It is therefore a healthy sign of maturity for our literature to find that, in the early 20th century, criticism as a literary art was beginning to be practiced by a considerable body of able men—intellectually and culturally equipped for the task. Criticism, as a literary art, tends to appear last in any culture, since effective criticism can function only when a diverse body of writings is available for appreciation and evaluation. And in the early century, the genteel tradition was under attack from many directions.

Early century criticism was characterized by one group that felt the necessity to bring a stubborn iconoclasm to bear in exposing the limitations of the genteel and Puritan bourgeois ideals of the past. These "radicals" were such men as Brander Matthews, F. L. Pattee, Van Wyck Brooks, George Jean Nathan, Lewis Mumford, Waldo Frank, H. L. Mencken, and others. Of the group, Mencken's work emerges as some of the best prose in American literature.

To balance the destructive force of the defenders of experimentation and the iconoclastic attacks on the genteel tradition, there sprang up a group of conservatives who were no less avid in holding to past values than they were in seeking an American philosophy for judgment of native literary, and social, values. This group included W. P. Trent, W. C. Brownell, Stuart P. Sherman, G. E. Woodburg, Paul Elmer More, and Irving Babbitt.

Since these first groups drew up their battle lines, many facets and theories have been explored, varying from the radicalism and Marxist theories of Max Eastman and Granville Hicks, through the liberal doctrines of Ludwig Lewisohn, to younger and rabid conservatives as Bernard DeVoto and Yvor Winters. In the last years, considerable attention has been focused upon appraisal and appreciation of the experimental movements of the early century.

Good taste and sound reason have not always been the result of much of the exploratory work of the last 40 years but those two requisites of any criticism worthy of the name are increasingly evident in recent years. The foundations of theory and practice have not yet resulted in clearly defined standards, but varied attacks have been made upon the problem from classical, romantic, realistic, and radical approaches. Much of the prejudice and biased and whimsical foundations laid down in our Puritan and genteel past have been broken down, and criticism in the last years is tending toward a level of distinction which the American intellectual sought in vain a few years ago, except in the older and more secure of European cultures.

THE VIEW AHEAD FOR AMERICAN CREATIVE WRITING

The end of such a brief review as this is rather like looking into the open expanse of a cornucopia, its walls narrowing rapidly in the background, but here overflowing with an abundance of the fruits of the many pens of American writers throughout the land. We know the scant and restricted production that resulted from the early harvest from the pens of the Puritans of Plymouth and from the Cavalier adventurers of Virginia. We have traced the increasing mass of American literature to the present. Among today's literary fruits, lying about in scattered disarray, we can only pick and choose what seems good, representative of American thought and life, and that which seems to have solid qualities necessary for its survival into time.

American literature has grown, in its 300-odd years, to command world respect and it has continued to portray faithfully the American scene, not necessarily restricted to the surface realities of any particular setting or group, but certainly cross sections of the inner pains and joys of a fledgling culture. The development of our literature has taken both a purely native direction and has faced outward at times toward broad universal values. It began with an extremely restricted Puritan theological view and it is only now emerging from an interwar period in which it reflected a world-wide disillusion and feeling of hopelessness for individual and collective man. Between those periods of restricted viewpoints, our writing has ebbed and flowed to reflect optimism and idealism, rugged and violent economic and political upheavals, tireless search for spiritual and ethical values, and equally tireless search for the unpleasant truths that hinder development of those very values in our land. Our writing has continued to reflect American interests and to preach the doctrine that young democracy can produce greatness in those elements of a culture that outlive any material usefulness.

The second half of the century will see an even larger reading public than exists today. New and broader bases of native criticism will consolidate its experiments to remove completely the one-sided genteel traditions of the past, and no monopoly or literary school or movement will control the major course of our writing. It is likely that the new masses of readers will have broader bases for judgment of literary values brought to a level of comprehension of all the graduates of our schools. It is also likely that our literature will be written for a wider audience than in the past. Democracy has proved that it can produce great writing; it must now demonstrate that wider educational facilities and the availability of broader critical advantages can bring about a public support and appreciation of a richer creative art.

Wars, economic want, and stultifying and oppressive ideologies have restricted free development of European literatures in this century. American literature has now reached a stage of richer development than its parent—English literature. In the coming years it will increasingly cease to imitate English and continental models, without ignoring the rich European heritage that it can never reproduce.

Past mid-century the extremely negative tone of our writing has diminished to weak but healthy proportions; the affirmative tone is the dominant one in most of the young writers and in many of the older ones who began writing in the interwar era. The experimenters of the early century were destructive, but the coming period will profit by the fact that they cut away much dry rot and loosened art from the restricted attitudes and forms of the past. Before that experimental period, our great writers, such as Melville, Mark Twain, Garland, and others, faced personal desperation in their desire to open wide their genius to full and free expression; our young writers of the period just beginning feel more of a spirit of personal inspiration to create to the fullest extent of their capacities and choice of directions.

Our literature has passed more than a mid-century marker in time; it has passed into a more democratic artistic atmosphere and a freer opportunity for continued greatness. The materials are present—the writers in greater numbers than ever before, the wider audience, rich and undeveloped materials, a new atmosphere toward critical good taste and sound judgment of our literary past and present—and, barring a world conflagration that could extinguish all civilization, it is likely that the next period will produce American books and writers who will rival and eclipse the greatness of the most creative representatives that have been named in this review.

APPENDIX A

Plot Summaries of Major Works

In the following section a digest is given of at least one example of each type of writing from our national literature, following the Revolutionary period. The summaries, together with critical notes, are geared to the main historical section and aim to present a rather full idea of the content of works, not discussed in detail in that section in order not to interrupt the continuity of the critical and biographical material. Representative examples of our more established 19th century writings are given detailed treatment. The briefer digests of 20th century writings are illustrative of the major trends and techniques in the treatment of literary themes in this century. They include both what may be considered as subliterary as well as those writings which seem to possess qualities which can cause them to endure as additions to our permanent body of American literature. The page numbers indicate the location of the discussion of the literary and social backgrounds in which the particular works or plot material were created.

1. **Washington Irving:** *Rip Van Winkle* and *The Legend of Sleepy Hollow* (tales from *The Sketch Book*)

Page 47. Irving began to publish his series of essays, tales, and sketches when he was in England in 1819. These tales of Irving, particularly those which dealt with the Dutch in upper New York, have become the most famous writings of Irving with Americans. They have established Irving as one of the creators of the modern short story. Irving's fame today rests almost entirely upon these sketches and tales in which he interpreted both the English and the American countryside. No anthology of the finest examples of the development of the short story today is complete without at least one of Irving's tales depicting the scenery and legend to be found among his Dutch neighbors of the upper Hudson River valleys. The characters of Rip Van Winkle and Ichabod Crane have not only become an integral part of American folklore but have become known the world over. Irving was our first writer to become popular among European readers.

Rip Van Winkle pictures a small Dutch village nestled among the Kaatskill mountains, along the upper reaches of the Hudson. Here dwells Rip who is a simple, good-natured man, and an obedient, hen-pecked husband. He was descended from a good old Dutch family, but there was in him little of the energy or of the martial character of his ancestors. He spent most of his time among children and dogs of the neighborhood.

One beautiful autumn day Rip and his dog, Wolf, climbed high into the mountains looking for squirrels. After a long day at their favorite pursuit among the mountain crags, Rip started for home when suddenly he heard his name called. He was astonished to find beside him a little man, dressed in the antique garb of the early Dutch settlers. The little fellow was trying to carry a keg of some sort of liquor and was glad to receive Rip's assistance in managing the unwieldly burden. He offered very little conversation as they ascended the mountain slopes. Soon Rip heard noises which appeared to him to be distant peals of thunder. Finally, they reached a level spot where Rip saw a group of little men, with bushy beards and dressed in short jerkins and breeches. The little men were playing at ninepins. Rip realized that the thunder which he had heard earlier was the crashing of the balls against the groups of wooden pins.

The curious little fellows ignored Rip and went right on with their playing. Soon the keg was tapped and the little men began to occupy themselves with guzzling huge flagons of the liquor which it contained. Curious, and not adverse to a drop or two, Rip poured a flagon of the liquor and tipped it down his throat. He was naturally a thirsty soul and soon attempted to repeat the draught. One taste led to another until his eyes swam in his head and he fell into a deep sleep.

When Rip awoke he found himself upon the same green knoll where he had first met the little man. He found his flintlock rusted away and that his clothes were in tatters. His beard had grown a foot long. Worried about what old Dame Van Winkle would say to him for passing the night in the mountains, Rip stumbled down the slopes and entered the town. The town had so changed that he had difficulty finding his own house. When he finally did locate it, he found it had fallen in ruins.

When Rip came into the village square he found the customary crowds of people but none whom he recognized.

> He looked in vain for the sage Nicholas Vedder, with his broad face, double chin, and fair long pipe, uttering clouds of tobacco smoke instead of idle speeches; or Van Bummel, the schoolmaster, doling forth the contents of an ancient newspaper. In place of these, a lean bilious-looking fellow, with his pockets full of handbills, was haranguing vehemently about rights of citizens—elections—members of Congress—liberty—Bunker's Hill—heroes of '76—and other words which were a perfect Babylonish jargon to the bewildered Van Winkle.

As the angered crowd of patriots, resentful of an old tattered stranger who entered the free precincts of an important election with a flintlock over his shoulder, was about to hustle Rip away to jail as a troublemaker or a "tory," a young woman, with a babe in her arms, pushed her way through the crowd and stared curiously at Rip. It was soon established that she was indeed Rip's only child who had been but a little girl when her father had left, twenty years before, for a day's sojourn in the mountains.

Rip's strange tale was told and retold and only the old men believed him and recalled that they had heard in their youth that old Hendrick Hudson and his crew came into the mountains every twenty years to revisit the scenes of their early exploits. One old man claimed that he, too, had seen the little men in antique Dutch garb playing at ninepins.

Rip was welcomed into the home of his daughter and her husband. Rip learned that his wife had died, years before, after breaking a blood vessel in a fit of passion at a New England peddler. Rip spent the rest of his days retelling his story at the inn until everyone in the town knew it by heart. And, even to this day, when peals of thunder are heard in the Kaatskills, the townspeople along the Hudson say that Hendrick Hudson and his crew are playing at ninepins. And all of the hen-pecked husbands in the neighborhood long for a quiet draught from the flagon that the players must be passing around in the little amphitheatre among the crags.

In *The Legend of Sleepy Hollow,* Irving recalls that the little valley near where he had his home was once a quiet and drowsy place, which had some sort of witching power over the minds of the good Dutch settlers. The dominant spirit that haunted the valley in those days was a human figure on horseback, without a head. It was known to all as the Headless Horseman of Sleepy Hollow.

Many had heard of the spectre but only Ichabod Crane, the schoolmaster, who looked like a scarecrow because of his green glassy eyes, his huge ears, and his long snipe nose, had actually met the famous horseman. Ichabod, with his kindly patience and his love of telling tall tales, was a welcome boarder in the homes of the parents of his pupils. Ichabod believed in ghosts and took delight in entertaining the family circles with tales of witchcraft and goblins which he had acquired in his reading of books written by early New England ministers. He took special delight in causing the young female members of the community to shudder and thrill at his awesome tales during the long winter evenings around the fireside, with apples and nuts roasting on the hearth.

Ichabod gave singing lessons around the valley in addition to his regular chores as schoolmaster. He was especially taken with the charms of a buxom Dutch girl, named Katrina Van Tassel. Not among the least of her charms was the fact that she was an only child of a wealthy burgher. He not only determined to capture the rosy-cheeked Katrina but also to inherit the more material charms which would be hers at her father's death. Katrina was also pursued by many other young swains of the neighborhood, including the very athletic Brom Bones. Ichabod Crane avoided any physical contact with his rival and all that Brom Bones could do was to hope that the day might come when he could find a subtle means to eliminate the schoolmaster from competition for the fair Katrina's heart and properties.

One Saturday night a quilting party was held at the Van Tassel manor to which all the countryside was invited. Ichabod borrowed a horse from his neighbor, a creature as lank and lean as himself, and the pair provided a ludicrous spectacle to the Dutch neighbors as they jogged along the country roads toward the festivities awaiting them at the Van Tassel mansion.

The party was a huge success. Ichabod paid court during the evening both to the wealthy burgher's rich foods and wines and to his lovely daughter. Ichabod was the last to leave and as he jogged along the dark country road all of his stories of ghosts and goblins passed through his mind and he became more sad and dismal as the effects of the rich food and heady wines began to wear off.

When he came to the bridge over Wiley's swamp, Gunpowder, his equine companion, balked and refused to cross. Then he saw the reason. On the other side of the bridge was standing a horseman, not an ordinary horseman but one whose body ended with his neck and whose head was held in the strange rider's hands in front of him. Ichabod, terrified, spurred Gunpowder past the horseman. As Ichabod and his equally frightened four-footed companion sped down the lane he realized that the headless horseman was following him, gaining at every step. At the bridge by the church the headless horseman was close upon his heels. As he turned his head to look, the figure drew back his own head and hurled it against Ichabod's body.

The next morning the Dutch neighbors found a shattered pumpkin near the bridge. Gunpowder was peacefully grazing in a nearby farmer's field, but Ichabod was nowhere to be found and was never seen in Sleepy Hollow again. The story of Ichabod Crane was told and retold wherever these Dutch settlers gathered and the man who laughed the most heartily was Brom Bones, the wealthy husband of the former Katrina Van Tassel.

2. James Fenimore Cooper: *The Last of the Mohicans*

Page 50. Cooper's five novels, which are the best representative examples of American fiction depicting the life of the early frontier, derive their collective title of *Leatherstocking Tales* from one of the nicknames of the principal hero, Natty Bumppo, a fearless woodsman who lived and fought in the epic struggles to advance the American frontier westward. *The Deerslayer* records Natty Bumppo's youth as a hunter brought up among the Delaware Indians. It follows the hero's early struggles to defend white settlers from the depredations of the enemy tribes, constantly at war with the friendly Delawares. In this novel Natty establishes himself as a perfect woodsman with cool nerve and unmatched resourcefulness. Natty also resists the restraints which civilization would put upon his freedom of action, including marriage to the lovely Judith Hunter, a girl whose family he has saved from the enemy Hurons, in order to be able to dedicate himself wholeheartedly to the hard life of a frontier scout.

The Last of the Mohicans, the second of the novels depicting, chronologically, the life of Natty Bumppo, opens as Major Duncan Heyward is engaged in the task of escorting Cora and Alice Munro from Fort Edward to Fort William Henry, where the girls' father is commandant. The party, including David Gamut, a singing-master, have put themselves in the care of a renegade Huron, named Magua, who pretends to lead them to their destination but, in reality, plans to deliver them into the hands of the enemy tribe. Before Magua can carry out his traitorous designs the little party meet the woodsman, Hawkeye, a name which Natty Bumppo has assumed, and his Mohican friends, Chingachgook, the Mohican chief, and his son Uncas. Hawkeye immediately recognizes the renegade Huron and forces him to flee into the forest.

Natty Bumppo, as Hawkeye, agrees to lead the party safely to Fort William Henry. That night Magua returns with a band of Iroquois and surprises the party. Hawkeye and his two Indian friends, realizing that they cannot win the fight because the enemy has stolen the canoe containing their ammunition, escape and swim downstream, leaving their newly found friends to be captured by the Iroquois. They return stealthily through the forest and fall upon the Iroquois just as the renegade Magua was attempting to force Cora to become his squaw. After several of the Iroquois are killed the remainder flee and Hawkeye returns to his task of guiding the party through the wilderness.

By stealth and trickery they manage to make their way through the French and Indian forces which are laying siege to the fort, under the French General Montcalm. Although Hawkeye steals away in the night to Fort Edward, help is refused by the commander there, and he is forced to return empty-handed. Colonel Munro is forced to surrender the fort to Montcalm who promises that the vanquished English may leave in safety.

As Colonel Munro and his charges are passing between long lines of French and Indians, an Indian darted toward one of the English women and snatched the colorful shawl in which her baby was wrapped. The Indian dashed the child to the ground as others of his savage companions threw themselves upon the unsuspecting English settlers. Montcalm stood by and did little to hold back his savage allies. Most of the helpless group was slaughtered. During the confusion the renegade Magua appeared again and carried Alice away in his arms. Cora ran after her sister with David Gamut close upon her heels.

Three days later Munro, Heyward, and Hawkeye, with his

two Indian friends, set out to trail Magua through the forest. After several days of hard pursuit, by canoe and on foot, they came upon David Gamut, wandering about aimlessly in the forest. Thinking him crazy, the Indians had let him wander from camp. In the bloody struggle which followed, Magua carried Cora to the top of a cliff, with Uncas, the Mohican, in close pursuit. Magua stabbed and killed Uncas just as Hawkeye arrived upon the scene. Hawkeye raised his rifle and shot Magua.

After the victorious, but sorrowful, little group had buried Cora and Uncas in the forest they made their way to the English fort. The book ends as Hawkeye returns to the wilderness to continue his struggle to bring peace to the frontier. Old Chingachgook, the last of the Mohican branch of the Delaware tribe, goes with him.

Cooper's novels *The Pathfinder, The Pioneers,* and *The Prairie,* in that order, carry Natty Bumppo through many adventures and hairbreadth escapes, until his death at the ripe old age of ninety-three. Many millions of Americans have read at least one of *The Leatherstocking Tales* and have thrilled at the perils and exploits of the dauntless Natty Bumppo. In 1954, Allen Nevins edited an admirable single-volume abridgment of the five novels in which today's reader may follow the best of the adventures, the ideas, and the philosophy of America's most epic hero of fiction, Natty Bumppo, from youth to old age.

3.   Herman Melville: *Moby Dick,* or *The Whale*

Page 57. Lewis Mumford, the eminent biographer of Herman Melville, states that the novelist has, "with Walt Whitman the distinction of being the greatest imaginative writer that America has produced: his epic *Moby Dick* is one of the supreme monuments of the English language." Only in the last forty years has the bias and condemnatory 19th century criticism been cleared away to reveal *Moby Dick* as one of the finest novels not only in American literature but one that can be placed beside the best writings of all time. On the surface *Moby Dick* is a finely written narrative of adventure on the high seas, and, beneath the surface of this swiftly moving narrative runs a deep current of symbolism, offering the reader a magnificent insight into human nature. Melville was deeply burdened with the problem of evil and the all-enveloping control which he felt it exercised in his own contemporary society. In the person of Captain

Ahab and in his disastrous pursuit of the whale that had once injured him, Melville set out to show the tragic consequences that may result when a man sets himself up as a god and tries to eliminate a force beyond the control of mere mortals. Melville uses the whale to symbolize evil; for him the ocean is life itself and Captain Ahab is the stubborn spirit of individual man grappling with the problem of evil. *Moby Dick* is a huge epic of the sea, artistically conceived and written down in a poetic prose, and deep within it lies a penetrating discussion of a universal human problem.

The story is told by young Ishmael, tired of his quiet existence as a schoolmaster, who longs once more to sail the seas as he had done in his youth. He comes to New Bedford one drizzly evening and puts up at the Spouter Inn, near the waterfront. He is quartered with a strange South Seas' islander who, at first, gives Ishmael the feeling that he is in the presence of a savage cannibal. The native Queequeg proves to be a friendly fellow, however, and tells Ismael that he is an expert harpooner.

The next day the two friends go aboard the whaler *Pequot* and are signed on as a part of the crew. Before boarding the ship they had heard strange reports of the mysterious Captain Ahab, who had lost a leg in a battle with a whale. For days the captain did not show himself on deck. When he finally did appear Ishmael was impressed by the stern and unrelenting expression on Ahab's face and by the curious artificial leg with which the captain hobbled about the deck. It had been carved from the jaw bone of a whale. Down one side of Ahab's face ran a deep livid scar which disappeared beneath the collar of his coat.

For many days the ship ran south and Ahab appeared rarely, to stand silently for minutes scanning the horizon with his long glass. Finally, one day, he called the crew together and nailed a gold piece to the mast which he declared would belong to the man who first sighted the white whale, known to the sailors as Moby Dick. Ahab had lost his leg in a battle with this particular whale and he had become a man obsessed with but one idea, to kill the whale and to destroy the evil that it represented. Starbuck, the mate, pleaded with the captain to abandon this pursuit which might result in disaster for them all.

Near the Cape of Good Hope a school of whales was sighted and the boats were lowered. Although a great deal of blubber was rendered into valuable oil, Captain Ahab seemed unenthusiastic and hastened to get the ship underway toward the Indian Ocean, where the white whale was last seen. As Ahab's obsession mounted, tension grew throughout the ship. Ignoring favorable signs of new schools of whales, the captain drove the ship forward and paused only to inquire of passing ships if they had news of the white whale.

Queequeg fell ill of a fever and it seemed that he would die. He ordered a coffin made for him in the shape of a canoe, a custom among Polynesian royalty when they felt that death was at hand. He recovered, however, and converted his coffin into a sea chest.

At last Ahab's calculations of the probable position in which Moby Dick would be found proved to be correct and the white whale was sighted. Boats were lowered and Captain Ahab, himself, rode in the lead boat. The great white sea monster plunged into one of the boats and splintered it; then Moby Dick headed into the open sea. The ship caught up with the whale again the following day and another boat was lost after three harpoons had found their mark in the creature's side. The Captain's bone leg had been snapped off. Once again the whale eluded his enemy, Ahab, for now the crew members were mere puppets drawn on by the controlling passion of the monomaniacal captain.

The third day saw the boats again in the water near where Moby Dick had shown his mighty bulk. Again he was harpooned and again he turned and splintered the boat from which it was thrown. The whale, enraged, turned toward the ship itself and plunged under it, tearing the timbers from its bottom. As the ship settled in the water, Ahab saw his opportunity and hurled his harpoon. It struck the mark but its coil of rope caught Ahab around the neck and he was hurled from the boat. The remainder of the crew in the one boat that was still afloat were sucked under the waves by the sinking ship.

> Now small fowls flew screaming over the yet yawning gulf; a sullen white suft beat against its steep sides; then all collapsed, and the great shroud of the sea rolled on as it rolled five thousand years ago.

Only Ishmael survived. He had been in Ahab's boat, and when it was sucked into the vortex of the sinking ship, he found himself grasping the only piece of the wreckage which shot back up to the surface—the coffin which the feverish Queequeg had ordered made for himself weeks before. Still clinging to the coffin, Ishmael is picked up by the *Rachel* "that in her retracing search after her missing children, only found another orphan."

4. Walt Whitman: *Song of Myself* (from *Leaves of Grass*)

Page 61. Walt Whitman, considered by many the greatest of all American poets, has also become an American legend and the literary man most identified with our expanding frontier, our budding democratic spirit, and our ideals of material greatness. Whitman's longest single poem and the one which best reveals the many facets, often contradictory, of his all-enveloping and robust Americanism, appeared in the first edition of *Leaves of Grass* (1855) simply as an introduction and without a title. In later editions, it was called *A Poem of Walt Whitman, An American.* Its present title appeared first in the edition of 1881.

The poem begins upon a note of equality for all people. Whitman is egoistic and proud of himself and equally proud of being identified with the same mold in which the reader and the things of nature are created.

> I celebrate myself;
> And what I assume you shall assume;
> For every atom belonging to me, as good belongs to you.

In optimistic vein the poet then catalogues the parts of himself and those of external nature in which he takes pride and joy. He classes the soul equally with the body:

> Clear and sweet is my Soul, and clear and sweet is all
>   that is not my Soul.
>   .   .   .   .
> I believe in you, my Soul—the other I am must not
>   abase itself to you;
> And you must not be abased to the other.

Whitman's belief in immortality is evident; his approach to it is through love, love of ones self and of all persons and things. He is mystic, optimistic, and believes in the indwelling presence of God.

The poet then turns to a catalogue of the people and the things which he loves in America and identifies himself with each of them.

> Comrade of raftsmen and coalmen—comrade of all who
>   shake hands and welcome to drink and meat;
> A learner with the simplest, a teacher of the thought-
>   fullest;
> A novice beginning, yet experient of myriads of seasons;
> Of every hue and caste am I, of every rank and religion;

Over and over in the poem Whitman returns to identify himself with all forms of life and to deny the importance of position, wealth, and social cleavage. He loves life when it is happy and he searches for the supreme value in all things which would give even to the lowliest forms of life and nature their reason for exalting themselves. He admits that he possesses the supreme ego and he calls to others to leave their hypocrisies, their whining, their scheming, their climbing over others, and attempt to scale the heights of pride, happiness, and joy that he takes in living.

Though Whitman preaches universality and equality and proclaims himself a mystic, he bows also to materialism and science, but only with a reservation that their importance is limited:

> I accept reality, and dare not question it;
> Materialism first and last imbuing,
> Hurrah for positive science! long live exact demonstration!
>
> .   .   .   .   .
>
> Gentlemen! to you the first honors always:
> Your facts are useful and real—and yet they are not my
>   dwelling;
> (I but enter by them to an area of my dwelling.)

That he is inconsistent and contradicts himself, Whitman is the first to admit. A poet that tries to encompass all things and all persons and their foibles and virtues must necessarily be contradictory:

> Do I contradict myself?
> Very well, then, I contradict myself;
> (I am large—I contain multitudes.)

He admits that his nature is somewhat more animal than reasonable and that he cannot be understood by all men, for his language is not the approved speech of all circles of society:

> I too am not a bit tamed—I too am untranslatable;
> I sound my barbaric yawp over the roofs of the world.

Whitman, in mid-19th century, speaks to the future generations at the close of his poem. Many in his lifetime refused him greatness because of his frank utterance, for his exaltation of the divinity of man's physical structure, for his pantheism, for his animism. But many in mid-20th century accept Whitman as a

great individualist and as our greatest poet; to many, Whitman's
ideas are his own, and whether or not they agree with those of
the reader, do not obscure his gifts of versatility of poetic expression of them.

> I bequeathe myself to the dirt, to grow from the grass
>   I love;
> If you want me again, look for me under your bootsoles.
>
> You will hardly know who I am, or what I mean;
> But I shall be good health to you nevertheless,
> And filter and fibre your blood.
>
> Failing to fetch me at first, keep encouraged;
> Missing me one place, search another;
> I stop somewhere, waiting for you.

5. **Edgar Allen Poe:** Three Tales *(The Fall of the House of
   Usher, The Pit and the Pendulum, The Murders in
   the Rue Morgue)*

Page 67. In addition to his abilities as a poet and as a literary
critic, Poe was our first master of the short story and his definition of the form as a distinctive literary genre was widely
accepted throughout Europe and Spanish America. Poe emphasized brevity and singleness of impression in the story. He
considered all other elements, plot, character development, detail, as secondary to the building of the single effect. Poe chose
the atmosphere of horror, dreariness, and melancholy as his
dominant mood and he deliberately selected incidents which
would assist in the creation of this effect.

The Fall of the House of Usher is considered one of world
literature's most perfect short stories. In it, Poe creates his
mood of horror and melancholy from the first line and builds his
series of minor climaxes, leading to the final horrible one.

> During the whole of a dull, dark, and soundless day in the
> autumn of the year, when the clouds hung oppressively low
> in the heavens, I had been passing alone, on horseback, through
> a singularly dreary tract of country; and at length found myself,
> as the shades of evening drew on, within view of the melancholy
> House of Usher.

The relator of the tale had not seen his friend, Roderick

Usher, since their days in school together. Recently a letter from his childhood companion had begged him to spend some weeks with him in an attempt to restore him to his former cheerful self. It seems that Roderick had suffered both physical and nervous collapse, a malady which had seemed to dog the steps of the direct heirs of the Usher estate.

The Usher mansion stands on the edge of a tarn, its stone decayed and fungus-grown. A zigzag crack runs down the side of the wall facing the tarn. For days Roderick's friend feels the gloom of the huge house settling upon him as he tries in vain to comfort his cheerless friend. In the same house Roderick's twin sister, Madeline, is wasting away from the same malady which afflicted her brother. The doctors are puzzled by her illness and finally consider that she is indeed dead and place her in the family vault; in reality she had fallen into a cataleptic trance.

As the days pass Roderick's sick mind and the gloom of the surroundings penetrate more and more into the visitor's nature and he begins to feel that he, too, will become a victim to the nameless fears which the House of Usher seems to exercise upon all the family members who have lived there.

One evening a severe storm sweeps across the tarn and envelops the house. Roderick, in a state of almost nervous collapse, comes to his friend's room. He seems to anticipate some horrible disaster. His friend picks up the first book to fall under his hand and reads to Usher, in an attempt to calm him. The book is a medieval romance. As the terrible episodes of the story unfold, noises are heard from deep within the mansion, which seem to accompany the ripping and tearing sounds which are described in the story. Roderick Usher faces the door, trembling and muttering in an unintelligible gibberish.

Suddenly the door is flung open and Madeline, in her shroud, appears before her brother. She runs to her brother, with blood streaming down her flimsy garment. Brother and sister fall to the floor, dead.

The visitor flees from the house in terror. In a sudden burst of eerie light, the visitor saw the zigzag fissure in the stone wall rapidly widening:

> . . . my brain reeled as I saw the mighty walls rushing asunder—there was a long tumultuous shouting sound like the voice of a thousand waters—and the deep and dark tarn at my feet closed sullenly and silently over the fragments of the "House of Usher."

The Pit and the Pendulum is another of the horror tales, in which a victim of the Spanish Inquisition tells of the horrible tortures he has endured. Finally, in a dead faint he is carried to a metal dungeon cell where, stumbling about in the dark, he barely ascapes falling into a pit. After sleeping fitfully, he awakens to find himself strapped to a wooden table. Above him a huge knife swings back and forth, descending toward his neck gradually. Just as the knife is about to touch his flesh, the rats, which have been swarming over his body, gnaw through the ropes. No sooner does he find himself free from this horror, than he realizes that the metal walls of his cell are closing in upon him and forcing him gradually, inch by inch, toward the edge of the bottomless pit. The French, who are besieging the city, burst into the prison and rescue the man as he totters screaming on the edge of the pit.

This story, along with other superb examples such as "The Masque of the Red Death," "The Tell-Tale Heart," and "The Black Cat," illustrate well Poe's singleness of purpose in building a mood of fear and horror toward a climax. The reader acquires the mood and is drawn on by the author, ignoring illogical incidents, to an ever higher pitch of excitement.

Poe introduced the detective story into American fiction, and created the first of a long line of fictional master sleuths with C. Auguste Dupin in _The Murders in the Rue Morgue_ (1841). The relator of the tale shares quarters with Dupin, who is gifted with extraordinary powers of deduction and analysis. The police of Paris have been unable to solve the brutal murders of a Mme. L'Espanaye and her daughter Camille in their upstairs flat in the Rue Morgue. The murderer evidently possessed superhuman strength and agility to have reached the apartment from the outside and to have mutilated the bodies in such a manner.

Dupin is persuaded to test his powers of ratiocination and attempts to solve the mystery. He looks over the scene and logically comes to the conclusion that the women were killed by an orang-outang. He inserts an advertisement in the newspaper which uncovers a sailor who admits that he had smuggled such an animal into Paris and that the ape had gotten away from him and had killed the women. The beast is captured and placed in a zoo.

Poe brings Dupin back in 1842 to solve _The Mystery of Marie Rogêt_. The similarity between Poe's detective and those of later writers, particularly the most famous of them all, Sherlock Holmes, is evident.

6. Harriet Beecher Stowe: *Uncle Tom's Cabin*

Page 77. As the writer prepares this digest, he takes note of a new book, *Goodbye to Uncle Tom* by J. C. Furnas, which is but one further proof that the tremendous influence of one of America's worst-written novels still lives on more than a century after Mrs. Stowe's "sojourn in the South," which resulted in the melodramatic and sentimental overflowing of words which captured the imaginations of generations of Americans and Europeans and gave the world a stereotyped concept of the Negro which is only now showing signs of being dissipated. Few present-day Americans actually read the book but also few fail to come into contact with the legend and the cliché expressions which have grown into the American conscience with regard to Uncle Tom, Simon Legree, Little Eva, Eliza, and the towsled little Topsy, who "just growed." All in the novel is, of course, highly exaggerated and dripping with a maudlin sentimentality but its plot and characters have been, perhaps, the most highly exploited of all American native fictional creations, and for this reason the novel deserves space in an historical review.

Mr. Selby finds his Kentucky plantation heavy in debt and he is forced to give up one of his slaves to satisfy temporarily his principal creditor. The creditor demands the pious and kindly Uncle Tom and Harry, the small son of Eliza, whose husband is owned by a neighbor. Eliza escapes during the night with her little son, hoping to reach the sanctuary of Canadian soil. The creditor, Haley, pursues her with bloodhounds but Eliza escapes across the Ohio River by jumping from one to another of the floating cakes of ice.

Uncle Tom, meanwhile, is shackled and placed aboard a steamboat bound for New Orleans. In spite of his handicaps Uncle Tom leaps after little Eva St. Clare, who has fallen overboard, and saves her. Mr. St. Clare, a kindly man, buys Tom and he is promised a happy life. Little Eva is in delicate health and Mr. St. Clare brings his cousin, Miss Ophelia, a whimsical spinster, to care for her. One of the most interesting characters in this portion of the book is the little pixy-like Topsy ("Ah wasn't bo'n; ah jes growed") who is given to Miss Ophelia to educate. Mrs. Stowe's Topsy has become fixed in the American mind as a sterotyped concept of a saucy and impudent child, towsled and dirty, but with crude humorous appeal.

The most tearful pages of the book record the sad death of little Eva. Shortly afterward Mr. St. Clare is knifed in an attempt to separate two fighting men. Mr. St. Clare had promised his dying child that he would free his slaves but he died before he could carry out his promise and Mrs. St. Clare sold the slaves at auction. Uncle Tom is bought by the cruel and drunken Simon Legree, who drives his slaves with a bull whip. Uncle Tom's kindnesses to the other slaves only cause him to receive more than his share of Legree's brutal treatment. He dies just as George Selby, the son of his first owner, arrives to buy him back.

The book ends with the happy reunion of Eliza with her husband and mother in Canada. George Selby frees all his slaves in memory of Uncle Tom.

7. John Greenleaf Whittier: *Snow-Bound*

Page 80. This long poem has proved to be the most popular pastoral idyl in American literature. Not only does it appeal widely to Americans because of its simple charm and its admirable description and characterization of a rural New England family circle in midwinter; it is an authentic study of social conditions of a section of rural America during the last century. The poet's masterpiece, it records his actual childhood experiences in a typical Quaker household.

> The sun that brief December day
> Rose cheerless over hills of gray,

The poem begins with portents of the coming snow storm and each member of the Quaker farm family is busily engaged in his assigned task in preparation for the night.

> And ere the early bedtime came
> The white drift piled the window-frame,
> And through the glass the clothes-line posts
> Looked like tall and sheeted ghosts.

When morning came the world was "a universe of sky and snow." But there was work to be done; a path must be cleared

to the barns to care for the imprisoned animals and chickens.
All day long the wind blew and that evening the family circle
gathered about the cheery fireside.

> . . . hovering near
> We watched the first red blaze appear,
> Heard the sharp crackle, caught the gleam
> On whitewashed wall and sagging beam,
> Until the old, rude-furnished room
> Burst, flower-like, into rosy bloom;
>
> .   .   .   .   .
>
> What matter how the night behaved?
> What matter how the north-wind raved?

The hot cider, baked apples, and nuts made the rounds as the
family passed the long evening with stories, darning socks, and
eating. Here the poem turns to long and thorough portraits of
the family members who are basking themselves before the fire,
the mother, the sister, the uncle, the maiden aunt:

> The sweetest woman ever Fate
> Perverse denied a household mate,
> Who, lonely, homeless, not the less
> Found peace in love's unselfishness,

Finally, to bed to lie for a while listening to the howling wind.
The next day teamsters open the country roads with oxen and
the doctor makes his rounds with sleigh bells jingling. Thus a
week passes for the farm group with no other contacts with the
outside world. When finally the carrier arrives with the weekly
newspaper, the spell is broken and the outside world rushes in
upon the little snowbound group. And the poet reflects, in
later years, that, in spite of the hustle and strife of living, such
happy memories always return now and then:

> The worldling's eyes shall gather dew,
>   Dreaming in throngful city ways
> Of winter joys his boyhood knew;

8. Nathaniel Hawthorne: *The Scarlet Letter*

Page 82. The scene of Hawthorne's masterpiece, which com-
petes with Melville's *Moby Dick* for the highest position among
American novels to date, is Puritan Boston of the mid-17th

century. Its theme is conscience and concealed guilt and their tragic consequences upon the lives of four people in early New England society. The author succeeds in maintaining a mood of mystery and the weirdness of deep psychological conflict throughout the book.

Roger Prynne, an aged scholar of Amsterdam, having determined to move to the New World, had sent his young wife Hester on before him. When he arrived in Boston, two years later, he found his wife in the pillory, a young babe in her arms, and upon her breast a scarlet letter "A" (for adultery) which she had been condemned to wear for the rest of her life. Prynne cautions her not to recognize him and takes up residence as a doctor under the name of Roger Chillingworth. Hester had refused to reveal to the authorities the name of the father of the child and she also refuses her husband the information. He determines to seek out the man and expose him.

Hester takes up residence in a hut on the edge of the wilderness and devotes her life to deeds of mercy. Her child, Pearl, becomes wayward and undisciplined. Hester, an outcast and forced to proclaim her sin by wearing the scarlet letter, earns a meager living by doing needlework for her neighbors. Her efforts to win back their approval by good deeds seem in vain. Years pass.

A young and respected minister, Arthur Dimmesdale, is in reality the father of Hester's child. Though at first he had joined his neighbors in sanctimonious condemnation of Hester, he gradually becomes burdened with the guilt and it gnaws upon his mind through the years, though pride keeps him from revealing it. Hester's aged husband discovers that Arthur is the father and, himself, becomes morose and degraded in his intent to harass and torture Dimmesdale into a public confession of his guilt.

Hester, observing the slow degeneration of Arthur, begs her husband to cease his persecution. Upon his refusal, she tells Arthur the true identity of the old physician and they determine to flee the colony and embark upon a ship for Europe. They arrange passage for four days later. The captain of the ship told Hester that Roger Chillingworth was also to sail on the same ship.

On Election Day, Arthur Dimmesdale delivers his sermon in the church, and upon leaving, he sees Hester and Pearl standing by the pillory where she had once endured such public shame. He, now almost demented, walks to them, and taking the mother and daughter by the hand, he mounts the pillory and calls for the attention of the crowd. He admits his guilt, rips off his ministerial garb and falls dying to the platform. Some people swore that, when he ripped the garb from his breast, a scarlet "A" was imprinted there in his flesh.

Chillingworth died shortly afterward, leaving his money to Pearl. After spending some time with Pearl in Europe, Hester returns to her little cottage. She continues to wear the emblem on her breast, now symbolic of her devotion to deeds of kindness and mercy in the minds of her Puritan neighbors. She proudly requested that her tombstone should bear only the inscription of the letter "A."

9. Henry Wadsworth Longfellow: Three Metrical Narratives
(Evangeline, The Courtship of Miles Standish, The Song of Hiawatha)

Page 85. Longfellow's simple narrative verse romances have had many millions of readers and continue in popularity with many people, a century since they were written, in an age that long since has repudiated the nostalgic sentimentality with which they abound. His *Hiawatha,* of course, continues to be a favorite of children, and the John Alden and Priscilla episode and Priscilla's famed "Why don't you speak for yourself, John?" have become symbolic of American individualism and form an indispensible part of every American child's fund of folklore and legend.

> This is the forest primeval. The murmuring pines
>   and the hemlocks,
> Bearded with moss, and in garments green, indistinct
>   in the twilight,
> Stand like druids of eld, with voices sad and pro-
>   phetic,
> Stand like harpers hoar, with beards that rest on their
>   bosoms.
> Loud from its rocky caverns, the deep-voiced neigh-
>   boring ocean
> Speaks, and in accents disconsolate answers the wail
>   of the forest.

Thus begins *Evangeline,* in unrimed hexameter verse, in the peaceful Arcadian village of Grand Pré, on the upper St. Lawrence in Canada, in 1755. Evangeline Bellefontaine, the farmer's daughter, is about to be married to Gabriel Lajeunesse, the son of the village blacksmith. It was during the French and Indian War.

One day the English commander of the area ordered the entire village to be cleared of its inhabitants on the charge that some in the area had given aid to the enemy. The houses are burned and the people are loaded aboard ships for transport into exile. Evangeline and Gabriel, the lovers, are put aboard separate ships. The inhabitants of Grand Pré are put ashore in little groups at various spots along the Eastern seaboard. Gabriel and his father make their way down the Mississippi to Louisiana where they become prosperous cattlemen. Evangeline, her father dead, wanders over the face of New England, seeking out groups of the exiles, hoping to find her lover among them. She followed up every rumor of the whereabouts of Gabriel but all ended in disappointment.

The seasons change and the years roll by and Evangeline, refusing an offer of marriage from young Basil who had helped her in her search, finally finds the ranch where Gabriel had lived. He had left several days before and they had apparently passed each other on the Mississippi. She follows him through the Ozark Mountains and into the woods of Michigan, reaching his camp sites sometimes only hours after he had abandoned them.

Finally, prematurely old and her beauty faded, she came to Philadelphia. During an epidemic that was raging there she becomes a sister of mercy and visits the sick in the hospitals. In one of them she finds Gabriel, dying; he recognizes his faithful sweetheart in his last moments.

> Still stands the forest primeval; but far away from
>   its shadow,
> Side by side, in their nameless graves, the lovers are
>   sleeping.
> Under the humble walls of the little Catholic church-
>   yard,
> In the heart of the city, they lie, unknown and un-
>   noticed.

Also in unrimed hexameters, *The Courtship of Miles Standish* takes the reader back to the early days of the Plymouth colony. Captain Standish, feeling himself too crude and rough for fine speeches, asks his friend, John Alden, to speak of his love to the maid, Priscilla. Alden, though secretly in love with the maid himself, cannot refuse his friend and goes to Priscilla's house where he eloquently extols the virtues and the bravery of Miles Standish. The Puritan maiden realizes that Alden loves her as he manfully strives to promote the suit of his friend:

> But as he warmed and glowed, in his simple and
>   eloquent language,
> Quite forgetful of self, and full of the praise of
>   his rival,
> Archly the maiden smiled, and, with eyes over-
>   running with laughter,
> Said, in a tremulous voice, "Why don't you speak
>   for yourself, John?"

Standish, furious with his friend for what he feels is a betrayal of trust, leaves on an Indian campaign and is later reported dead. John and Priscilla meet often and plan to marry. Captain Standish belies the false report of his death by appearing at the wedding to ask forgiveness of the happy couple.

The Song of Hiawatha has often been referred to as the American Indian "epic" poem. Its simple unrimed trochaic tetrameter lines, with their lilting repetitious melody, are in imitation of the Finnish epic poem, _Kalevala_. Longfellow also borrowed much of the spirit of the Finnish poem and some of the episodes are strikingly similar in both poems. _Hiawatha_ concerns a North American Indian legend of the warrior hero that the Great Spirit sent to unite the various tribes in peace. In it Longfellow has woven the beliefs, the songs, the customs, and the stories and legends of the American Indian.

Wenonah, deserted by her lover Mudjekeewis, the West Wind, bore a son whom she called Hiawatha. The lad grew up in the wigwam of Nakomis, his grandmother, who had fallen to earth from the full moon. The young Hiawatha learns all of the arts and skills of the Indian and comes to know all of the secrets of nature.

> Then the little Hiawatha
> Learned of every bird its language,
> Learned their names and all their secrets,
> How they built their nests in Summer,
> Where they hid themselves in Winter,
> Talked with them whene'er he met them,
> Called them "Hiawatha's Chickens."

When he learned how his father, the West Wind, had deserted his mother he resolved to seek him out and punish him. In the land of the West Wind, he and Mudjekeewis fight for three days. Finally they become reconciled and Mudjekeewis sends Hiawatha to earth to unite his peoples. On the way, Hiawatha stops in the land of the Dakotahs and meets the lovely daughter of the arrow maker, Minnehaha. He bears her away as his bride.

> Over wide and rushing rivers
> In his arms he bore the maiden;
> Light he thought her as a feather,
> As the plume upon his head-gear;

Among Hiawatha's deeds had been the defeat of the Corn Spirit, which resulted in his learning the secret of the growth of this indispensible food for his peoples, the destruction of Pearl-Feather who visited death and disease upon the Indians. With the aid of his friend, Kwasind, he had cleared the rivers and streams of debris and sand bars so that his people could sail upon them in safety.

During a severe winter, during which famine came upon the tribes, Minnehaha died. During the next spring the first white men came into the Indian country. After talking to the priest among them, Hiawatha advised his peoples to keep the peace with the white men, else they would perish. At last, Hiawatha, his mission finished on earth, sailed into the sunset to the Land of the Hereafter.

10. Francis Bret(t) Harte and Joel Chandler Harris: Masters of the "local color" tale

Page 101. Bret Harte became the most famous of the local colorists of the Far West. His melodramatic tales deal with romantic incidents from life among the gold camps of California during the days of '49. *The Luck of Roaring Camp,* perhaps the most known and most loved of his tales, tells of the death in childbirth of Cherokee Sal, a prostitute of the gold-mining settlement of Roaring Camp. The child is christened Thomas Luck and is adopted by the lawless miners of the camp. When a flood sweeps down upon Roaring Camp, Kentuck, one of the roughest of the miners, is drowned in a futile attempt to rescue The Luck.

In the same vein of sentimentality, *The Outcasts of Poker Flat* relates how young Tom Simson and Piney elope to be married and are forced to take refuge from a snowstorm with a rather dubious group of characters who have been driven from Poker Flat by the irate citizenry. The group includes Mr. Oakhurst, the gambler, "The Duchess" and "Mother Shipton," prostitutes, and Uncle Billy, a suspected sluice-robber and confirmed drunkard. Days went by and the snow only piled higher. Mother Shipton starved herself to death, saving her rations of food for Piney. Piney becomes ill and Mr. Oakhurst gives the only pair of snowshoes to Tom in the hope that he can reach the settlement to bring help for Piney. Oakhurst dies in the snow and that night the Duchess attempts to keep Piney warm with her own body, as both die.

Page 103. Joel Chandler Harris, with his Uncle Remus series, became the most popular of the Southern local colorists. His humorous stories of such animals as Brer Rabbit, Brer Fox, and Brer Wolf, who talked in the dialect of the wooly-headed and kindly old Uncle Remus, a former slave, have given millions of readers the world over their concept of life and customs on the southern plantations. The first Uncle Remus story appeared in 1879, and by 1906 Harris had issued six collections of the songs, tales, and sayings of Uncle Remus, our greatest collection of Negro folk literature.

A typical tale concerns Brer Rabbit, Brer Fox, and the Tar-Baby. Brer Fox spent most of his time trying to catch Brer Rabbit and one morning it seemed that he had succeeded. He made a very human-looking figure from tar and set it upon the road. Brer Rabbit came along and, in an attempt to make acquaintance with the stranger, got his paws stuck in the tar The more he struggled, the more he became stuck. Brer Fox came from the bushes and began to gloat over his helpless enemy. As he prepares to build a fire to roast Brer Rabbit, the sly rabbit begs the fox to do anything he likes except throw him into the brier patch. The fox, thinking he can make the rabbit suffer even more before roasting him, flings the rabbit into the brier patch. Brer Rabbit, of course, gets the Tar-Baby stuck in the briers and scampers away, flinging insults at the foiled Brer Fox.

> " 'Bred en bawn in a brier-patch, Brer Fox—bred en bawn in a brier-patch!' En wid dat he skip out ez lively ez a cricket."
> "Did the fox ever catch the rabbit?" said the little boy.
> "I hear Miss Sally callin'," said Uncle Remus. "Yer better run 'long."

11. Mark Twain (Samuel L. Clemens): *The Adventures of Tom Sawyer* and *The Adventures of Huckleberry Finn*

Page 112. These two classics of American literature were created by Mark Twain largely from his recollections of his childhood days along the Mississippi. They live not only as great stories for young and old alike in the United States but as our most charming of "local color" prose, depicting with native humor and keen insight the life and customs of a portion of early America, which have long since changed. The books are superb fantasies of boyhood and are masterpieces of adult recreation in writing of the nostalgic memories of one of our greatest writers.

Tom Sawyer lived with his kindly but stern Aunt Polly in the dreamy little river town of St. Petersburg, Missouri. The mischievous Tom is carried through one prank after another in the early pages of the book, suffering the just punishment meted out by Aunt Polly, usually provoked by Tom's tale-bearing half-brother, Sid. The episode where Tom induces his friends to whitewash the fence by persuading them that it is great fun is perhaps the prank most remembered by millions who have read the book.

When the pretty little Becky Thatcher, with the lace pantalets, moves next door, Tom renounces his love for his former sweetheart and turns his amorous attentions to the new girl. When Becky snubs him he plays hookey from school and roams the woods and the river bank with his friend, Huck Finn, the ragged and lovable son of a ne'er-do-well town drunkard. Huck and Tom are in the graveyard at midnight when they witness a quarrel between three grave robbers, Injun Joe, Muff Potter, and Doctor Robinson. Injun Joe stabs the Doctor and Muff Potter is later brought to trial for the crime.

For days Tom and Huck are panic-stricken at the thought of what Injun Joe might do to them if he found out what they knew. They run away to Jackson's Island to become pirates. Finally, their sense of fair play gets the best of them and they appear in a dramatic manner in the courtroom to accuse Injun Joe, who escapes by crashing through a window. Tom is now a hero in Becky Thatcher's eyes and gradually loses his fear of Injun Joe.

Later, on a school picnic, Tom and Becky become lost together in a cave beside the river and wander for hours. They discover that Injun Joe is hiding there. The next day they find an exit, some five miles from the spot they had entered the cave. A search party returns to the cave and finds Injun Joe dead. Tom and Huck return to the cave and find a great deal of stolen money that Injun Joe had buried there. Since the owners are never found, the money is held in trust for Tom and Huck, who had been adopted by the Widow Douglas. Tom and Huck are town heroes. The only fly in the ointment for Huck is that he now has to wear clean clothes. But Tom consoles him by promising that he will form a pirate gang and make Huck the chief buccaneer.

Huckleberry Finn concentrates less on melodramatic incident and more upon an authentic local color portrayal of the Mississippi River region and on character portrayal, and is usually considered to be a more integrated account than *Tom Sawyer*. Huck Finn, himself, narrates his experiences, beginning with the attempt on the part of Huck's drunkard father to kidnap the boy from the Widow Douglas and secure his money. Huck escapes and starts down the Mississippi on a raft, accompanied by the runaway slave, Jim. They travel by night and tie up to the bank by day. The raft is hit by a steamboat on one occasion and Huck and Jim become temporarily separated only to be reunited in the midst of a feud between the Grangerfords and the Shepherdsons.

Again on the river, Huck and Jim take aboard the raft two eccentric river characters who pretend to be an English duke and a French king but are, in reality, a couple of sharpsters. They stage a fake show in one town and flee before an angry mob from whom they have taken several hundred dollars. The fake Duke and King pretend, on another occasion, to be the genuine uncles of three poor girls whose father has just died and left them a considerable sum of money. Huck feels sorry for the girls and exposes the fake uncles.

Shortly afterward the King, having learned that Jim is a runaway slave, turns him in to a Mrs. Phelps for the reward. Huck goes to Mrs. Phelps, who is in reality Tom Sawyer's Aunt Sally, and pretends to be Tom Sawyer. The real Tom arrives and the two boys concoct an elaborate plot to aid Jim to escape. Finally, after Tom had been shot in the leg in the escape effort, it is revealed that Mrs. Watson, Jim's owner, had died and left Jim free in her will.

Back home again Huck learns that his father had died and that his money was safely in the hands of Judge Thatcher. When Huck Finn finds that Tom's Aunt Sally is anxious to take him in order to try to civilize him, he is tempted to run away again. He had had one taste of "sivilizing" with the Widow Douglas and one such horrible experience should be enough for a boy of free will.

12. William Dean Howells: *A Modern Instance* and *The Rise of Silas Lapham*

Page 118. Howells, a pioneer in American realism, wrote many novels to bear out his theory that the novel should present real life faithfully. His novels, though short of a full and authentic realism, are pioneer works of American literature in the analysis of character and in the presentation of social problems.

A Modern Instance (1881) studies the problem of divorce and of the flaws of character that lead to unhappiness in marriage. The Hubbards' marriage takes place in a country town in Maine, where Bartley Hubbard, vain, selfish, and unscrupulous, marries Marcia, a passionately jealous country girl. Bartley, a journalist, takes his bride to Boston. Gradually Bartley's carefree manner, his loose business practices, and his philandering begin to bring out Marcia's chief character flaw, jealousy, and the rift between the couple becomes wider. Finally, Bartley leaves his wife and child, after Marcia learns that her husband was responsible for the degraded condition of Hannah Morrison, a girl of whom she had been jealous years before. Hartley disappears and is not heard from for two years. When he finally turns up in an Indiana town and sues for divorce, Marcia's father, a judge, succeeds in getting the decree set aside. Later Bartley is killed in a brawl in Arizona. A young minister from one of Boston's older families, Ben Halleck, had been in love with Marcia for years. The implication at the end of the book is that Marcia and Halleck are about to come to a decision that they are now morally free to marry.

The Rise of Silas Lapham (1885), the most popular novel of Howells, is the study of the moral regeneration of a crude, self-made man, who comes to dwell among the genteel Brahmin society of Boston. Colonel Silas Lapham, born on a Vermont farm, has become wealthy as a paint manufacturer. He comes to Boston with his family and persuades his wife and two daughters to take their places in Boston society. The Coreys, a poor but high-born Brahmin family, are forced to accept financial aid from Silas. Young Tom Corey and Penelope, Lapham's older daughter, are in love but Penelope refuses him when the immature and flighty younger daughter makes a scene, thinking Corey was in love with her. The Lapham and Corey families are both angered at the scandalous scene and Silas, drunk, reveals his crude upbringing at a dinner party. He has been speculating heavily, and when forced to lose his fortune or enter into a dishonest business scheme, his innate honesty causes him to face ruin. This is the making of Silas Lapham, who sacrifices wealth and social position rather than compromise his sense of integrity and fair play. The Brahmin Corey so admires the honest qualities of the Laphams that he encourages young Tom and Penelope to marry. They go to New Mexico to live in an atmosphere where their social distinctions will not cause them to face embarrassment and unhappiness.

13. Stephen Crane: *The Red Badge of Courage* (1895)

Page 136. Crane's novel attracted a great deal of attention around the turn of the century in both America and England. It was a penetrating study of the mental reactions of a young soldier who faced battle for the first time. Crane, only twenty-four, had derived his knowledge of war from his reading of European novels with naturalistic leanings, such as Tolstoy's *War and Peace.*

The novel follows young Henry Fleming, a farm boy from New York filled with patriotism, who volunteers for action in the Union army. Filled with visions of heroic actions, young Fleming swaggers about and brags of deep patriotism. He is thrust into action in the Battle of Chancellorsville and is overcome with panic. He runs from the field. He is beset with all the mental torture of the coward who faces certain death as he runs about, trying to avoid the battle but seeming to encounter only situations that increase his fear. Finally, faced with the sight of his wounded comrades, and having received a scratch himself, his fear vanishes and an indomitable courage enters his spirit. He snatches up his company's colors and leads a successful charge against the enemy. When the battle is over he feels serene and quiet in his new-found manliness: "He had rid himself of the red sickness of battle. The sultry nightmare was in the past. He had been an animal, blistering and sweating in the heat and pain of war. He now turned with a lover's thirst to images of tranquil skies."

14. Frank Norris: _McTeague_ (1899)

Page 137. This novel was a pioneer in a long line of American fictional works during the first decades of the present century which followed the French deterministic theory of realistic fiction—a naturalism in which man is a victim of his inherited evil traits and has little choice of freedom of will to rise above the sordid circumstances in which he finds himself. It was the first notable example of our literature's era of "brutal" novels.

McTeague, born in a mining camp to a ne'er-do-well father, is given educational opportunities by his mother in the hope that her son would rise above the sordid conditions of his boyhood surroundings. The boy becomes a dentist in San Francisco. His friend Marcus Schouler introduces McTeague to his cousin, Trina Sieppe, with whom he is in love. McTeague courts and wins the lovely Trina, who has just won $5,000 on a lottery ticket. He is angered that Trina invests the money instead of spending it on luxuries for the two of them. Marcus, more and more angered at the loss of what might have been his fortune, provokes McTeague repeatedly and, at a picnic, in a supposedly friendly wrestling match, bites off the lobe of McTeague's ear. McTeague retaliates by breaking his former friend's arm.

Marcus succeeds in getting McTeague barred from his profession for falsifying his dental license. Gradually Trina is becoming more miserly and McTeague more surly and violent as a result of the loss of his dental practice. They become poverty-stricken and take a miserable flat in the slums. McTeague finally murders Trina to get her savings and flees across Death Valley. Schouler catches up with him and is killed, but not before he succeeds in handcuffing their wrists together. McTeague starves to death from thirst, trying to drag the dead body across the burning waste.

Page 138. _The Octopus_ and _The Pit_ (1901 and 1903) are the first two of a projected trilogy of novels about wheat. Here Norris has produced two of the best of our early social novels and forerunners of the "muckraking" school. In _The Octopus_ the wheat farmers of California are shown to be controlled by the monopolistic railroad interests, necessary for the moving of the wheat to the eastern markets. All of the many characters that move in and out of the novel are but instruments in the hands of Norris to show how the railroad interests rob the farmers of their profits, principally through control of local law-making bodies. Behrman, the railroad agent and the symbol of the evil that threatens the producers of the necessary crop, is finally crushed under an accidental wheat slide as Magnus Derrick, the leader of the farmers, is finally ruined and forced to seek employment with the railroad.

The Pit, the stronger of the two novels, is concerned with speculation in wheat on the Chicago Board of Trade. Laura Dearborn counts among her suitors Sheldon Corthell, a young and wealthy artist, and Curtis Jadwin, a seemingly honest and powerful capitalist. She marries Jadwin but feels neglected as her husband devotes more and more of his energies to money-making. At times she is tempted to go away with Sheldon but comes to realize that she loves her husband in spite of his neglect of her.

Jadwin spends all of his time at "the pit," where speculation takes place in wheat. The gambling fever seizes him and he makes rapid gains and finally comes to have a "corner," or complete control, of the wheat market. An unpredictable bumper crop of wheat in the West ruins him financially. Meanwhile Laura has decided to run away with Corthell. When Jadwin returns home in physical collapse she stays with him and the couple, all their properties sold to satisfy creditors, leave for the West to build life anew.

15. Theodore Dreiser: *An American Tragedy* (1925)

Page 139. This long novel represents the height of popularity of the naturalistic technique in the American novel. Until after 1930 it was hailed by many critics as the great American classic. Today this early enthusiasm has cooled, and although the novel is still recognized as a powerful social document on inequality of social opportunity and lack of privilege of an era of American life, it is considered a rather disarranged mass of reportorial detail and little likely to become one of America's classics of fine literature. The story is based on a New York murder case.

Clyde Griffiths grows up in poverty in a family of evangelists. Revolted by drab existence he becomes a hotel bellboy. His popularity and increasing tips go to his head and he becomes dissipated. One night, in a borrowed car with a loose girl for whom he had just bought an expensive coat, he runs over a little girl and flees to Chicago to escape the consequences. There he meets his wealthy uncle, Samuel Griffiths, who runs a collar factory in New York state. The uncle is attracted by the boy's polished manners and takes him into his factory. There Clyde forms an intimate relationship with Roberta Allen, an employee in the department he heads.

About this time he falls in love with Sondra Finchley, wealthy and of a leading family in local society. Suddenly Roberta discovers herself to be pregnant and demands that Clyde marry her. He begins to form plans to do away with her and begs her to go with him to a nearby lake resort. They row out into the lake. Clyde's courage deserts him. The girl rises in the boat and it tips over, throwing them both into the water. Although he could have rescued her, Clyde swam to shore alone, leaving Roberta to drown. He is accused of murder and is brought to trial. After a long trial Clyde is convicted and sentenced to death. The novel ends as the young man is electrocuted after signing a statement that he had repented his sins.

16. Brief Digests of Other Famed 20th Century Naturalistic Novels

Page 140. The century has produced hundreds of novels which have followed the technique of French naturalism with its deterministic leanings, highlighting brute animal nature, the futile struggle of man with his circumstances, and the hopeless and pessimistic approach to life. These novels are filled with sharp, realistic detail. The naturalistic novel passed its peak of popularity in the 20's but notable examples are being produced past mid-century. Following are very brief digests of the principal elements in the plots of a few of these novels employing the technique of naturalism.

Jack London (1876-1916)

The Call of the Wild (1903) is the story of the dog, Buck, half St. Bernard and half Scotch shepherd, who is stolen from his home in California and shipped to the Klondike and cruelly whipped and trained to be a sledge dog. After a cruel struggle with the other dogs Buck becomes the leader of the team. When his master is murdered by Indians, Buck responds to the primitive instincts which have been aroused in his nature and goes into the wilderness to fight his way to the leadership of a wolf pack.

The Sea Wolf (1904). Humphrey Van Weyden, a wealthy play boy, is picked up by a sealing ship when the ferryboat on which he was crossing San Francisco Bay is rammed. The captain is Wolf Larson, ruthless and cruel. Before they reach the sealing grounds Van Weyden, now hardened by the brutality of Larson, has witnessed many deeds of almost inhuman cruelty on the part of the captain. A girl, Maude Brewster, is rescued from a wrecked ship and becomes the object of Larson's attentions. When the ship, *Ghost,* is wrecked Van Weyden and the girl escape to an island. They return to the hulk of the ship, now washed up to the beach, and find Larson, still alive and blind. He tries to kill Humphrey but becomes paralyzed and unable to move. At last the lovers are rescued and make their way back to civilization. *The Sea Wolf* is a high point in American literature's wave of "brutal" novels.

F. Scott Fitzgerald (1896-1940)

The Great Gatsby (1925) is concerned with the disillusion and debauched life of the era following World War I. James Gatz, from miserable surroundings, has risen by sinister business dealings to great wealth. Now masquerading under the name of Jay Gatsby, Gatz lives mysteriously in a mansion on Long Island where he entertains lavishly with his ill-gotten gains. Gatsby persuades his former mistress, Daisy, to live with him again. Daisy's husband had as his mistress, Myrtle Wilson. Daisy, driving Gatsby's car, fatally injures Myrtle. Myrtle's garageman husband is told by Daisy, who is now back in the good graces of her husband, that Gatsby had killed his wife. The garageman shoots Gatsby and then himself. The "great" Gatsby's funeral was only attended by his one friend, Nick, his aged father and one curiosity seeker.

John Dos Passos (1896-)

U. S. A. (1938) is composed of a trilogy of novels which tell the story of the United States in the early century, dwelling upon the disillusionment and sense of futility that governed the lives of the many characters that weave in and out of the three novels. *The 42nd Parallel* (1930) attacks American commercialism through character studies of various types of disillusioned Americans, all treated with the pessimistic bias of naturalism. *1919* (1932) continues to weave in new characters and incidents from the World War I period, the entire pattern being treated from the definite Marxist leanings of the author. The Big Money (1936) carries the author's gigantic study of American society into the interwar period. The only character treated here who is "successful" is one who allies himself wholeheartedly with the opportunistic standards of the era.

This trilogy, covering an enormous sweep of the American scene and employing a variety of experimental fictional devices, is the author's attempt to penetrate into the social pattern of the first three decades of the 20th century. His major theme is degradation of character as influenced by crass commercialism, which Dos Passos considered to be the rotten core causing the whole social structure to decay.

James T. Farrell (1904-   )

Studs Lonigan is the collective title of Farrell's trilogy of novels: *Young Lonigan* (1932), *The Young Manhood of Studs Lonigan* (1934), and *Judgement Day* (1935). Farrell, a disciple of Dreiser, gives us a highly detailed account of the gradual degeneration of young Studs Lonigan, a healthy and decent lad, raised in the slums of Chicago's East Side. Studs gradually gives way to his sordid environment and, by the time he is fifteen, his ideas are sex, gangsterism, and drink. His early Catholic religious training has not been strong enough to combat the foul circumstances surrounding him.

As Studs reaches young manhood, the incidents in Farrell's detailed study give way to a more penetrating analysis of Studs' mental reactions as he yields more and more to the environmental influences which are undermining his character. He is acutely conscious of his burden of sin but this seems to drive him further in the mire. He increases his drinking, and though he has managed to escape serious clashes with the law, he continues in the same gang spirit to flaunt social decency.

By the time he is 27, Studs has become depressed and morose. He feels that life has passed him by. His heart is troubling him and he feels lonely. After an affair with Catherine Banahan, he asks her to marry him in the hope that he can begin a clean life and wash his soul of sin. Events, however, continue to bring failure to him. He dies, unemployed and with a pregnant wife, during the depression.

Ernest Hemingway (1898-   )

Hemingway, the Nobel Prize winner for literature in 1954, has alternated between the "brutal" story, the cynical analytical technique of naturalism, and pure poetic romance.

The Sun Also Rises (1926) concerns a group of American and English expatriates who wander over the face of Europe seeking an escape from their terrible disillusionment brought on by the war. The surface story is one of violence as the typical "lost generation" group, one by one, deteriorates spiritually and physically. But underlying the story is Hemingway's attempt to formulate a positive attitude.

A Farewell to Arms (1929) contains the beautiful and poignant love story of an American ambulance driver and an English nurse. It also shows the shattering effects of the war upon individuals and the succession of disastrous events that finally end in the death of the wife in childbirth and the utter completion of the disillusionment of the hero, Frederic Henry.

For Whom the Bell Tolls (1940) is a powerful account of the Spanish Civil War. Robert Jordan is an American, fighting with the International Brigade on the side of the Spanish Loyalists. All the characters and events are developed around one small mission: the blowing up of a bridge to prevent its use by the enemy. The bridge is successfully blown up but it is evident that this small bridge is no longer of any use to the enemy. Jordan and his small group are killed. Again the surface incidents are violent and lead to the feeling of pessimistic futility. But, again, Hemingway attempts to leave the impression that such local struggles are unimportant in a longer view toward freedom and unity among the peoples of the world.

The Old Man and the Sea (1952) portrays the pride that can come to the spirit of a man who fails in outward accomplishment but who has given his best efforts in the struggle. It is the story of the luckless old Cuban fisherman who finally succeeds in making a big catch, a huge marlin. He lashes the marlin to the side of his little boat and his long pull to shore is the record of the old man's struggle against the sharks who are continuously tearing away pieces of the fish. When he reaches port only the skeleton of the marlin is left but the old man, exhausted by his epic struggle, sleeps peacefully, dreaming of his success in securing the greatest marlin that he had seen in his lifetime as a fisherman. In this novelette Hemingway shows that he has abandoned the deterministic bias of French naturalism, but has retained the reportorial and detailed approach of the naturalists.

Erskine Caldwell (1903-   )

Caldwell became famous with _Tobacco Road (1932)_ and has followed his success with many novels and short stories dealing with the ignorance and squalor of the sharecroppers of Georgia. Caldwell deals with his sordid subjects with humor and a simple and lucid prose style. _Tobacco Road_ is composed with episodes in the life of Jeeter Lester and his miserable and half-starving wife and fifteen children. Jeeter refuses to leave his barren land and tries continuously to borrow money to plant cotton. He and his wife, Ada, die in the old shack when it burns to the ground one night.

Another popular Caldwell account of Georgia is _God's Little Acre (1933)_ in which Ty Ty Walden, a mountaineer, spends his time digging for gold. The episodes of the book are all cut from the same cloth, a series of sordid events involving greed, loose morals, and violent deaths. Ty Ty has dedicated the proceeds of one acre to the church but continues to shift the location of the compromised acre when he wishes to dig for gold in the particular spot he had previously set aside.

Thomas Wolfe (1900-1938)

Wolfe's best novels are bitter and pessimistic portrayals of life in the South. The details are highly autobiographical. _Look Homeward, Angel (1929)_ concerns Oliver Gant, a stonecutter who is the prototype of Wolfe's own father, a stonecutter in North Carolina. The novel carries Eugene Gant from birth to young manhood and a decision to leave the sordid environment of his childhood. _Of Time and the River (1935)_ finds Eugene at Harvard, relates his sordid love affairs, and ends with his wandering through Europe, aimless and disillusioned. _The Web and the Rock (1939)_ and _You Can't Go Home Again (1940)_ change the central character to George Weber, a struggling writer, but the incidents and the atmosphere of the books continue in the same vein as in the earlier novels: restless wandering, fruitless love affairs, and a growing disillusionment with nations and individuals. The four books are considered to be a detailed psychological self-penetration into the hopeless spirit of the author himself.

William Faulkner (1897-   )

Faulkner, winner of a Nobel Prize in 1950, also analyzed deterioration of character in the South in his best novels, although more objectively than Wolfe. *The Sound and the Fury* (1929), perhaps his best known novel, continues the bitter picture of moral decay among Southern aristocratic families that Faulkner had exploited in his earlier novels. The technique is unusual in that the story is partly told by an idiot member of the Compson family. All the family members are subnormal in one direction or another.

Faulkner's later novels continue the same pessimistic portrayals, employing various experimental techniques. *Intruder in the Dust* (1948) shows that Faulkner, like Hemingway, is becoming more optimistic in his outlook. The story itself concerns the murder of a white man and the imminent lynching of Lucas Beauchamp, a Negro. Lucas has white friends who hurry to find evidence to prove the Negro innocent before the mob can reach him. Lucas is saved and the guilty brother of the murdered man is caught. During the story, Faulkner projects his theory that the hope of the South lies in its educated youth.

Richard Wright (1909-   )

Wright, generally considered to be America's leading Negro writer, has been concerned in most of his writing with the folklore and accumulated culture of the Negro race. His famed naturalist contribution is *Native Son* (1940). This novel tells the story of Bigger Thomas, a Negro born in the Chicago slums. Thomas is embittered as he struggles to compete in a white man's world. Finally, he seems to be gaining some status when he goes to work for a wealthy realtor. He is patronized by the Dalton family and, confused and drunk, he kills the daughter. Before he is caught, he also kills his Negro sweetheart, Bessie. He concludes before his execution that the circumstances in his environment could never have been altered.

James Jones (1921-   ) and **John O'Hara** (1905-   )

From Here to Eternity (1951) of Jones and *Ten North Frederick* (1955) of O'Hara are ample proof that the popularity of the naturalistic novel has not died completely in the United States past mid-century. Both novels are distinguished for their wealth of exact detail and psychological penetration into the lives of frustrated individuals.

From Here to Eternity, a controversial novel, is an analysis of depravity at all levels of regular army life in Hawaii, just prior to the Pearl Harbor attack. It has shocked many readers with its exact reproduction of the habits and speech of soldiers.

Ten North Frederick is O'Hara's sixth novel and most critics consider it his best. In it the author is concerned with the analysis of the character of Joseph Chapin, Gibbsville's leading citizen, now dead. To the world Chapin had lived an exemplary life and had accumulated an honest fortune. O'Hara proceeds to destroy the illusion by moving realistically back to analyze the ambitions, the failures, the frustration, and the sordidness of the inner lives of the family that had built the house at 10 North Frederick and had won social approval.

17. Upton Sinclair: *The Jungle* (1906)

Sinclair is the foremost pioneer in the branch of the American social novel that has acquired the name of "muckraking" school. Most of the novels in this classification employed to a considerable degree the naturalistic technique, especially the element of detailed and factual reporting. The "muckraking" school of novelists concentrated their attention upon exposés of the corruption and evil practices which writers considered to be present in many American institutions at the turn of the century.

The Jungle is a story of the immigrant workers in the stockyards and slaughterhouses of Chicago. The story begins with the young and strong Jurgis Rudkus who comes to America from Lithuania with high hopes of making his fortune. From the first Jurgis finds that he is swindled by his employers in the meat packing plant. The working conditions are horrible. At the end of a year his disillusionment is complete but he has no choice but to continue. He marries his betrothed from the old country. Finally all the members of the little Lithuanian group have sickened and died. After his wife's death, Jurgis takes to drink and joins the socialists. The sensation created by Sinclair's book caused Congress to enact new legislation regulating the meat packing industry.

18. Other Representative Early-Century Social Novels

Winston Churchill (1871-1947)

Page 144. In 1906, after writing a number of popular historical romances, Churchill turned his facile fictional style to the analysis of flaws present in the American system. In *Coniston (1906)* Churchill studies Jethro Bass, a rude local political boss of the last century, and how he rises from local to state-wide power by favoring the large railroad interests. *The Inside of the Cup (1913)* concerns the control of religion by capitalist interests. In it John Hodder, a fearless and idealistic minister, is deprived of his post because he has dared to criticize a wealthy member who is responsible for blocking improvement of slum conditions for his own gain. Churchill's other novels, as the two mentioned here, are better written and are more intellectually conceived than the vast majority of those of the "muckraking" school.

Robert Herrick (1868-1938)

Herrick, like Churchill, brought a keen sense of intellectual observation to his novels. Also, like Churchill, he is concerned with exposés of the twisted ethics of institutions rather than some specific institution or person. *The Common Lot (1904)* is a fine study of a young architect who lets himself be bribed to erect buildings for his contractor friend which do not meet building specifications. He builds a rickety hotel, in which he has been given an interest, which burns, killing eight people, and finds his career ruined. *The Memoirs of an American Citizen (1905)* is a thorough analysis of the career of an American businessman who climbs over his weaker competitors by unscrupulous methods to gain control over the meat packing industry. His wealth and power gain him the election to the U. S. Senate and he goes to Washington to attempt to promote laws favorable to monopolistic business interests.

Jack London (1876-1916) and Ernest Poole (1880-1950)

London and Poole approached the subject of economic revolution. They both believed in a radical form of socialism (with organized workers in complete control of government and the instruments of production and distribution) but their approach was from widely varying viewpoints. London was sympathetic with Marxist socialism, as he was also sympathetic with the "superman" philosophy of Nietzsche and approaches his social novels from an emotional and sympathetic attitude rather than from knowledge. Poole, on the other hand, studied carefully our economic past and present and makes his analysis of the future ideal from more logical bases of evolution.

The Iron Heel (1907) is London's outstanding "prophetic" novel, in which he shows the middle and lower economic classes fighting to survive under an oppressive capitalistic dictatorship. Labor and middle-class security seem to be almost extinct when the rather superhuman social revolutionary, Ernest Everhard, rises and leads his group to victory.

The Harbor (1915) of Poole follows the career of Bill, son of a small shipowner. After toying with the idea of becoming an author through college and an extended stay in Paris, Bill returns to New York and marries Eleanore, the daughter of an industrial engineer. His father-in-law converts him to the viewpoint of big business and they work upon a plan for organizing the harbor facilities into an efficient and unified industrial port. Through his friend, Joe Kramer, a labor leader who had married his sister, Bill comes to see that the plan will create a monopoly and destroy the rights of the workers. He turns his energies as a writer toward a precisely opposite point of view than the one he had expressed in his earlier writings.

19. William Allen White and Booth Tarkington: Defenders of the American Small Town

Page 145. White's *A Certain Rich Man* (1909) is a representative novel of the group of writers who defended American village life in romantic-realistic stories which have happy endings and justify the life and ideals of the small town. Here a local boy, John Barclay, becomes the town banker in Sycamore Ridge, Kansas, and gradually gains monopolistic control over

local politics and transportation facilities. He also manufactures
inferior flour and sells polluted water to the city. His wife dies
of typhoid and causes a complete change of conscience in the
leader. He restores the savings of those he has swindled, gives
up his mills, and permits his daughter to marry the poor man
she has loved. He drowns in a successful attempt to rescue
Trixie Lee, a prostitute.

The Gentleman from Indiana (1899) is typical of many
Tarkington novels which, in a semirealistic vein, extol the virtues of solid material success and social approval in the small
town where the major virtues of American democracy reside.
In this story John Harkness prefers to become a small town
newspaper editor rather than to go on to greatness in the outer
world. He wins friends and the admiration of the "best" people
by his manliness and his fearless attacks on local political corruption and petty gangsterism. After many displays of bravery
and fearlessness, during which he almost suffers loss of life, he
marries the girl of his choice and is rewarded by the local
citizenry with a nomination to Congress.

20. Sinclair Lewis and Sherwood Anderson:
Attackers of the American Small Town

Pages 145-147. The attack upon the idyllic concept of small
town life was begun as early as 1883 with Ed Howe's _The Story
of a Country Town_ and passed another landmark with _Spoon
River Anthology,_ the famed collection of naturalistic portraits
in verse of small-town people, which appeared in 1915. But it
was after 1918, when the early muckraking movement had
passed its peak of popularity, that a concerted attack was begun
upon the American village. Some of the century's best creative
writers produced their best works in this particular phase of
American realism devoted to the social novel.

Main Street (1920), a satirically realistic portrait of Gopher
Prairie, Minnesota, brought Lewis wide acclaim both in the
United States and in Europe. There is little plot. Carol Mil-
ford, a librarian, married Dr. Will Kennicott and comes to
Gopher Prairie. She cannot adjust her progressive and intellectual spirit to the drab dullness and lack of culture which she
finds in the smug little community. She tries to organize a
community theater in her first attempt to do something about
the cultural level of the town. She is met with the chill of oppo-

sition. She leaves her husband and takes a job in Washington, D. C. After two years she permits her husband to come for her and returns to the pettiness of Gopher Prairie, now somewhat resigned to take up the dull routine of spiritual stagnation.

Babbitt (1922) concentrates upon the character of the middle-class successful business man. George F. Babbitt is a prosperous real estate man of Zenith, a go-getter type, conventional and stereotyped in all of his relations with society. At the age of forty-six he comes to a realization of the dreariness of his existence and tries to change himself. He becomes radical in his views and openly has an affair with one of his female clients. The illness of his wife and the chilling attitude which his fellow townsmen are taking toward him cause him to drop back into his former comfortable, if dull, existence. However, as the book ends he encourages his son in his intention to leave school and elope.

Arrowsmith (1925), perhaps the third most famous novel of Sinclair Lewis, discusses the smug complacency and commercialism that the author finds in the medical profession. After years of attempting to maintain his ideals in the face of the publicity-minded and money-conscious superiors he must work with in clinics and hospitals, Martin Arrowsmith finds peace only by retiring to a lonely Vermont farm where he can continue his research and manufacture a serum which he has perfected.

Winesburg, Ohio (1919) of Sherwood Anderson is a collection of 23 stories which created a sensation in the literary world, second only to that accorded to the _Spoon River Anthology_ of Masters in 1915. Anderson employs the naturalistic technique and probes beneath the surface of the lives of frustrated individuals, caught in the stultifying and conventional morality of a small town. He describes his characters as "grotesques." One of the outstanding portrayals is simply called "Hands," dealing with the teacher Wing Biddlebaum and his innocent fondness for caressing living things. His almost absent-minded touching of one of his students finally causes him to be driven from the town as immoral. "Godliness" concerns the religious fanaticism of the old farmer, Jesse Bentley. To escape her father's domination his daughter leaves the farm to marry a second time, leaving her little son. When the boy is fifteen the old man, who had prayed for years for the destruction of his Philistine neighbors, is killed by a stone from the slingshot of his grandson, David.

21.   John Steinbeck: *The Grapes of Wrath* (1939)

Page 148. This novel, written in an almost poetic prose, is the classic social novel to be written about the economic depression of the 30's. Steinbeck, himself bitterly indignant at the miserable conditions to be found among the migrant farm workers of the large areas of his native state, California, has given American literature its most beautifully written social novel.

The Joad family, desperately miserable in the Oklahoma Dust Bowl, set out for California in an old dilapidated car. The story of the migration is superbly told. Grampa, lusty and foul-mouthed, and Granma, religious to the point of fanaticism, die on the road. Finally, the "Oakies" reach the San Joaquin Valley and their disillusionment begins. They are hounded by officers and labor contractors. They are herded into cramped and ill-smelling quarters and the men are paid miserably small wages for long hours of hard work. During a strike Tom Joad kills a man among the vigilantes who are attempting to break up the strike and has to leave the family. Steinbeck injects shocking scenes into the book, the most controversial being the one in which the daughter, Rose of Sharon, having given birth to a dead baby, nourishes a dying man with her milk. Facing starvation, Ma Joad, always the optimistic member of the clan, says: "We ain't gonna die out. People is goin' on—changin' a little, maybe, but goin' right on."

22.   Edith Wharton: *The House of Mirth* (1905) and *Ethan Frome* (1911)

Page 151. Though Mrs. Wharton's principal novels are of "genteel" social groups in New York, Boston, or Europe, her main interest is not in the study of the bases for the conventions and customs of these groups but in the psychological and spiritual reactions of her characters to their environment. Mrs. Wharton is not a social novelist and shows little interest in reform; her desire is to present faithfully the inner conflicts of individuals and to create an artistic and integrated work. She succeeds admirably in both purposes.

The House of Mirth gave her a wide reputation and is typical of the majority of her work. Lily Bart is 29 and unmarried in spite of her beauty and the refined manners of her aristocratic

New York ancestry. An orphan, she lives with her aunt whose stern principles have resulted in a quiet and monotonous existence for the girl. At a party Lily loses heavily at cards and permits the host, the wealthy Gus Trevor, to pay her bills. When Gus later makes advances upon her honor she realizes that she had compromised herself by accepting the money. While trying to decide whether to marry Simon Rosedale, a rich Jew, or the man she does love, Laurence Selden, who has no money, she is invited on a yachting trip to the Mediterranean. She is accused by the host's wife of being her husband's mistress. Though innocent, appearances cause her to be snubbed by New York society and virtually disinherited by her aunt. She commits suicide just as Selden arrives to clear her honor by marrying her. Lily Bart, who had done no evil act but who had violated the artificial moral code of her social group, paid with a broken spirit and, finally, death.

Ethan Frome (1911), representing a departure from Mrs. Wharton's novels of high society, is a novelette depicting a grim series of incidents on a bleak New England farm. Ethan, from sheer loneliness, marries Zenobia, seven years older than he and a whining hypochondriac. Ethan finds that he is more lonely than ever under the domineering and complaining Zenobia. When Mattie Silver, Zenobia's pretty cousin, comes to live with them, the older woman becomes intensely jealous of the friendship between Ethan and Mattie. She finally orders Mattie to leave. As Ethan takes Mattie to the station, he realizes he loves her. She accepts his love but, as their situation seems hopeless, they decide to suicide and take off down a steep hill and steer their sled into an elm tree. They do not die but are crippled and spend their lives under the dominating care of Zenobia. As in Mrs. Wharton's other novels, circumstances have brought the natural inclinations of individuals into conformance with the social conventions.

23.   **Willa Cather:** _My Ántonia_ (1918) and _Death Comes for the Archbishop_ (1927)

Page 151. Like Edith Wharton, Miss Cather was an excellent prose stylist. Unlike Mrs. Wharton, her novels are less satirical in her approach to the realities of life. Both women are less than true realists, however, since they concentrate upon the inner life of their characters and tend to poetize and refine the more brutal and violent aspects of life.

My Ántonia is the story of the hardships and joys that come into the life of Ántonia Shimerda, the daughter of Bohemian immigrants who take up the hard pioneer life of the Nebraska prairies. Their land is bad and Mr. Shimerda, who is a dreamy and music-loving man, suicides in the face of the hardships. Ántonia takes over the burden of the household, doing not only most of the work at home but hires out as a maid in the town. The simple and trusting country girl is deceived and abandoned by a railway employee and returns home with her child. The story is told by Jim Burden, a childhood friend of Ántonia. When he returns to the little Nebraska community twenty years later he finds Ántonia, comfortably married to the friendly and industrious Anton Cuzak and raising a large family. She still has her strength and pioneer courage to face into the future. As Miss Cather puts it: "She was a rich mine of life, like the founders of early races."

Death Comes for the Archbishop is a story of the early pioneering efforts of the Catholic Church in the area that was later to become New Mexico. The story follows the missionary work of Bishop Jean Latour and his vicar, Joseph Vaillant. Friends since childhood in France, the two missionaries combine the qualities of intellect and courage of Latour and the practicality of his vicar to overcome the suspicion of the Indians and the opposition of the Spanish priests to organize the new diocese of New Mexico. Vaillant finally goes to Colorado and Archbishop Latour dies, convinced at last that his forty-year task had been entirely worth while. The strength of the novel lies in its poetic prose and its skillful delineation of the characters of the two holy men, one intellectual and skeptical and the other doggedly practical and faithful.

24. Booth Tarkington: _The Magnificent Ambersons_ (1918)

Page 152. This novel is simply one of many novels of the century which lightly touch a surface reality and depend a great deal upon sentimentality and emotionalized situations for their popularity. Some critics have called the Tarkington type of novel "middle-class" fiction and the term can well be interpreted to mean a novel aimed at a large mass of readers and one which is subliterary but does not descend quite to the level of sensationalism and melodramatic incidents. Tarkington, one of our most popular novelists of the century, had a great deal of ability at characterization, especially in analysis of the foibles and personality traits of women.

The Magnificent Ambersons, a Pulitzer Prize winner, concentrates attention upon Isabel, the daughter of old Major Amberson, who made a fortune in the Gilded Age period and had established his family in a secure position in an Indiana town. Isabel quarreled with her sweetheart, Eugene Morgan, and entered into a loveless marriage with Wilbur Minafer. Years later Morgan, a widower, returns with his daughter Lucy. Isabel has a son, George. The children fall in love and the parents feel their old affection returning. When Isabel's husband dies, George becomes possessive toward her and prevents her remarriage to Eugene Morgan. After the mother's death, George finds himself penniless and friendless. Morgan, meanwhile, has become wealthy and socially prominent. George is injured in an accident and Eugene comes to his aid. George and Lucy's father are reconciled by their memories of the woman who had been so dear to both of them.

25. Representative Historical Novels with Regional Interest

Page 154. Beginning with the local colorists of the late 19th century, regionalism (the extensive use of the customs, language, and characteristics of a particular area of the United States) has been one of the strongest native elements to establish itself as a continuing force in our literature. In this century many of our finest writers, whatever their literary techniques, have been identified, in at least a part of their work, with particular regions. (See above digests of works by William Allen White, Booth Tarkington, Sinclair Lewis, Sherwood Anderson, John Steinbeck, Edith Wharton, Willa Cather, Erskine Caldwell, Thomas Wolfe, William Faulkner.)

In this century the popularity of the regional novel, treating the contemporary scene, has been equaled (or surpassed) only by a form closely allied to it: the historical novel, which, almost invariably, emphasizes the same regional aspects as the contemporary type, only with a shift to some period in the country's past. On the higher levels of artistic creation the regional novel, dealing with the contemporary scene, has won much greater critical esteem than the corresponding levels of historical fiction, one reason perhaps being the near impossibility for even the most scrupulous novelist to keep an aura of romantic glamour from the fictional treatment of the great and near-great events and personages of our national history. On a subliterary level, in this century, the historical novel has won greater reading audiences than any other types, except perhaps the detective story, the western, and the "confessions" type of feminine fiction.

Below are short digests of representative historical novels of recent years, all of which show a regional interest in addition to the main historical narrative. Their fate, as enduring classics of American literature, is dubious, but their popularity in this period, in terms of numbers of readers, is fact. The greatest blossoming of historical novels, dealing with the U. S. scene, which would seem to have the most enduring values, were written from about 1925 to The World War II period.

To Have and To Hold (1900) by Mary Johnston. Along with Winston Churchill, Mary Johnston was one of the early pioneers of the historical novel, having written some fifteen idealized romances of life in various periods of the history of Virginia. After Johnston and Churchill (*The Crossing* (1904), dealing with the early Kentucky and Tennessee frontier and the part it played in the Revolution, is considered his best effort) the historical novel was to wait almost twenty years until its next, and greatest, flowering.

To Have and To Hold deals with the lovely ward of the English king, Jocelyn Leigh, who escapes a marriage to the hateful Lord Carnal by concealing herself aboard a shipload of English women who are going to the Virginia colony in 1621 to becomes wives of the settlers. Ralph Percy, aristocratic and adventurous, selects her by lot and they are married. Love is growing between them as Lord Carnal arrives and Percy foils all of his enemy's foul schemes to do away with him. An order arrives from England for the arrest of Jocelyn and Ralph and they flee in a small boat and are cast up on an island. The island proves to be a stronghold of pirates, and Percy, pretending to be a buccaneer himself, assumes command of the band. He refuses to lead the band against an English ship and his crew mutinies. After another shipwreck, the couple are rescued, only to find that Percy is accused of piracy and is about to be hanged. Jocelyn saves him by convincing the authorities that he is innocent. Finally, after adventures among Indians in Virgina and the death by suicide of the evil Lord Carnal, the couple return to England, now free to enjoy their happiness together.

Giants in the Earth (1927) by Ole Rölvaag, a Norwegian

immigrant, is the epic saga of pioneer life in South Dakota. Considered to be one of the most authentic of the century's historical novels, Rölvaag's account is factual and sympathetic. Per Hansa had followed the sea in his native Norway. In America he experiences the hard life of wresting a bare living from the soil. He is devoted to the land but his wife is ill suited to the hardships of pioneer life. She longs for Norway and Per is gradually changed from his optimistic attitude to one of stubborn silence by her lamentations. His wife finally turns to religion and becomes fanatic. One night during a blizzard, when a neighbor is near death in their house, Per's wife nags him into going out into the storm to seek a minister for she considers the last rites to be more important than the risk of her husband's life. Per is swallowed up by the blizzard and is never heard from again.

The Great Meadow (1930) by Elizabeth M. Roberts is a story of pioneer life in Kentucky in the 1770's. Diony Hall, daughter of a scholarly Virginia farmer, is 17 when she marries the lanky Berk Jarvis and begins her trek into the wilderness toward the frontier of Kentucky. The novel is a study of women's part in the conquering of the western frontier. After months of hard work the Jarvis family is almost deprived of its women when Diony and Elvira, Berk's mother, are gathering nuts outside the stockade as a party of Shawnee Indians fall upon them. Elvira is scalped and Diony is beaten and left as dead. After Berk leads a raiding party against the Indians and is reported dead, Diony finally marries Evan, a hunter. Diony, at the end of three years has two children, one by Evan and one by Berk. Berk, who had been a captive of the Indians, escapes and returns home. Evan again takes up his solitary life as a hunter as Diony returns to her true love. Different than most historical novelists, Mrs. Roberts employs the stream-of-consciousness technique and follows the thoughts of the heroine during much of the novel.

Drums Along the Mohawk (1936) by Walter D. Edmonds concentrates attention upon Revolutionary times in the Mohawk Valley of upper New York state. The story opens in July, 1776, as Gilbert Martin and his wife, Magdalena, come to Deerfield to take up a plot of land. The inhabitants of the Mohawk Valley only hear vague rumors of the Revolutionary fighting. Their sympathies are with the American rebels but their little militia concentrates its efforts on making the settlers safe from Indian raids. One particular raid of Senecas and renegade whites compels Gil and his wife to leave their plot of land and ride to Fort Schuyler. Gil is forced to become a hired man as all of his possessions are lost. The little local militia are busy with raiding parties of both Indians and British. Finally, when the war is over, Gil takes his wife and children back to Deerfield to begin life again on their plot of land.

Gone With the Wind (1936) by Margaret Mitchell, awarded the 1937 Pulitzer Prize, is set in Georgia during the Civil War and the period of Reconstruction. This sensationally popular novel tells the story of Scarlett O'Hara, a high-spirited and willful daughter of an Irish immigrant. When Ashley Wilkes, with whom Scarlett is in love, marries his cousin, Melanie Hamilton, Scarlett marries Melanie's brother from spite. When Charles dies in the War, Scarlett returns to the abandoned family plantation, Tara, and determines to make it prosper. She marries her sister's fiancé for his money. Her husband is killed in a duel when his wife's honor is slandered. Scarlett, at 27, meets and attracts the unscrupulous and dashing war profiteer, Rhett Butler. She continues to love Ashley, however, and after a period of quarreling, Rhett leaves her. Melanie dies and Ashley has become indifferent toward Scarlett's attentions. She finally realizes too late that Rhett Butler was the only man she had known who could have conquered her spirit and brought happiness to her. The book devotes much of its attention to the fall of Atlanta to the Northern armies and to the harsh realities of plantation life during the immediate postwar period.

26. Pearl Buck: _The Good Earth_ (1931)

Page 156. Pearl Buck, in several books, has made a serious effort to present a realistic picture of Chinese peasant life during the present century. She won both the Pulitzer Prize (1931) and the Nobel Prize (1938).

The Good Earth concerns the poor peasant, Wang Lung, who marries O-Lan, a kitchen maid. They labor side by side and face hardships, famines, floods, and disease, as they gain a semblance of prosperity, only to lose it again. Three sons and a daughter are born to O-Lan. When Wang Lung finds some jewels in the house of a rich man that had been raided by revolutionists, he buys more land, and with prosperity, he takes a second wife, Lotus, a former prostitute. O-Lan, now out of favor with her husband, continues to keep the household until her death. When Wang Lung is near death he is sad that one of his sons is a revolutionary leader and that the other two do not love the soil and have taken up life in the city.

Pearl Buck wrote two sequels to *The Good Earth: Sons* (1932) and *A House Divided* (1935), the trilogy of novels being known as *The House of Earth.*

27. James Branch Cabell: *Jurgen* (1919)

Page 156. Pearl Buck attempts a thoroughgoing realism in her approach to contemporary Chinese peasant life. Among the better writers of the mass of exotic fiction of the century, who divorce themselves from the familiar and the contemporary and project their plots into the pure realm of the imagination, James Cabell is outstanding. Cabell does not create his fanciful scenes in order to escape the realities of today; he does so in order that his satire and social criticism of today's world may appear more pointed by contrast.

Jurgen, Cabell's masterpiece, takes the reader into a mythical medieval land called Poictesme, completely equipped as to cities, political subdivisions, social and religious institutions. Jurgen is a fifty-year-old pawnbroker whose old shrewish wife, Liza, has been carried off by Satan. In response to social pressures to look for her, Jurgen meets the centaur Nessus and is carried to the garden between dawn and sunrise where he is given his wish to relive a portion of his youth. In this illusion he is rejoined by his youthful sweetheart, Dorothy, but finds that the desires he had built up in his older imagination did not satisfy when he achieved them. From this point Jurgen has many merry adventures among the great ladies of myth and legend. He visits both Hell and Heaven. When he at last regains his middle-aged body, he continues the search for his Liza. When Koshchei, the Prince of Darkness, offers him great beauties of the past instead of his old shrewish wife, Jurgen refuses. He had had a fling at reliving his youth and had made the same false decisions that he had made during the same period of his natural life. He is content to return to his unexciting, but comfortable, middle-age life with Liza.

Jurgen, which bears the subtitle *A Comedy of Justice,* is an escapist romance of love and adventure. But, at the same time, it is a clever allegory, filled with satirical jabs at modern civilization and its conventions, and it is a philosophical view of life. *Jurgen* and a number of Cabell's other tales of Poictesme are fanciful romances, written on an intellectual level.

28. Eugene O'Neill: Three Pulitzer Prize Plays

Page 184. O'Neill, American Literature's only dramatist to gain fame on a world-wide basis, won the Pulitzer Prize four times and became the Nobel Prize winner for his drama in 1936.

Beyond the Horizon (Pulitzer Prize for 1920) is a tragedy of frustration, based upon the mistaken choices made by two brothers, Robert and Andrew Mayo. Andrew is practical, hard-working, and loves the soil; Robert is of delicate health, of a poetic nature, and a dreamer. Andrew, as a matter of course, was planning to marry Ruth, a neighboring girl with an invalid mother, and take over his father's farm. The play opens as Robert, who is about to depart on a sea voyage with an uncle, meets Ruth and the two decide that they are in love. He decides to remain on the New England farm. Andrew, disappointed and angry, decides to leave with the uncle.

During the following three years, Robert becomes sick and disillusioned with the farm work. Ruth, now realizing that she does not love Robert, becomes a nagging and frustrated wife. She longs to see Andrew again. When Andrew returns for a brief visit, Ruth finds that he has gotten over his love for her. Andrew leaves for the Argentine. The farm continues to deteriorate. Finally, their child dead, Robert and Ruth sink into a slovenly, miserable existence with each other. Robert is dying with tuberculosis when Andrew returns five years later. He begs Andrew and Ruth to marry and bring the farm back to prosperity as he runs down the country road, toward the point "beyond the horizon." He falls dead as the sun rises over the distant hills.

Anna Christie (Pulitzer Prize for 1922) opens in the waterfront saloon of Johnny-the-Priest as old Chris Christopherson, a coal barge captain, waits for his daughter Anna, whom he has not seen for fifteen years. Years before he had sent his young daughter to relatives in the Midwest to protect her from the coarse life she would encounter at her father's side. In reality, Anna had been seduced by a cousin when she was sixteen, had lived as a prostitute in St. Louis, and had developed an intense hatred for men. However, old Chris fails to see the coarseness and vulgarity in Anna which is evident to others. He welcomes his daughter and invites her to come with him on the coal barge.

On the open sea Anna begins to be filled with a renewed desire to live. She regains her health and much of her former beauty. The barge picks up a boat of shipwrecked sailors. Among them is Mat Burke, an Irish stoker, who falls in love with Anna. Chris feels that Mat is too rough and coarse for his daughter. Anna then relates her past life to the two men. Both are shocked by the story and leave the girl. Mat soon comes to the conclusion that his love is all that matters and he goes to Anna to ask that she wait for him as he had signed on for a voyage while he was drunk. As it turns out, Chris also returns to Anna after he had signed on for a voyage on the same ship. Anna promises to have a home ready for the two men when they return. The sea, "dat ole davil sea," from whose wicked influence Chris had tried to protect his little daughter, thus came to be the means of her regeneration in later years.

Strange Interlude (Pulitzer Prize for 1928) is a long experimental play in nine acts in which O'Neill has his characters deliver long asides which reveal their inner thoughts. In this play and in his _Mourning Becomes Electra_ (1931) O'Neill adapts to drama the stream-of-consciousness technique.

Nina Leeds is persuaded by her father, a New England professor, to postpone her marriage to Gordon Shaw until he returns from World War I. Shaw is killed and Nina becomes neurotic and hates her father. She becomes a nurse in a hospital for disabled soldiers and gives herself to one after another of the men under the insane delusion that she is fulfilling a duty to Gordon Shaw.

Dr. Edmund Darrell, who loves Nina but does not wish to risk a setback to his scientific career, thinks that motherhood would cure her of her obsession. He encourages her to marry Sam Evans. Shortly before she is to have Sam's child, Nina learns from Sam's mother of insanity in the family. She has an abortion. She later conceives a child by Dr. Darrell. Sam believes that the boy, Gordon, is his own and a very close affection grows between the boy and his supposed father. The boy never develops any real affection for his mother, and after Sam dies suddenly, goes out of Nina's life. Nina finally marries Charles Marsden, a novelist with a strong mother fixation. He gives her the friendship and companionable affection for which she had been starved in her life with Sam and her son Gordon.

In May, 1957, O'Neill was awarded a Posthumous Pulitzer Prize for his drama, _Long Day's Journey Into Night._

APPENDIX B

Dictionary of Literary Terms

The following glossary of terms includes brief definitions of the items indicated by an asterisk (*) in the main historical sections. In addition, the student will find here many other items dealing with the study of literature which he may care to review without the necessity of locating them in voluminous histories or anthologies. The terms in this volume are restricted to those which pertain particularly to the study of American literature. Terms pertaining to the English backgrounds for American creative writing may be located in similar sections included in the author's volumes on English literature.

Accent. The stress given to a syllable in a word or a phrase. A series of accents, according to a predetermined pattern, gives a line of poetry a definite artistic expression of emotional and rhythmical language. *See* Poetry.

Adaptation. The literary process by which writing throughout the ages achieves continuity and variety. It is the creation of individual expression through use of inherited or already created material. Longfellow, for instance, adapted not only the meter but much of the spirit and content of the Finnish epic *Kalevala* in the creation of his original poem, *Hiawatha*.

Age. A long, but indefinite, period of political or cultural history, distinguished by real or fictitious characteristics, and usually named for particularly important characteristics or for real or imaginary personages. Examples: *The Colonial Period, The New England Writers, The Imagist School, The Gilded Age, The American Renaissance.*

Allegory. Allegory is created in a literary work when one or more meanings, in addition to the literal one, are to be derived by the reader. Thus, in narrative, objects, ideas, incidents, or people are represented indirectly to the reader by means of personification or symbolism. The reader is intended, therefore, to understand not only the expressed events in the narrative but also the hidden truths or meanings. Allegory, as a major device, has been comparatively rare in modern literatures, where narrative tends to be more objective and direct in its expression of ideas. However, allegory has become a very definite element present in much of modern symbolism. A notable example of allegory in American literature is Melville's

Moby Dick, where the author portrays a struggle between man and his fate. "All visible objects are but as cardboard masks." Concepts of good and evil are buried as allegory beneath the surface events of the adventure narrative. Unless masterfully presented, modern readers have little patience with fables, parables, and other literary forms with involved hidden moral meanings. Notable, and controversial, recent works which involve allegory are T. S. Eliot's *The Waste-Land* and William Faulkner's *A Fable.*

Alliteration. *See* Poetry.

Amphibrach. *See* Poetry.

Anapest. *See* Poetry.

Antithesis. *See* Poetry.

Artificiality. In literature, this term would mean any writing which is deliberately and consciously affected and artistic. In form, the expression would be elaborate, ornate, and courtly or aristocratic. In theme, such writing would deal with unrealistic or fantastic subject matter.

Ballad. In the older sense, ballad poetry was folk verse, usually always narrative and employing a very direct and simple metrical form. The popular or folk ballad was composed to be recited or sung and treated some dramatic or timely episode in the lives of the common people during the European Middle Ages. Few appeared in written form before the 16th century, when humanists and literary men began to collect and publish them from oral tradition. The "literary" or "art" ballad is a composition of a cultured poet in imitation of the simple charm of the earlier popular folk ballad. American literature is rich both in adaptations of European ballads and in original poems in imitation of traditional ballad form and subject matter. The romantic poets, particularly Longfellow, have given us many charming ballads.

Belles-Lettres. Poetry, fiction, and other imaginative literature which is intended to be enjoyed for its own sake rather than for a purpose of imparting information or instruction. *Belles-lettres* refers to aesthetic or elegant writing or to studies and criticism which apply to writing as a fine art.

Blank Verse. As originally conceived, blank verse was a form of rhymeless poetry, the lines consisting of ten syllables each, with accents on the even-numbered syllables (iambic pentameter). This form was used almost exclusively by Shakespeare and Milton. In more recent poetry the term seems to extend to any metrical unrhymed form, executed with artistry and genius, such as that found in many American poets such as Whitman, Masters, Sandburg, and others.

Brahmin. In its basic meaning, a worshiper of Brahma, a member of the high priestly order of Hinduism. In America, it is a satirically humorous term applied to any member of New England aristocracy, an untitled class distinguished for its emphasis on class differences. Brahmin literature would refer, therefore, to works by members of the class or by others with a common tendency to exalt the traditional and genteel ideals of this particular group in American society. In the romantic period, for instance, Longfellow and Holmes were Brahmin poets; Whitman and Whittier were not.

Brook Farm. An agricultural community established in 1841 near Boston by a group of transcendentalists. The basic purpose of the utopian experiment, which lasted six years, was to give its members a chance to live their lives according to their beliefs. All labor and profit was shared among the members. Although many of the New England writers of the period, including Emerson, Dana, Channing, Alcott, Dwight, Thoreau, and Hawthorne, were influenced greatly by the ideals of brotherly cooperation and the promotion of the physical, intellectual, and moral benefits to be derived from this form of communal living, only Hawthorne, Dana, and Dwight actually lived there. Hawthorne gives us an intimate description of Brook Farm in his novel, *The Blithedale Romance.*

Caesura. *See* Poetry.

Calvinism. A system of theological thought which derived from the teaching of John Calvin (1509-64), a great early French Protestant reformer, and which formed the basis for the religious doctrines practiced by the early settlers of New England. Calvinistic philosophy (and especially its more extreme interpretation, Puritanism) had a very profound, and almost controlling, effect upon the early development of American literature (*See* Puritanism). Reactions against Calvinistic doctrine (*See* Transcendentalism) had equally profound effects upon American literature during the 19th century. During the last 400 years much of the literature of England and a considerable portion of all of American literature have reflected Calvinistic thought and conduct, or reactions which protest its rigidity.

Calvinism was founded upon these basic ideas: (1) Man is a depraved creature and incapable of exercising free will since he has inherited the corruption attendant upon Adam's fall; (2) Man is saved only if, through Atonement, he is elected through God's wisdom to be among the "chosen few"; (3) Although the Church and the State are theoretically separate, the Church, through its elected (or chosen) few, must advise the State in all things. These principles and many others of a similar nature guided the course of the vast majority of Colonial writing. Hawthorne's *The Scarlet Letter* (1850) is the first great work of American literature to protest the effects of the Calvinistic doctrines upon the human heart and mind.

Chronicle. The term implies a sort of historical miscellany which lacks the documentation and critical attitude of historians and tends to be incomplete, inaccurate as to detail, and sketchy. The chronicle often departs from its historical thread and treats material which is purely fictional. Most of the accounts of the early New England settlers tend to be more accurate than those of the Virginia settlers, though much that is personal opinion and romance is present in the so-called *histories* of both regions.

Classic, Classicism. As applied to literatures, the terms usually refer to the meaning attached to them among the Renaissance writers who considered only the great works of Greek and Roman literatures as being worthy of imitation and emulation in their own efforts. Therefore the form and content of those works was *classical* and anything produced in imitation of that form and content was also *classical.* Therefore, from this angle, the terms would mean a return to the forms and ideals of the ancient literatures. Later movements which imitated the ancient classics and produced works on classic themes are known in the various literatures as neoclassical ("new classical") schools of writing. All the world's major literatures returned to classical form and content in the early 18th century, following the lead of France, which produced a brilliant neoclassical literature during the last third of the 17th century.

The term classical, as applied to modern literatures, would imply "disciplined" writing, emphasis on form rather than on content, technical perfection rather than experimentation, precision and objectivity over emotional expressiveness and individuality, rational thinking over imaginative and wild fantasy. The style must be clear, lucid and restrained, controlled and intellectual, moderated and decorous.

Broadly, the term "classic" would cover any piece of literature in any period which, in the opinion of critics over the years, had achieved a solid and recognized position for its excellence and universal appeal. This would, of course, be true even for the works of romantic writers. Every literature takes pride in its own "classics," models of artistic expression from its own literary past. *See* Romantic, Romanticism.

Column, Columnist. Increasingly, during the 20th century, much fine American writing is to be found in the columns of newspapers and magazines. Many of the columnists of this century have achieved reputations as fine creative writers dealing with a multitude of subjects of interest to the average American. Many writers, such as Clifton Fadiman, George Ade, Franklin P. Adams, Don Marquis, Christopher Morley, Dorothy Thompson, Mrs. Franklin D. Roosevelt, and many others, have approached fine literature in this century with their humorous, critical, and satirical commentary upon social, political, and aesthetic questions of the day. Their efforts are to be compared favorably with those of the writers of the last century who achieved permanent places in our literature with both formal and informal, or familiar, essays—such writers as Emerson, Holmes, Lowell, and Mark Twain.

Comedy. Comedy is opposed, in literary theory, to tragedy. Comedy is a light form of drama and is designed to amuse and entertain, and almost invariably ends happily, at least for the admirable characters. A play which ends without any deaths has traditionally been considered comedy. However, tragedy does not necessarily imply that there will be bodies lying about the stage; it simply implies deep conflicts, with a great deal of serious sorrow and sadness prevalent in the action. We may call plays *tragicomedies* when there is a mixture of the tragic and the comic elements present. Comedy may be fantasy, on an utterly idealized plane, with no connection with human lives, or it may involve serious human psychological and social problems. Comedies may be highly exaggerated matter, designed to thrill audiences in a sensational manner (*melodrama*) or they may be somewhat realistic exposures of the customs of social groups, such as the *comedy of manners* or the *satirical comedy*. They may be analyses of the human mind, such as *psychological comedy,* or description of the inner workings of family relationships, such as *domestic comedies.* Comedy which is designed to appeal somewhat to the intelligence and is highly subtle and sophisticated, is often designated as "high" comedy;

comedy designed to produce raucous laughter through its absurdly complicated situations (such as *farce comedy*) or that which is bawdy and broad in its grotesque characterization and crude lines, is often distinguished with the term "low" comedy. *See* Drama, Tragedy.

Convention. The term as used in literature would imply rules, devices, or styles of expression which, through usage and custom, become accepted and recognized means of literary technique during particular literary periods or ages. Convention in poetry long decreed that lines of verse must conform to definite rhyme schemes and certain metrical devices (*See* Poetry). During recent years, however, poets have insisted on freedom from these traditional usages in an effort to create a "new" or "free" poetry with a wider scope and range for the expression of thought and emotion. Much of this rhymeless type of verse (for instance, that of Whitman) was viewed for years with suspicion by many critics who are only now coming to recognize and accept it as legitimate literary expression of the highest type. Many literary conventions perish within a particular age or group of writers; others, such as the use of the chorus or the soliloquy in drama, have been revived with new freshness and appeal by succeeding groups of writers since they were first used as effective dramatic devices by the ancient Greeks.

Couplet. *See* Poetry.

Criticism, Literary. The art of judging qualities and values in creative writing. A competent critic is one who makes a disinterested endeavor, through good taste and sound judgment, to learn of and to propagate the best writings of others. Sound criticism presumes a wide background of culture and learning on the part of the critics. From the days of Aristotle, in ancient Greece, principles have been laid down and rules have been promulgated upon which literary critics of the ages have formulated the aesthetics upon which literary taste in particular periods has been molded. Scholars and critics of later periods have been engaged in a constant process of re-evaluation of the criticism of prior periods. Thus much foolish and biased opinion is discovered and eliminated from the general body of criticism of the literatures of the past.

American criticism, before Edgar Allen Poe (1809-49), tended to be very haphazard and prejudiced. There was little analysis involved in the work of early American critics, who, for the most part, attemped to act as moralists, condemning or praising literary production for what they considered the evil or salutary effects the writing might have upon the souls of the readers. Poe knew literature and attempted to make his judgments from close analysis of the works and from the critical system he had evolved in his acute mind. His opinions were clear and fearlessly expressed.

In the late 19th century our dominant critics were largely novelists (Howells, Garland, James) and highly influential in the advance of an American realism, based on European models. But in the early decades of the 20th century many trained minds leaped into the critical arena with startling questions: What in American life had prevented the continued growth of a literature of scope and maturity that such writers as Whitman, Melville, and Hawthorne had promised —a literature that had shown few such signs of challenging the best production of European literatures? With such questions as this and many others there arose a lively give-and-take of opinion from various groups, generally divided into traditionalist, or conservative, and experimental radical camps. Today a complete and disinterested analysis of the mass of critical material that has been produced during the past 40 years has not been completed but it is already evident that American criticism has come to stand on its own feet. The aim of the majority of the trained younger critics is an aesthetic disinterestedness in seeking the truly universal and permanent values underlying a mass of American writing which had been subjected too often in the past to forces which twisted a general concept of "culture" into narrow paths of Puritanism, national pride, intolerance for the unpopular, the domination of art by science and industrial materialism, control by a "genteel" aristocracy, blind subservience to foreign influences, and other cultural defects inherent in the rapid and violent changes in a fledgling democracy.

Dactyl. *See* Poetry.

Dadaism. A school of art and literature which flourished among young and radical literary and art groups in European capitals during the period of disillusionment following World War I. The purpose of their work seemed to be to disrupt any logical relationship between thought and expression, to demolish all traditional concepts of the past. They proclaimed that art had been too feminine ("mama") and should become masculine ("dada"). The dadaist groups produced much that is to be considered pure insanity in painting and in writing. Dadaism was an extremist fad stemming from symbolism. It directly influenced the rise of Surrealism and contributed a great deal of inspiration to the experimental techniques in literature which rose in the twenties (*See* below under Impressionism, Stream of Consciousness) and whose permanent values to literature are questions of much critical discussion today.

Deism. A system of religious philosophy which holds that a personal God created the world but reveals Himself neither in nature nor in religious experience. It holds that God rules the world by established laws and will judge mankind at the end of the world but that He does not participate in temporal affairs. This rationalistic religious movement was popular in the 17th and 18th centuries. Famed European advocates were Voltaire and Rousseau in France and Herbert in England. In America, Jefferson and Franklin were to be counted among the Deists. *The Age of Reason* by Thomas Paine is the most notable American book explaining the philosophy of Deism. The importance of Deism to American literature lies in the fact that it was an early reaction against Calvinism and greatly influenced the rise of the great Unitarian and Transcendental (*See* below) movements in New England during the early 19th century.

Dial, The. The quarterly magazine of literature, philosophy, and religion published by the Transcendentalist Club of Boston from 1840–1844. Ralph Waldo Emerson was editor during the final two years of its existence. Many important contributions to the American essay were first published in *The Dial,* among the contributors being Emerson, Thoreau, W. H. Channing, Theodore Parker, and C. A. Dana.

Didactic Writing. Writing which is dedicated essentially to teaching lessons or moral truths. All writing, of course, to a certain extent will contain truth. But when the beauties of expression are suppressed to make the writing a vehicle of teaching, such writing comes within the term *didactic*. Most of the best American writing of the Colonial and Revolutionary periods is didactic. Much of 19th century literature of the New England group, particularly that of the Transcendentalists, comes within the meaning of the term. In this century, a large part of our literature has been dedicated to social, economic, and political reform, and is, therefore, largely didactic.

Dimeter. *See* Poetry.

Drama. As a literary genre, drama requires a story, or series of actions, a setting, and actors to impersonate the characters in the story. The form is dialogue with a certain amount of descriptive interpolations giving information as to setting, character description, and action. According to Aristotle, drama is "imitated human action." Much drama in literature is designated "closet" drama, not written basically for the purpose of being acted on the stage. This type of drama is usually very philosophical, has very little action, and is aimed toward the enjoyment of readers, rather than that of viewers. It is doubtful if many authors have aimed their plays entirely toward a reading audience, but much drama in American writing had seldom been staged because of difficulty and expense of staging and the prospect of small viewing audiences. Notable plays of this century which have come to be considered by many as "closet" drama, because of impracticability of staging, are *Strange Interlude* (1928) and *Mourning Becomes Electra* (1931) of Eugene O'Neill.

As applied to the theater, drama covers all types of work designed for performance. Therefore its most elementary expression is in mimic of actions and of vocal expressions of the characters involved in the dramatic composition. Most of drama in the United States is written basically for performance in the commercial theaters of New York. As literature, most of dramatic composition in the United States is subliterary and unlikely to survive as classics of our literary heritage.

Dramatic Monologue. A type of narrative poetry in which a single character speaks throughout the composition. The speaker comments upon an incident or dramatic moment of his life, and during his relation he reveals his own characteristics or those of other persons. Robert Browning was a master of the dramatic monologue in English literature. Many American poets of the 20th century have used the form with great effectiveness: Carl Sandburg, Edgar Lee Masters, Amy Lowell, E. A. Robinson, Robert Frost, and others.

Elegy. Usually a poem in which the content is a lament for the dead. However, any lyrical expression of sorrowful thoughts upon the subjects of life, love, and death is called an elegy in modern poetry.

Epic. Traditionally, the term *epic* was used in literatures to designate long narrative poems of a dramatic character dealing with the real or fictitious relation of notable actions carried out in a heroic manner, guided by the inspiration of some powerful social or supernatural force. The early European *folk epic* developed from popular songs or ballads relating great deeds of a central hero. Such a poem in

English literature is *Beowulf*. The later Renaissance *artistic, literary,* or *art epic* had a single author who composed his poem in a grandiose style, weaving his action and characterization around some noble central theme of patriotic or heroic interest. In English literature, Milton's *Paradise Lost* is a superb example of the art epic. In America, Timothy Dwight produced an ambitious, but artificial and monotonous, epic poem, *The Conquest of Canaan* (1785), based on the biblical Joshua. Joel Barlow wrote an equally artificial epic poem, *The Columbiad* (1807), based upon the life of Columbus and the glories of the New World. During our Revolutionary and early national periods several *mock,* or *burlesque,* epic poems were produced. Here the authors used modern themes of insignificant importance within the framework of noble grandeur and heroic atmosphere. Trumbull's *McFingel* (1782) and Barlow's *Hasty Pudding* (1792) are famed examples of mock heroic epic poems in American literature. Longfellow's *The Song of Hiawatha* (1855), from our romantic period, has been called an American Indian epic. In recent writing, Stephen V. Benét's book-length narrative poem of the Civil War, *John Brown's Body* (1928), has some of the qualities associated with the epic but lacks the unity, the grandiose style, and the inspiration of the great traditional epic poems of world literatures of the past. Benét's poem is better qualified as a novel in verse.

Essay. The term is loosely used to cover any brief piece of writing, preferably prose, which is expository and informative. Generally, the following characteristics define the essay: (1) it is reflective in its approach to matter, (2) it is brief, (3) it does not tell a story, but may employ narrative episodes to further the didactic purpose, (4) it may be *informal* in that it reflects the viewpoints, tastes, and feelings of the author in a whimsical, humorous, or warm-hearted manner, or it may be *formal* in that it is a serious study of almost any phase of human interest, (5) it does not require plot or characterization and does not require any particular completeness or unity of structure.

Euphuism. An elaborated and highly colored style of writing, depending upon strings of similes and complicated patterns of antithesis, alliteration, and metaphorical comparisons for its fanciful effects of language. The term arises from the style employed by John Lyly in his 16th century romances *Euphues* and *Euphues and His England*. Modern readers tend to look upon this type of complexity of language as artificial and stilted. But, since the 16th century Lyly, the same elegance of form, and sometimes abstruseness of meaning, has appeared in various European literatures and is known by various terms, such as *gongorism, marinism, preciosité, baroque,* etc., and has reappeared in various periods. Many of the symbolists and exponents of "free verse" of this century have adopted much of the euphuistic style.

Expressionism. *See* Impressionism.

Fiction. That which is imagined or invented in contrast with that which is true and factual. In strict literary usage, the term usually refers only to the novel or the short story, though it is recognized that much of the material employed in those genres could be true in fact or from the actual experience of the author. *Nonfiction* is used to designate reference works, history, biography, and literary criticism. *Poetry* and *drama* are normally considered as separate classes in literature.

Figures of Speech. *See* Poetry.

Fin de Siècle. From the French, meaning "end of the century." This term pertains to or is characteristic of the end of the 19th century, which was generally, in literatures, a transitional period when traditional ideas and conventions were being abandoned and there was evident a great deal of confusion and erratic search for new ideas and artistic objectives to take their place. "Fin de siècle" writing was not wholly worthless or decadent as some critics tend to label it. During the period, literature tended to become highly experimental. There was a general feeling of emancipation from the bonds of the past and much of the writing of the era reflects propaganda for new, and in some cases, radical movements and revolutionary social aspirations. In American literature, the "nineties" showed a new wave of late-romanticism, of uncertainty of direction in poetry, and of the beginnings of the early 20th century movements toward naturalism and a "muckraking" realism in fiction. It was generally a period of lull and little accomplishment between our gilded age and the contemporary movements. The term "fin-de-siècle" is often associated with other end-of-age transitional periods when one set of values seemed to be dying and another set of values had not yet become thoroughly established.

Foot, Metrical. *See* Poetry.

Free Verse, or *vers libre.* The term designates a definite attempt of the poets of the second and third decades of this century to break with the formal metrical conventions of the past and to give poetry a new spontaneity and freedom. The resulting experimentation was highly irregular metrical patterns, departing radically from the tradition metrical feet of English poetry and giving more importance to cadence, assonance, and alliteration for its effect. The new verse tends to be sensual and to employ subtle effects of rhythm. This poetry depends upon occasional rhyme or no rhyme at all but tends to concentrate upon the stanza or the strophe, rather than the metrical foot or the verse line, for its effect. *Free verse,* although it received little critical attention in America before the symbolist, impressionist, and imagist movements of Europe and England, had been practiced in the last century by two of our greatest poets, Walt Whitman and Emily Dickinson. *Vers libre,* in American literature, was neither practiced widely by poets nor accepted by the traditionally minded critics until after 1912. And it was only after that date that Whitman and Dickinson have been recognized as two of the most outstanding poets of the entire course of our literature. And though excesses have been many in this new poetry, it has nonetheless added much to the spontaneity and variety of present-day verse, which the traditional forms could not have achieved alone. The new poetry has not replaced the traditional forms but it is obvious, at mid-century, that it has brought to the total body of poetry a new and enriched set of values. It is yet too early to predict what directions those values may take in the future of poetic art.

Frontier Literature. Until 1890, a very large portion of American writing, from the settlements on the Atlantic seaboard in the early

17th century, was directly concerned with recording the activities and the spirit, the struggles and the conquests and the defeats of the American frontier as it gradually pushed westward. After 1890, this influence, though it continues to the present day to occupy writers, is largely a historical interest. After this date the free lands of America had largely been settled. This large portion of native American literature reflected the optimism of the individual that he could conquer and control his environment. Thus it is that this large body of "frontier" literature accounts for much of the color and spirit of the total body of American literature, and at the same time accounts for much of the low-spirited and pessimistic tone of our writings in the period immediately following 1890, when American writers turned so whole-heartedly toward the disillusioned and deterministic pessimism that characterized the literatures of the Old World during the period.

Genre. A word meaning a *kind* or a *type*, which has been adapted in a literary sense, to indicate a classification according to style, subject matter, or manner of treatment of literary matter. Sonnets form a *genre* because of their set poetic form; drama is a *genre* of literature because of its manner of treatment of subject matter; "frontier" literature could be called a distinctive *genre* of American literature because of the common subject matter treated in all its examples.

Genteel Tradition. An important term, peculiar to American literature, which refers to the code of particular customs and prejudices which characterized the upper class of New England society during the 19th century. This upper-class Brahmin (q.v.) respectability, based on family position, money, and custom determined to a great extent the course of much of our best writing during the last century and influenced the bases of our literary criticism until well into this century. The genteel tradition, centering in Boston, has often been compared to English Victorianism of the same period. To the representatives of both traditions "truth" in writing must conform to the good manners and regard for appearances of "respectability," as the leaders of upper-class society defined it. These groups, both in England and in America, demanded that unpleasant social facts be suppressed in the interest of good taste and that none of the taboos of the class with regard to sex, religious traditions of morality, and profaneness and vulgarity of language be violated in the printed word. The tradition insisted that human justice was God-given to His chosen representatives and that open discussion of disconcerting social problems was mean and vulgar. The genteel tradition in American letters was challenged from many directions after 1840 and gave ground slowly. Only in this century has its hampering influence upon the development of a "free" American literature been broken to give rise to a new critical system of assessing literary values other than on the basis of the prejudices of a particular sector of the population.

Gothic Novel. In the neoclassic age, the Gothic romance or novel came to be so named to indicate any such writing dealing with horrors, suspense, and sensational adventure, which offended the classic taste for simplicity, dignity, and sentimentalism. The form of writing, dealing with terror, violence, murder, and mysterious workings of exaggerated fancy, acquired its name in European literatures from the Gothic architectural patterns of pointed arches and vaults, slender spires and buttresses, and the dungeon keeps of the Middle Ages. This architectural style was looked upon by the neoclassics as primitive and savage and therefore an apt title to affix to the new sensationalism which was popular in the novel in the late years of the 18th century. Our first genuine American novelist, Charles Brockden Brown, adapted the Gothic pattern to his novels with American backgrounds, the most famous of which is *Wieland* (1798). Hawthorne and Edgar Allen Poe were our major fiction writers of the romantic period whose tales bear the distinctive imprint of the Gothic romance. The Gothic elements of horror and suspense continue to account for a large portion of our subliterary "popular" fiction to the present day.

Graveyard School.   The term refers to a group of English poets, about mid-18th century, who wrote long, gloomy poems dealing with melancholic and doleful thoughts of life and death. This group of poets attempted to raise gloom to the level of pleasurable emotion. The "graveyard" school of English poetry had a good deal of influence on our early romantic poets, particularly Bryant.

Heptameter, Hexameter.   *See* Poetry.

Humanism, The New Humanism.   The term humanism is generally applied to the attitude of mind which developed in Europe after the Middle Ages and which laid emphasis on the importance of the interests of the individual in his earthly life rather than, as in the Middle Age teachings, considering this life solely as a period in which to prepare oneself for the life to come. The Renaissance humanists took as the inspiration for their writings and studies the classical literatures of Greece and Rome.

The New Humanism, in American letters, refers to the movement in philosophy and criticism which flourished in the 1920's and gave rise to such important writers as Irving Babbitt and Paul Elmer More. The New Humanism reacted against naturalism in writing as stressing the base and sordid aspects of human nature, the false and only half-truthful philosophies and beliefs which professed to be "scientific," and the extremes of orthodoxy in religion. The movement sought to guide American thought in the direction of a middle course, avoiding the extremes of realism (a deterministic naturalism in particular), the worship of science, and the dictates of orthodoxy in religion. It stressed the importance of reason and human will and urged restraint in all phases of ethical, artistic, and intellectual considerations. In its attacks on traditional criticism, it stressed avoidance of major emphasis on either the excesses of realism or those of romanticism. The more radical opponents of the movement attacked it on the ground that it was a last-stand defense of the "Genteel Tradition." A notable work of criticism of the movement is *The Genteel Tradition at Bay* (1931) of George Santayana. The best book that summarized the principles of the group was a symposium published in 1930: *Humanism and America*.

Hyperbole.   *See* Poetry.

Iambus, Iambic.   *See* Poetry.

Imagism.   Usually is used in reference to a movement within the ranks of the advocates of the New Poetry. In America the group rose to prominence in the period from 1912 to 1914. The leader of the group was Amy Lowell, who had received her enthusiasm in the direction of revolt against conventional concepts in England, where she had associated with Ezra Pound and his group of young enthusiasts for French symbolism. The imagist verse concentrated upon the creation of sharp and precisely delineated images, coldly unsentimental, to provide in the mind of the reader a clear and unclouded picture of the subject being treated. Imagist verse sought to employ exact terms from common speech and to suggest ideas rather than to give them complete expression. No subject was barred as unfit for treatment; only the traditional verse patterns and the cliché expressions of the past were to be avoided. Imagist verse continued in popularity until after the death of Amy Lowell in 1925 and the contributions of the early experimental phases of imagism have added much to the versatility of present-day poetry. H. D. (Hilda Doolittle), John Gould Fletcher, Robert Frost, and Carl Sandburg are outstanding American poets of the century whose work has, at least in part, been influenced directly by the principles of *Imagism*.

Impressionism.   In literature, the term *impressionism* is generally used to cover the various aspects of *symbolism, imagism,* and, in the novel, *stream-of-consciousness* techniques. This particular technique attempts to record the impression of experience upon the consciousness of the artist. Rather than dealing with the objective characteristics of things and happenings the writer explores inner meanings and presents for the reader characters and moods as they impress themselves on his particular temperament. In English poetry, T. S. Eliot, and in the novel, James Joyce and Virginia Woolf, are masters of the new technique. A pioneer of the impressionistic technique in the American novel was Stephen Crane, followed by such masters as John Dos Passos and Thomas Wolfe. In American poetry, Amy Lowell, Carl Sandburg, Conrad Aiken, Wallace Stevens, and Marianne Moore are counted among the impressionists in American literature of the 20th century.

An outgrowth of the experimental techniques of early-century dramatists and novelists of Europe and of the impressionistic writers was a contrasting technique called *expressionism*. Here the artist attempts to present external nature as intellectual abstractions, giving emphasis to some quality present in the subject being treated. Impressionism deals with actual external appearances of reality as they are relayed to the reader through the personal mood of the writer; expressionism presents external reality, not only modified by the artist's personal temperament but also as distorted (usually) by the writer's mental concept of the reality, usually a concept formed by overconcentration upon the quality or qualities of the reality which appeal to the writer. Both impressionism and expressionism are phases of the artist's view of reality, the first giving the primary impact of the reality upon the emotional temperament and the second giving the later intellectual concept formed by that impact. A further extension of both techniques would lead to *surrealism, dadaism,* and other forms of delving in the subconsciousness. Among Americans to employ the expressionist technique in drama were Eugene O'Neill (particularly in *The Hairy Ape* and *The Emperor Jones*), Elmer Rice in *The Adding Machine,* and George Kaufman and Marc Connelly in *Beggar on Horseback.*

In all these 20th century experimental techniques, literature is following in the footsteps of similar and more developed experiments in painting, music, and in the medical and psychological fields, in psychiatry, and in extensions of the theories of Freud and his disciples. They are all attempts to interpret and translate into the printed word the dreams, thoughts, and subconscious impressions which are a part of the inner world of the individual. These literary techniques are still in a highly experimental stage, and in any such period, the average reader is likely to dismiss them as insane or as hoaxes. But such writers as Strindberg in Sweden, Lorca in Spain, Eliot and Joyce in England, Wedekind, Kaiser, Toller, Capek, Werfel, Kafka, and others, in central Europe, and our chief exponent of the expressionist technique, Eugene O'Neill, are pioneers in new directions for literary expression and merit the respect of readers who may not yet be able to understand them thoroughly.

Knickerbocker Group. A name given to writers in New York during the first quarter of the 19th century who were instrumental in causing New York City to forge ahead of Boston as the country's leading literary center—a position which it has never lost since that time. These writers had little in common except that they were associated with the same geographical area. The name Knickerbocker (that of an early Dutch family in New York, was made famous by Washington Irving in his whimsical *Knickerbocker History of New York* (1809). Aside from Irving, other outstanding members of the group were William Cullen Bryant and James Fenimore Cooper.

Literature. While the term would broadly cover all the preserved writings belonging to a given language or people, it is generally limited in its artistic concept to include only writing which has purpose beyond the mere compilation of information and which is characterized by an artistic form. *See* Belles-Lettres.

Local Color Literature. In American writing, the term is particularly apt to refer to a whole genre of writing, coming into prominence after the Civil War, which, in fiction and verse, portrayed particular sections of the U. S. for the entertainment and enlightenment of readers of the whole country. The local colorists emphasized the setting and the character of particular sections of the country, carefully reproducing the dialects, customs, dress, and peculiarities of culture and geographical features to be found there. The local color writing of the late 19th century tended to be colorful and romantic; the more realistic regionalism of this century gives more authenticity to the areas and peoples portrayed. The local color literature is perhaps to be considered our outstanding native development. Its major shortcoming as literature is its scant appeal to readers in other parts of the world.

Lost Generation. Refers to the generation of men and women who came to maturity during World War I. Many of this group, returning from the war disillusioned and facing the social upheavals which resulted, felt themselves alien to their environment and sought to portray their feelings of futility, aimlessness, and lack of spiritual focus in writing. Notable "lost" generation writers in this country were Ernest Hemingway, F. Scott Fitzgerald, and many of the experimental poets, such as E. E. Cummings.

Lyric Poetry. The term *lyric* in poetry always implies a musical quality, since all early lyric poetry was intended to be sung. Lyric poetry today is any verse which is highly personal and emotional and which is a sincere expression of feeling. There may be ideas and thought, or even narrative elements, in lyric poetry, but they are definitely subordinated to the expression of subjective emotion of the poet, couched in metrical language, which is designed to appeal to the emotional, rather than the intellectual, in the mind of the reader or hearer. Much of the New Poetry of this century is a distinct challenge to the traditional concept of *lyric* in poetry; it is yet too early to determine if criticism will come forward with a new pattern of terminology with regard to poetry.

Melodrama. A play or dramatic spectacle which employs startling and sensational action and lurid, emotional, and exaggerated language in order to play upon the emotional and sentimental reactions of the audience. Integration of plot, character development, or dramatic motivation are definitely secondary to the exaggerated incidents of the action, designed to inspire horror, joy, deep feelings of pity and sorrow. This type of play is usually full of hairbreath escapes, oppressive villains, noble heroes, and sorrowing families who are rescued, usually, in the nick of time, with all ending happily for the "good" people and sadly for the "bad" individuals. The term *melodramatic* may be applied to any form of writing in which the sensational and the spectacular predominate.

Metaphor, Meter, Metonymy, Monometer. *See* Poetry.

Muckraking Movement. In American literature, refers to the intense interest which our writers took in the investigation of corruption in business, politics, and other American institutions during the period from 1902 to the outbreak of World War I. Hundreds of novels, essays, and journalistic studies appeared during this period, in which sweeping and allegedly biased charges were made against individuals and institutions. Upton Sinclair, author of perhaps the best of the "muckraking" novels, *The Jungle* (1906), continued his attacks in fiction until 1937, when he wrote *The Flivver King,* a study of the automobile industry.

Mysticism, Mystical Writing. All literatures in all ages have shown recurring movements and individual writers concerned with man's attempt to communicate directly with the divine spirit. The expression of this faith in the possibility of man's contact with the spiritual elements of nature or with some concept of deity is known as mysticism. American literature has had no well-defined literature of mysticism as compared with English, Spanish, and German literatures. The Puritan poetry of the Colonial period was concerned with the purely orthodox beliefs of Calvinsim and even the nature poetry of Bryant, differing from that of the English Wordsworth, simply regarded nature as a manifestation of the beauty and power of God. The philosophical writings of the Transcendentalists (*See* below) placed reliance on the intuition and the conscience as a means of contact with a higher force and as a source of knowledge and thus came within the definition of mystical writings. William Vaughn

Moody (1869-1910) is our greatest mystical poet. Much of the New Poetry of this century shows mystical learnings, particularly that of Carl Sandburg. Poetry which becomes involved in psychological and theological analysis of man's place in the universe and his ultimate destiny is often referred to as *metaphysical* poetry. This verse is highly intellectual and appeals more to the reason than to the emotions.

Naturalism. The term is usually applied to a literary movement of the 19th and 20th centuries which was initiated in European literatures by impulses from the extensive development of biological science in the early 19th century. This type of literary technique is really an extreme phase of literary realism which studies human society and the lives of men with more of scientific objectivity than does the casual observation, "life-as-it-is," technique of realism. The subject matter of naturalism tends to be some social problem or vice, selected usually from the lower strata of society, which is analyzed and studied with more or less of a scientific "case study" method. The characters usually are selected to represent the vices or the weaknesses of a particular group, and their backgrounds and lives are presented in careful and meticulous detail. The characters are developed with exaggerated emphasis upon their social importance, and their environments and background play a much more important part in their destinies than do their individual wills and desires. American naturalism stemmed from the French Zola and has tended to be largely dominated by the pessimistic determinism which the French writer employed in novel after novel from 1875 to 1890. The biological determinists hold that man's actions are determined by his heredity and that he has little choice in the course of his destiny. Beginning with Crane, Herrick, and Norris at the turn of the century, naturalism (usually of the pessimistic determinism of Zola) has dominated at least a part of the work of most of our major novelists of this century, including Dreiser, Sherwood Anderson, Lewis, Faulkner, Dos Passos, Farrell, Hemingway, Caldwell, and Wolfe.

Neoclassicism. *Neo*-classic writing would be a conscious literary attempt at a revival or a modern interpretation of the ideals and forms of ancient literatures, particularly those of Greece and Rome. All modern revivals of "classic" spirit are simply returns to more order and discipline in writing and less of the individual and imaginative spirit that prevails in periods of romanticism. Modern classic writing tends to be colorless and unimaginative, but intellectual and clever. Beginning with a classic revival among French writers in the last half of the 17th century, all European literatures went through a period of neo-(new)classical writing. In English literature the term refers to the movements of the Restoration period and to the majority of the literature of the 18th century. Much of our Revolutionary writing and that of our first years as an independent nation were imitations of English neoclassical authors, and stressed the order, logic, restrained emotion, correctness, and "good taste" of the writings of Addison, Pope, and Swift.

New Poetry, The. A term used quite often in American criticism to describe the aspects of the various experimental tendencies which led to a marked revival in interest in poetry in the United States about 1912. (*See* Free Verse for specific characteristics of the New Poetry.) The term tends to emphasize the fact that, with the new writers, poetry became less conventional and aristocratic and began to utilize colloquial language and to treat the common, everyday objects of American life. Thus such poets as Sandburg, Lindsay, Masters, Frost, and others, treated all the aspects, rural and industrial, of the nation and attempted to interpret American life in a vigorous and genuine language that could be understood by all classes of readers.

Nobel Prize For Literature. An award of approximately $40,000, given each year by the Swedish Academy in Stockholm for what the committee judges to be the most eminent work in "idealistic" literature. The literary award (one of five such prizes made possible by the will of Alfred Bernard Nobel, the famed Swedish chemist) is not necessarily given for a particular work but rather to the individual, regardless of nationality, whose literary achievement has been outstanding on a world basis. American writers who have won the Nobel Prize for literature are: Sinclair Lewis (1930), Eugene O'Neill (1936), Pearl Buck (1938), William Faulkner (1950), Ernest Hemingway (1954). T. S. Eliot, who won the prize in 1948, was American born and educated, although most of his work has been produced since he became a British subject in 1927.

Novel. A novel is usually considered a fictitious prose tale, of considerable length, in which an integrated plot, professing to be a cut from real life, is woven around characters and situations. This definition, of course, is highly inadequate, since we classify as novels many fictional works which do not tell a story and which have very little action. But, by and large, the novel is written to entertain the reader, to present a problem, or to enlarge upon some ethical question, or to present a realistic cut from life. It tends to be long (from 75,000 words up) and to be an integrated whole as to plot, characterization, and purpose. Since the 18th century development of the modern novel, this form has become the most popular branch of English and American writing, being challenged in reader interest only by the short story. For the most part the novel has continued to treat adventure and love as its two major themes. The American novel in this century has leaned very heavily toward being a vehicle for social criticism, to analyze character, or to teach truth, particularly with regard to social mores and manners. The best American novels of the century are highly introspective and analytical.

Octave, Octometer. *See* Poetry.

Pentameter, Personification. *See* Poetry.

Poetry, Poetic Figures, Meter, Basic Forms, Free Verse Technique. Poetry embodies the most imaginative expression of writing. Its language is distinguished by its patterns of rhythmical words and phrases. It is the crystallization in language of the beauty and the musicality of imaginative thought and of the poet's powerful emotional reaction to the sensory impressions which life and fancy have engraved upon his mind. Poetry is ethereal and imaginative; hence any exact definition of it is likely to be equally ethereal. Thousands of poets have attempted to define their own medium. Wordsworth called it "the spontaneous overflow of powerful feeling recollected in tranquility." Poe termed it, "the rhythmical creation of beauty." Emily Dickinson, one of American literature's most beloved poets and one most adverse to set formula and restrictive conventions, had this infallible method for recognizing poetry: "If I read a book and it makes my whole body so cold no fire can ever warm me, I know that is poetry. If I feel physically as if the top of my head were taken off, I know that is poetry. These are the only ways I know it. Is there any other way?" But, though the most expressive medium of creative literature cannot be imprisoned within any set formula, most poets, critics, and perceptive readers would agree that, regardless of form, poetry must have rhythm, some regular or cadenced beat of accents, some recurring pattern of echoing sound, whether or not ryhme is present. Briefly and nontechnically this article will attempt to build up a few of the basic ideas of English and American poetry, both for the traditional forms and for the "free verse" or New Poetry.

Language of English Poetry. To build up musically, rhythm, and imaginative ideas, the poet resorts often to symbolic expressions to carry his meanings outside the realm of reality, these expressions being known as *figures of speech.* The most common of these are:

1. *Simile.* A comparison, where a resemblance between two things is noted with *as* or *like,* e.g., *like silk is her hair.*

2. *Metaphor.* An implied comparison, where words or phrases actually denoting characteristics of one thing are used in reference to another thing to suggest a likeness or analogy between the two things, e.g., *to see the world in a grain of sand or heaven in a flower.*

3. *Synecdoche.* A figure which uses a more comprehensive term to represent a less comprehensive one, or vice versa, e.g., *A fleet of twenty sail; Now, all hands to the task.*

4. *Metonymy.* The substitution of one object or thought for another, closely associated with it because of some common quality assigned to both, e.g., *The pen is mightier than the sword.*

5. *Personification.* Where human characteristics are given to inanimate objects or ideas, e.g., *See how my sword weeps for the poor king's death.*

6. *Alliteration.* A repetition of the same sound in consecutive or almost consecutive words, e.g., *the moan of doves in immemorial elms, and murmuring of innumerable bees.*

7. *Hyperbole.* An exaggeration for the sake of emphasis, e.g., *rivers of blood; waves mountain high; oceans of love.*

8. *Antithesis.* The balancing of one opposing term against another for the purpose of heightening effect through contrast, e.g., *fair is foul, and foul is fair.*

The above common figures show only a few of the many devices by which the language of poetry is made to appeal to the feelings and to provoke mental and emotional reactions on the part of readers through skillful molding of the vocabulary of the language into imaginative thoughts and ideas.

Meter of traditional English poetry. A second essential to verse is the rise and fall of stress in a poetic line which produce the melody or rhythmical grouping in the flow of poetic language. Poets of the past in every language have developed certain definite patterns of stress. American poets, of course, inherited the traditional English patterns, which are known under the general term *meter*. Traditionally, a single metrical unit in English verse is a *foot*, so called because Greek verse was originally measured by the time of the rise and fall of the "step forward and step backward" in the dance. A foot may contain from 1 to 3 syllables. Each type of foot bears a special name, according to the stressed or unstressed syllables it contains . When one counts, or scans, poetic feet, a *breve* (∪), or other mark, may be used to mark the unstressed syllables and a *macron* (—), or other mark, may be used to designate the stressed syllables. The common poetic feet used in traditional English poetry are:

The *iambus* ∪ –	The *spondee* – –
The *trochee* – ∪	The *pyrrhic* ∪ ∪
The *anapest* ∪∪ –	The *amphibrach* ∪ – ∪
The *dactyl* – ∪ ∪	

Poetic lines are classified according to the number of feet in a line:

Monometer: 1 foot	*Pentameter:* 5 feet
Dimeter: 2 feet	*Hexameter:* 6 feet
Trimeter: 3 feet	*Heptameter:* 7 feet
Tetrameter: 4 feet	*Octometer:* 8 feet

The meter of most of the lines from the great English and American poets, prior to the rise of the "free verse" movements, may be scanned by some combination or combinations of the above elements. For instance, Whittier in *The Clear Vision* uses the *iambus* in a *tetrameter* line. His meter is thus *iambic tetrameter* in the two lines here:

> I did | but dream. | I nev | er knew
> What charms | our stern | est sea | son wore.

A line from Longfellow's *Hiawatha* shows the reversal of stress to give a *trochaic tetrameter* line:

> Then be | gan the | deadly | conflict.

Since Longfellow uses this form throughout the long poem, the constant repetition of the same swinging rhythm tends to become monotonous. Great poets vary their patterns ordinarily to build up harmonies of sound by means of their variations. Here Burns uses in his *tetrameter* line, 3 *amphibrach* feet and an *iambus:*

> Flow gently, | sweet Afton, | among thy | green braes.

Melody and caesura. In addition to the technical aspects noted above, the poet (whether operating within the traditional metrical patterns or not) is also concerned with the melody or the over-all tone quality of the poetic line. In order to give the line the flow of language or the swing he desires, he must be careful in his cho'ce of words and phrases which will have the proper combination of vowels and consonants to give the mood he intends to create in the reader. Thus not only his ideas but the very choice of words and phrases will give impressions of sadness, gentle delicacy, roughness, gayety, or madness.

Also in almost every line of poetry of 3 or more feet, there is provided a slight rhythmical pause, indicated by the poet by a break in the sense of the line. This pause is know as a *caesura*. If the pause follows an accented syllable, the caesura is called *masculine;*

if it follows an unaccented syllable, it is known as *feminine*. The following 2 lines from Milton shows both uses of the caesura in *iambic pentameter* lines:

Vain war with Heaven ‖ and, by success untaught,
His proud imaginations ‖ thus displayed.

Stanza forms. A number of poetic lines *(verses)* make up a division *(stanza)* of the entire poem. Of course, a stanza may constitute the entire poem, or the composition may comprise many stanzas and not necessarily of the same length in number of lines. Stanzas are commonly known by the number of verses they contain:

> The *couplet:* 2-line stanza
> The *triplet:* 3-line stanza
> The *quatrain:* 4-line stanza
> The *quintet:* 5-line stanza
> The *sestet:* 6-line stanza
> The *septet:* 7-line stanza
> The *octave:* 8-line stanza
> The 9-or-more line stanza

In the above mentioned types of stanzas *rhyme* may or may not be considered necessary. Even before the "free verse" movements much famous poetry had been written in which there was no end rhyme. This verse (in which most of the work of Shakespeare and Milton is written) traditionally has been called *blank verse*. Conventional rhyme in English is secured almost invariably by a repetition of sound produced by similarity of sounds (same vowels and consonants) in two or more words *(swallow-follow; love-above)* placed at the ends of two or more lines of the stanza. Occasionally poets have rhyme occur within lines.

When a stanza contains more than 2 lines, we usually look for the rhyme pattern by assigning letters of the alphabet to the end-rhyming words. Thus a 4-line stanza (quatrain) with end words rhyming *zone-flight-alone-aright* would rhyme *abab* (see page 52). A 6-line stanza (sestet) with end words rhyming *grow-retreat-blow-greet-here-tear* would rhyme *ababcc* (see page 26).

Attention has been called in this section to only a very few of the possibilities for variations within the comparatively fixed patterns of traditional English versification. The variety of forms possible with the traditional feet and the line-rhyme patterns are legion and American poets throughout our library history have used them to give us a rich store of immortal American verse. But within the past century, many American poets have left the traditional forms, in at least a part of their production, to follow both European and native American experimental techniques which we know by the general terms "free verse," New Poetry, and various other more specialized names.

Characteristics of free verse. In *free verse* the rhymic form is not based upon any precise meter but upon some pattern of cadence or by the harmonious recurrence of certain elements within the poetic unit. The aim, then, in free verse is general rhythm throughout the unit, or *strophe*. In Greek drama *strophe* indicated the turn which the chorus made from right to left as the ode or choral lyric was being recited. Traditionally the word has been used as synonymous of *stanza*. The word has been adopted by the writers of free verse to indicate the complete cycle of cadenced rhythmic verse necessary to complete the emotion or effect desired by the poet. The strophe might well be the entire poem or a series of strophies might be necessary to round out the entire poem. Thus the unit in free verse is quite different than the *foot and line* pattern of traditional metrical verse. Free verse is sometimes called *strophic verse* to indicate this distinctive characteristic.

The late 19th and 20th century experimentations with free verse are, of course, not new discoveries in the world's writing. Old Hebrew poetry was composed upon the principle of balance and rhythm, employing the strophe measure instead of rhyme and meter. The Psalms, The Songs of Solomon, and the Book of Job in the *Bible* were written in "free verse."

The periods immediately behind us in American literature have produced much in both the conventional "meter and line" patterns of English poetry and in the "cadenced strophe" of the free poetry that will live to become a part of our permanent body of verse classics and much that will be cast aside by time and neglect. At mid-century much of the more radical experimentation of the earlier free verse movements has calmed and the work of the younger poets shows again a greater measure of the conventional patterns. "Free verse" has not eliminated the conventional pattens of poetic expression; it has simply added the necessity to give more critical attention to the search for the values of the underlying pattern of vigor and enrichment that the New Poetry brings to focus in the contemporary age—basically not a revolutionary pattern at all but one that ancient great poets considered as conventional in their times.

Proletarian Literature. A term which is applied to writing which has as its underlying theme the exposure of injustices and economic inequalities of society. Its purpose, aside from artistic considerations, would be the arousing of public indignation toward the bettering of the conditions under which the proletariat (the lowest classes economically) exists. It is easily seen that "proletarian" literature tends toward injecting an element of propaganda, for better or worse, into aesthetic writing when it is produced by the best creative artists of an age. A great portion of American writing, especially in the 1920's and 1930's, would fit the classification of "proletarian" literature.

Pulitzer Prizes. A series of annual awards in journalism and letters, created by a fund set aside for the purpose by a bequest of Joseph Pulitzer, an American journalist and philanthropist who died in 1911. He founded the Columbia School of Journalism and designated that the Advisory Board of the school select yearly the various works produced in the U. S. that would be judged as "best" in their respective fields. In the field of American letters the bequest provided for awards to the following: a novel, preferably dealing with American life; an original play, preferably dealing with American life; a book on U. S. history; a biography "teaching patriotic and unselfish services"; a volume of verse. The Pulitzer prizes have come to be the most known of all the various literary awards which are made within the United States. There has been, quite naturally, a great deal of controversy at times among critics generally with regard to the Pulitzer selections. The restrictions noted above would tend to make much creative writing ineligible for awards. It is noted by some critics that awards usually go to writers who treat conventional themes and to those with established reputations among the general reading public. William Faulkner, for instance, received the Nobel prize in 1950, after having produced novels over a 25-year period, many of which were acclaimed as outstanding creative works by literary critics, without having received a single Pulitzer prize. It is well recognized, of course, by students of literature that no contemporary literary prize will add to the creative values which a literary work possesses at the time that it is issued in the final form which the author gives to it.

Puritanism. This term is used rather loosely and in at least two distinct meanings. In England, Puritanism became a term which designated a group within the Established Church of England who desired to reform the Church in the direction of the principles of Calvinism. The Puritans soon became politically minded and sought to establish the power of Parliament and to destroy the royal party's theory of the divine right of kings in England. In the American Colonial period, Puritanism represents for us the moral code and the system of preaching in the churches of New England from 1620 to the beginning of the 19th century. This system of Puritan morality, really a very strict interpretation of Calvinism (q.v.), invaded all phases of social and political life of the New England Colonies. Puritanism, with its emphasis on the depravity of man and its insistence upon an unnatural self-denial and individual consciousness of sin, invaded the whole social structure of early America, and for the most part, gave us a barren and depressing literature for the first century and a half of our literary history.

Puritanism, as a system of morality, has given ground slowly in our national development and in its repressive influence upon the creative arts. It is only in this century that the "genteel" attitudes in criticism have been broken down. Today, for most Americans, *puritan* and *puritanical* are symbols of a morality that verges upon intolerance, an oversensitive conscience laden with a burden of sin, an undue repression of normal human enjoyment, an intellectual and aesthetic narrow-mindedness, a threat against freedom of thought and its individual expression in all forms of artistic endeavor.

Pyrrhic. *See* Poetry.

Quatrain, Quintet. *See* Poetry.

Realism. A general term applied to all literary work which attempts to present the actualities of life without coloration induced by subjective prejudices, idealism, or romantic fancy. It is an attempt to depict life-as-it-is in an entirely honest manner. The purpose of the realist is a truthful representation of material in both its surface and its inner aspects, avoiding no aspect, pleasant or unpleasant, sordid or noble. True realism deals with the commonplace and the ordinary and avoids the unusual in life. But, unlike the camera, which records only surface appearances of things as they are, the true realist delves into underlying motivation and structure of material to attempt to present the whole truth. True realism, of course, is seldom achieved wholly in creative writing. It is simply a technique or attitude, as opposed to the romantic attitude, with which the realist approaches his material. (*See* pages 131-135 for a discussion of the various shadings of the realistic technique; *See also* Naturalism above.)

Regional Literature. Writing in which the geographical setting is of major importance, portraying a particular section of the country in its depiction of the atmosphere, the people, problems, customs, habits, and speech of the particular community or district treated. (*See* pages 134, 236 for a discussion of American regional writing of this century; *See also* under Frontier Literature and Local Color Literature above.)

Renaissance, American. A term used by some anthologists and literary historians to indicate the period of American literature between 1830 and 1870. The term "renaissance," of course, is ordinarily applied to the literary and art movements which characterized the transition period from the medieval to the modern age. This period of a flowering in art and literature began with the Italian humanists and creative writers in the 14th century, and its influence spread into France. About the time of the discovery of America (1492) the revival of interest in learning, based largely upon the ancient Greek and Roman classics, had penetrated into every corner of Europe. When the Pilgrim settlers came to the shores of New England (1620), the Renaissance influence had passed its peak in England. The term is used in America to indicate the period, some 200 years later, when the young United States was beginning its first great period of cultural awakening and American writers were beginning to produce the first truly native writings. It was the great period of the New England writers of the 19th century. The term "renaissance" is thus used to indicate the first truly great developments in our national literature.

Romance. In the medieval age the term *romance* came to apply to the vernacular languages which developed from the Latin spoken in the provinces of the Roman Empire in Europe. And, applied to literature, the term passed over to the type of tale which began to develop in the courts of these provinces in the new vernacular Romance languages. This tale, either in verse or in prose, was one of knights and the ideals of chivalry. It spoke of love and refined living, of monsters and of adventures, of nobility and courtesy. Today, in fictitious narrative, in verse or prose, tales in which the imagination is unrestricted continue to be called romances, as contrasted with realistic matter in which actual life is faithfully reproduced.

Romanticism. In general, an attitude toward life or a literary technique which tends to produce writing marked by individualism, fancy, imagination, color, and revolt against tradition. Writers, imbued with the spirit of individual worth, tend to seek their themes in the realm of the unusual and fanciful and to express freely their feelings and emotions. They tend to oppose rules and conventions in writing and to create new and original forms in which to give vent to their ideas and emotions. Romanticism, as an attitude and a philosophy, can exist and has existed among writers in any period. But we generally refer to the late 18th and early 19th centuries when we speak of romanticism as a major world literary movement. In the United States the romantic movement began as a tardy imitation of the English, French, and German movements and tended to continue throughout most of the century, giving away to realism as a major trend only in the last years of the century. (See pages 38-44 for a fuller discussion of romanticism and of its particular American characteristics.)

Satire. Literary satire is writing intended to incite contempt, amusement, or disgust on the part of the reader toward some theme which the author is holding up to ridicule. A true satirist will attempt to improve institutions and conditions by pointing out their weaknesses, and by means of humor and wit, he will lightly prod and prick at those weaknesses until readers responsible for the perpetuation of those weaknesses will seek their improvement. Hence satire may take a very light, humorous, and mischievous direction and provoke laughter on the part of those being satirized. On the other hand, it may take the direction of an expression of bitterness and libelous ideas; it may be vindictive and abusive. Satire has been common to all literatures from ancient times to the present day.

Sentimentalism. In literature, this quality would denote an excess of emotional appeal in writing, a mawkish tear-jerking type of writing which deliberately places characters in positions calculated to cause intense emotional reactions on the part of readers (or audiences in the case of drama). A wave of sentimental fiction and drama swept through European literatures during the 18th century. English sentimental novels, mostly written by women, were eagerly read in the American colonies and many imitations of the English sentimental novel were produced in America during the late 18th and the early 19th centuries. The sentimental romance accounts for a considerable portion of the subliterary fiction produced in this century.

Septet, Sestet. *See* Poetry.

Short Story. A brief prose narrative, varying in length from a few hundred words to upward of 15,000 (as compared with the average-length novel of some 75,000 words). Tales, sketches, fables, anecdotes, myths, and various other short narrative forms are found from the earliest recorded writings, but the modern short story as a definite genre in literature was first given definitive structure by Edgar Allen Poe. In 1842, Poe set down his critical concepts of what the short story should be. Since Poe's day, the short fictional form has undergone many experimentations by many of the world's best writers but Poe's basic requirements have changed little. He conceived the form as being brief enough to be read in a single sitting so as not to disturb the single dramatic effect which he saw necessary in such a brief form. Poe believed that all characters and situations should be utilized to further the single effect. Naturally, the characters and incidents must be few. This idea of the form has been the conventional one to the present day for most stories written for the magazine market. In this century, however, there has been much experimentation in the realistic and naturalistic techniques toward concentrating the purpose of the short story on characterization and atmosphere and less upon the plot as an end in itself. But, despite the fact that many of our better writers have produced highly polished and artistic short stories, the vast majority of the stories written are produced for the seemingly insatiable public demand for magazines which carry the "formula" story, packed with romantic thrills or a highly sentimentalized love interest. Economic necessity, perhaps, has caused many of our better fiction writers to cater to this mass demand and to the quick financial return which magazines with large circulations promise to the writers who conform to the conventionalized requirements of the reading public.

Simile, Spondee. *See* Poetry.

Stream of Consciousness Technique. In literature, a 20th century literary technique derived from the vocabulary of psychology, in which character and events in narrative are presented through the mental images, emotional reactions, and thoughts of the main personages. The author attempts to follow the uninterrupted flow of conscious reactions and associations which pass through the minds of his characters as they act externally during a period in their lives. Famed English novelists who have employed the technique are James Joyce *(Ulysses)* and Virginia Woolf *(Mrs. Dalloway).* Eugene O'Neill used the technique through long asides and soliloquies in his lengthy plays, *Strange Interlude* (1928) and *Mourning Becomes Electra* (1931). Melville and Poe, in the last century, utilized the technique, and in this century, Sherwood Anderson, John Dos Passos, William Faulkner, Elizabeth Madox Roberts, Ernest Hemingway, Conrad Aiken, James T. Farrell, and others have employed the technique occasionally.

Symbolism. As an attitude of the human mind in its approach to the material of thought and idea, symbolism has existed since the beginnings of writing. Symbolism is basically the presentation of ideas, objects, and life in general, through means of imagery, metaphor, and subtle beauties and musicality of expression. As such, *symbolism* is opposed to *realism* in that realism presents things as they are and symbolism presents things through indirect impressions. Most of the beauty of poetry is achieved through some form of symbolism.

As distinct literary movements bearing the name of "Symbolism," France led the way between 1870 and 1886 when a group of poets, in reaction against realism (and its extension into naturalism), concentrated their work toward the achievement of sound and rhythm in their poetry so as to leave sensory impressions upon the mind of the reader rather than the details of reality. The hiding of the basic ideas, objects, and emotions under abstraction and vagueness of clustered metaphors and images led more and more to the mere *suggestion* of ideas rather than their expression.

All world poetry of the 20th century has been strongly influenced by the French movement (and its extension into the pre-Raphaelite poetry of England). Some modern schools of symbolism have carried abstraction and vagueness of meaning to the extent of literary insanity. Others have used it to add a deep richness of color and fancy to their verse. The "free" verse of this century is a direct consequence of the symbolist movements. For, whatever the particular branch of experimentation has been called, *imagist, surrealist, dadaist, vers libre, impressionist,* etc., the result is an adaptation of the symbolist technique to the expression of ideas and feelings. Aside from the continued use of traditional patterns, American poetry of this century has passed through many and varied individual styles and experimentation under the banner of New Poetry. Despite the impression that many readers get that much of this poetry is insane and worthless, there is much reason to believe that the long-term gain will be a new freshness and vigor in American verse that seemed to be lacking in the traditional patterns of the poets in the late 19th century and the first decade of this one. In America, Walt Whitman and Emily Dickinson were precursors of many eminent 20th century poets who have employed the basic symbolist technique in their experimental patterns.

Synecdoche. *See* Poetry.

Tetrameter. *See* Poetry.

Tragedy. Aristotle first defined tragedy as "dramatic representation of some serious action, arousing pity and fear." This basic idea of tragedy has changed little through the years. It is now considered that tragedy is a struggle and conflict of wills which ends disastrously for a leading personality or personalities. The struggle might be a conflict of wills of different individuals, a conflict of will with circumstances within the enivronment, or the revelation of some fundamental inner conflict of will of the "tragic" personality. Despite the attitude of early modern tragedians (influenced unduly by the tragedies of the Roman writer, Seneca) this form does not require that there be deaths and murders. It is sufficient that the conflicts be very serious and that the consequences be deadly important. There may be comic moments in tragedy but they are interspersed to lighten, for a brief time, the concentration of the audience upon the serious conflict being unfolded. The audience reaction to tragedy is intended to be thoughtful, sad, or pitying. Of course, tragedy does not have to be embodied in a dramatic form. Tragic elements may be found in any of the literary genres.

Transcendentalism. The notable New England movement in religious philosophy, which had such a decided influence upon much of our best literature of the period beginning about 1840, received its name and initial impetus from the philosophy of the German Kant's *Critique of Pure Reason* (1788). Kant, and other German writers who followed Kant's reasoning, such as Herder, Jacobi, and Schelling, influenced greatly the early English romantics, particularly Coleridge, Wordsworth, and Carlyle. The New England group, headed by Emerson, not only absorbed the basic notion of Kant of the importance of transcendental human experience—intuitive and personal revelation that goes beyond the senses in the determination of right and wrong—but they borrowed other ideas from Eastern religions and philosophers and from both ancient Greek and modern philosophies.

The New England Transcendentalists preached that man's relationship to God was a personal matter and was established directly by the individual rather than through the medium of "chosen" representatives and ritualistic proceedings. This latter idea was basic to Unitarianism (q.v.). The group held that man had within himself the essence of divinity and urged the development of individual self-trust and self-reliance as opposed to a dependence upon tradition and authority. Feeling was exalted above logic. The group advocated that man live close to Nature and resist commercialism in all forms (*See* Brook Farm).

The Transcendental Club of Boston met from time to time from the year 1836 and published a magazine with articles by various members for a time (*See Dial*). Although the Transcendentalists did not constitute a close-knit organization, the movement had two tremendous influences upon American thought and upon literature. The ideas of the group did much to strike a final blow at an already weakening Calvinistic Puritanism and gave a new and fresh impetus to the development of our first truly national body of literature. Emerson, Thoreau, Alcott, Bryant, the Channings, Margaret Fuller, Elizabeth Peabody, Longfellow, Hawthorne, Whittier, Whitman, and Melville were some of our writers of the period who were directly associated with the movement or whose writings reflected much of the spirit of individualism, self-reliance, and humanitarianism that had been little evident in the first 200 years of our literary history.

Trimeter, Triplet, Trochee. *See* Poetry.

Unitarianism. The term designates the creed of a religious sect which came into importance in America about 1820 and which did much to liberalize the Calvinistic preaching in New England and to pave the way for the general cultural and intellectual awakening which we so strongly associate with Transcendentalism. Thus, although a religious creed, Unitarianism (whose basic doctrine discarded the belief in the Trinity and held for the unity of God and for the human-divine character of Christ) attempted to combine humanistic reasoning with supernaturalism. Its influence in breaking down the traditional Calvinistic attitude and in making possible the rise of culture based on reasoning, common sense, and individual judgment gives it importance in any consideration of the forces responsible for the rise of a new and enlightened era in the development of our literature. Unitarianism and Transcendentalism are inseparable and direct causes of the so-called American Renaissance (q.v.) in our literature.

Vers Libre. *See* Free Verse; *also* Poetry.

Victorian. The term is sometimes used as synonymous of "genteel" (*See* Genteel Tradition). In general, the term designates English literature of the age of Queen Victoria (1837-1901). Since much of the writings of that age reflected the attitudes of English Victorian society, closely paralleling those of the upper ranges of New England society of the same period, the term, as "genteel," has come to represent hypocritical, complacent, and narrow concepts of respectability and decency in human society.

Index

The comprehensive *Table of Contents* gives references to the major divisions of American Literature and cultural history. This Index locates specific items within those major divisions and draws attention to the portions of the text giving the most concise information for the review of a particular subject. Boldface figures indicate main references. The letter A indicates a plot summary in Appendix A. The letter B indicates a definition of the particular literary term in Appendix B. All titles are italicized.